David Robbins

To Hudson

DAVID ROBBINS

THE VELVET GRIND
SELECTED ESSAYS, INTERVIEWS, SATIRES (1983–2005)

Edited by Lionel Bovier & Fabrice Stroun

JRP|Ringier, Zurich, & Les Presses du réel, Dijon

TABLE OF CONTENTS

SECTION II
INTELLECTUAL SHOWBIZ

Tree trimming, removal, shrub pruning, stump grinding. No job too natural. (214) 442-7883

120 PUBLIC NOTICES

FREE! David Robbins has been generous with his ideas about art and comedy for twenty-five years. The same pioneering urge that created such works as *Talent* (1986) and the *Ice Cream Social* (1993-?) now leads him to break the bonds of the artworld, push on, pursue other ways of thinking, other rewards.... As a goodbye present he's giving away those few of his works that remain at Feature, a gallery that has happily presented the products of his imagination for the past twenty years.

On Saturday, November 12*, the framed works will be placed at the curb in front of the gallery and made available free of charge. Mankind, bring your minivan, and help celebrate freedom by obtaining a free momento thereof!

*Rain date: Saturday November 19

124 FOUND ITEMS

Young cat. Impressive resilience. Fast. Sassy. Answers to "Here, Kitty." 334-3328

Curb Giveaway announcement card, 2005

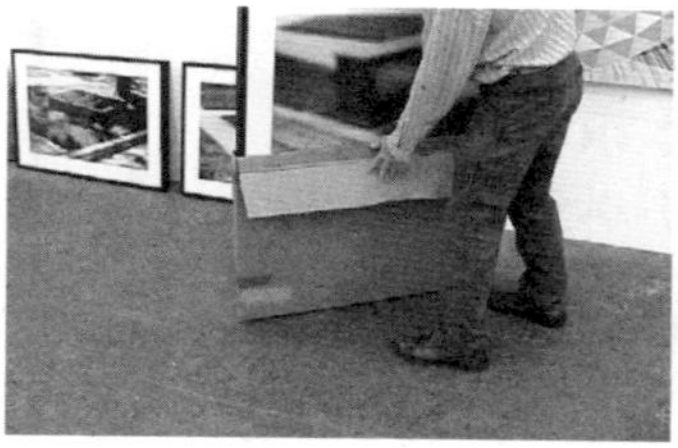

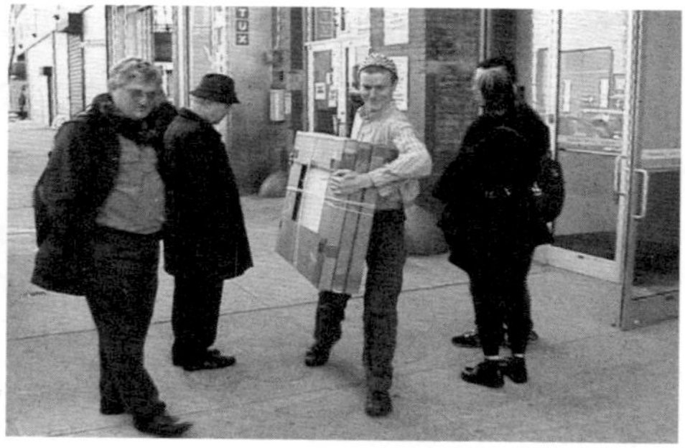

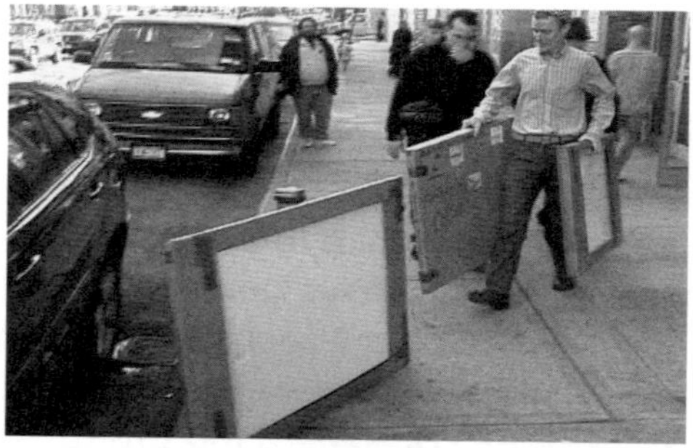

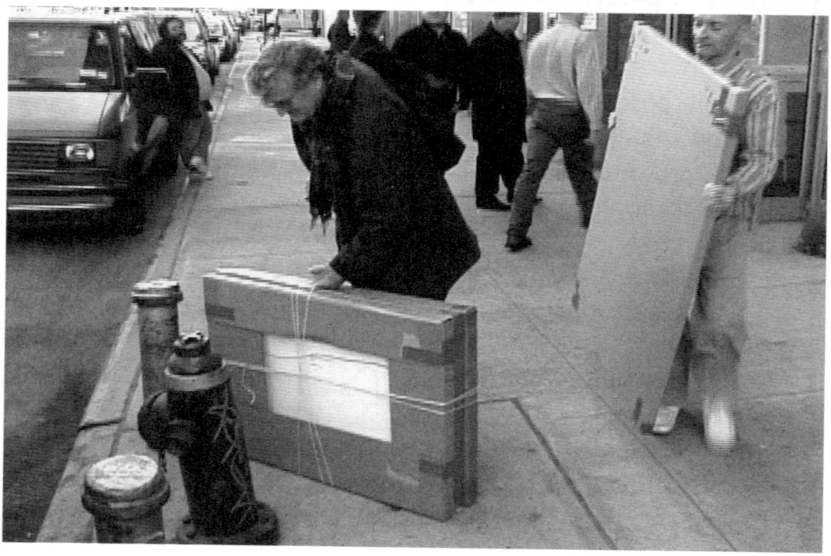

Curb Giveaway, 2005
video stills

Introduction
Lionel Bovier & Fabrice Stroun

THIS FOURTH VOLUME OF THE "POSITIONS" SERIES—WHICH AIMS TO QUESTION ARTISTIC AND CURATORIAL PRACTICES FROM THE SINGULAR POSITION OF AN ARTIST WHO WRITES BOTH ON HIS/HER OWN WORK AS WELL AS THAT OF OTHER ARTISTS—STANDS OUT IN MORE WAYS THAN ONE. This anthology includes short fictions alongside the essays and interviews that have been the series' fare to date, and is structured as to produce an experience akin to reading a novel. Through the progression and interplay of the texts, the author gradually emerges as a character in a kind of real-life *Bildungsroman*, set in a world of specialized image-producers.

Selected for their narrative gist as much as for their keen critical analysis of the makeup of American culture, taken together these writings yield a coherent narrative of the profound transformation of Robbins' artistic itinerary from downtown New York post-punk-DIY conceptualism in the early 1980s, to, today, a willing participant in the research-and-development branch of a hyper-lubricated, market-driven, all-encompassing entertainment industry. Divided into two distinct thematic and chronological poles, "The Children of Barthes and Coca-Cola" and "Intellectual Showbiz," the anthology reproduces the above indicated evolution of recent American art history and the profound transformation of the status of the artist that it implies. At the same time, this coming-into-being "fiction" is not another account among many of success (or failure) in New York City. As its title indicates, The Velvet Grind points to a much slower day-to-day equilibrium between privilege and discipline, between decadence and weariness on the one hand, and industriousness, deliberation, and long-term commitment on the other.

Producing images (mostly photographic) and objects (imbued with a comedic quality rather than any stylistic or thematic consistency) alongside texts, Robbins' practice concurrently develops two lines of investigation. Occasionally the two tracks do converge, yielding direct correspondences between words and actions, but for the most part they remain essentially independent productions.

Like many other artists of his generation, at the onset of his career David Robbins posited mass-media entertainment as the definitive perspective of American culture. Andy Warhol, who broke ground on the edifice that would come to occupy Robbins' work, is thus a recurring presence in his texts. That Robbins' first job in New York was as a Warhol Factory assistant partially explains why he did not seek to duplicate Warhol's revolutionary self-legitimization strategies in any way shape or form.[1] Rather, his brief Factory stint, little more than a year of service, gave him a head start toward "my own thing—whatever that might turn out to be. At Andy's, I saw what art-world glamour was. Talk about starting at the top! You didn't get bigger than Warhol. And seeing it up close liberated me from having to pursue that experience. I could look for something else, build another model."[2]

"Let's not be afraid to make something that isn't art," Robbins would write in 1993. "There will always be plenty of slaves to the superego of art—a fact that should free the rest of us to risk the pursuit of new territory. Actually, this pursuit is almost an obligation, if we take seriously the idea that, at this point in history, art, the widest cultural aperture, is less about the invention of pictures and objects than about the invention of behavior."[3] His rejection of the art-world star system exemplified by Warhol didn't stem, then, from a purist neo-conceptual posture or a puritanical aversion to the market.

Instead, as is evidenced from the texts collected here, it was a logical outcome of the artist's idiosyncratic use of mass-media culture as a horizon of the Great American Imagination.[4] Why be content to be a great American artist or a great American entertainer, he asks more than once in this volume, when one could possibly embody the Great American Imagination?

As the sum of hopes the spirit can spatially (geographically) conceive of, the notion of the Great American Imagination has always implied some kind of physical spanning of the American vastness and so, in 1995, after residing in Europe (Brussels, Cologne, Graz, Naples ...) during most of the previous seven years, Robbins repatriated not to New York but to his native Midwest.[5] The Midwest is known as the place where American artists come from, certainly not where they move to. Yet, halfway between New York and Los Angeles, the Midwest, a place that stands on the margins of dominant cultural production, geographically incarnates the hybrid "third option"—neither art nor entertainment—advocated by the artist from the very beginning of his public life. Writing from Milwaukee where he currently resides, the artist states: "The most highly evolved Midwestern imaginations are quite conscious that they represent and embody an alternative to the dominant models of culture making celebrated in and promoted by the magazines and TV shows produced in the current centers. Being officially 'out of it' and in the middle of the country, Midwesterners enjoy a natural, deep-dyed perspective on the seamlessly managed professional culture of the often dubious commercial product that is ceaselessly lobbed at them from the coasts. The model of emergent Midwestern contemporary culture is based in part on plasticizing, activating, and exploiting that perspective to risk something new."[6] At the end of the day, the Great American Imagination appears within the following pages as a structural—and ultimately political—paradigm rather than an existential one. The narrative that can be garnered from this anthology is one of a progressive move away from the centers of cultural production, and toward marginal territories that exemplify the day-to-day usage of this said production; a move away from the mediated images of the individual as envisioned by pop culture—"the expressive side of marketplace culture"[7]—and toward works that not only investigate but also produce social, or rather socializing, events.[8]

Yet, if The Velvet Grind does provides a narrative of the transition between the most sophisticated picture-based practices of the 1980s to the "relational" 1990s and digitalization's promise of expanded behavioral freedom, Robbins' Midwest—which the artist likens to a kind of American Scandinavia—bears little resemblance to Dominique Gonzalez-Foerster's Brasilia, Pierre Huyghe's neo-modernist outskirts of Paris, Philippe Parreno's images of the deep sea, or the collectively-conceived decors for the appropriated Manga character Ann Lee. Contrarily to his younger French forebears' colonization of liminal territories, Milwaukee, or for that matter, Brussels, do not set stages for any kind of romantic projection. This, deflating side of his sensibility had shown up early, in the most well-known piece from his days in New York, Talent (1986). A series of 18 photographs of a generation-and-a half of up-and-coming New York-based post-Conceptual artists taken by a professional headshot photographer whose lens was usually directed at hopeful actors, Talent already stood in sharp contrast to Jeff Koons' Luxury and Degradation portraits of a fresh bourgeois-class-in-the-making shown in New York that same year. Freedom, which Robbins repeatedly couches in terms of "full access to my own imagination," never emerges in his work as a known quantity, as an internalized socio-cultural allegory of success, but as a concrete, physical provision for action. What he does with this freedom, liberating creative forms from fixed contexts and positioning new contextual horizons for artists' productions, is only hinted at by this book: it happens here and there, today and tomorrow, in the art world and elsewhere.

POSTSCRIPT

Fabrice Stroun

On the morning of Saturday November 12, 2005, I set out to return from New York to Geneva. On the way to JFK, I asked the driver to take a detour through Chelsea in order to see Robbins' latest piece of theater. A few days prior, I had received a public notice from the artist's gallery announcing that he was taking his leave of the art world, and that all of those works still consigned to his New York gallery would be placed on the sidewalk for the taking, free of charge. A compulsive collector myself, I had at first imagined taking something. But once on site, rather than join the fray, I strangely found myself unable to do so. Was it really necessary to burden myself with one more object? Why not instead unload all of my suitcases full of artists' books and editions and leave them on the sidewalk as well? Yet, contrarily to Huebler's famous statement about the fact that there are too many objects in the world as it is—so why bother adding new ones!—Robbins' flyer doesn't so much embody a "radical" position as a satirical one. It didn't call for a critique of the art system, be it for its fetishism or the ever-expanding comedic character that regulates the incestuous commerce between artists, critics, curators, collectors, and dealers; rather it produced (as in theater) a comedy. In the end, the joke is on me. I should have taken something. I didn't—an exhilaratingly funny and liberating thought that has nagged me ever since.

NOTES

1. There is no doubt that Warhol's successes and failures in the matter far exceeded those of his 1980s followers, whether they were acting from within the art world (Jeff Koons), or outside of it (Robert Longo). In "Pops" (a short version of which appeared in Artforum, October 2004, as "Biz Kid"), an autobiographical reminiscence of the artist's days at the Warhol Factory, Robbins concludes: "Warhol's art, occupying an intersection of the trajectories of formidable social and technological forces, happened to be about a society then in the process of discovering its modern scale … Hoping to replicate Warhol's impact is as foolhardy as expecting the repetition of modern mass culture's Christopher Columbus phase of self-discovery."

2. From a conversation with the artist, May 25, 2006.

3. "The Dr. Frankenstein Option" reproduced in this volume, p. 209-227.

4. To reinvest in earnest in the concept of the American imagination, while fully engaging in the most radical transformations undertaken by his generation to the status of artist, the work of art, its institutional validation, and its concomitant exchange value—transformations that we have come to categorize under the general category of "postmodernism" (and which include the loss of aura of the work of art, the critique of "authenticity," the ironic deflation of the grand narrative of the historical avant-garde, etc.)—may seem strange, so much have we come to identify this decade as one of an anxiety-ridden désenchantement. Yet, this historical construction excludes a gamut of artists for whom the collapse of modernism's utopian principles has been experienced as joyous and productive comedy. As it turns out, the majority of these artists started their careers at Nature Morte, a gallery run by two artists, Peter Nagy and Alan Belcher, and for whom Robbins acted as a kind of in-house writer. The fact that, with very few exceptions, almost all of these artists had stopped producing art altogether or had moved out of New York by the mid-1990s accounts for their absence from today's descriptions of the ideological debates of that era. Reflecting back on this decade in the pages of Artforum, Robbins wrote: "the most lasting contribution of the East Village Conceptualists, intangible, but appearing everywhere since, may turn out to have been a discourse of happiness—affirmation of the present and receptivity to the future." ("ABC TV," reproduced in this volume p. 103-112).

5. By the time Robbins reached New York, the Great American Imagination had deteriorated, after its hedonistic transformations in the 1960s and its subsequent embodiment of the deception of that decade's unrealized dream (Hunter S. Thompson's Fear and Loathing in Las Vegas), into the resulting self-alienation and psycho-pathological obsession with greatness (Tom Wolfe's 1972 essay "Why They Aren't Writing the Great American Novel Anymore") that characterize our collective memory of that decade's self-serving excesses. Robbins' earnestness, of course, is steeped in critical irony: any possibility of self-transformation, of personal growth, can never be experienced apart from the chain of associations that lead back to the mass media's exploitation of it. Consequently, Robbins is able to de-psychoanalyze this whole narrative of ideological disintegration, or more precisely, to put in quotation marks the pathological "feelings" that accompany it.

6. From "Notes on a Midwestern Makeover."

7. See note 3.

8. This two-step progression is made evident when one compares, for example, "Art after Entertainment," a prospective text written in 1989, when Robbins was still making photo-based work ("I am calling for the planting of the flag of a third culture that might draw upon the virtue of both contexts, art and entertainment. By processing entertainment through the sensitive faculties of art, we can discover the patterns of entertainment culture in order to determine those aspects of mass media culture most worth preserving. And by injecting the experimentalism of art into entertainment, we can produce more satisfying models of entertainment and eventually blackmail our irresponsible entertainment culture into becoming a civilizing force," reproduced in this volume p. 129-142,) and the latter writings related to his Ice Cream Social project (1993-onward), republished by JRP|Ringier in 2004, and which serves as an addendum of sorts to the present volume.

SECTION I
THE CHILDREN OF BARTHES AND COCA-COLA

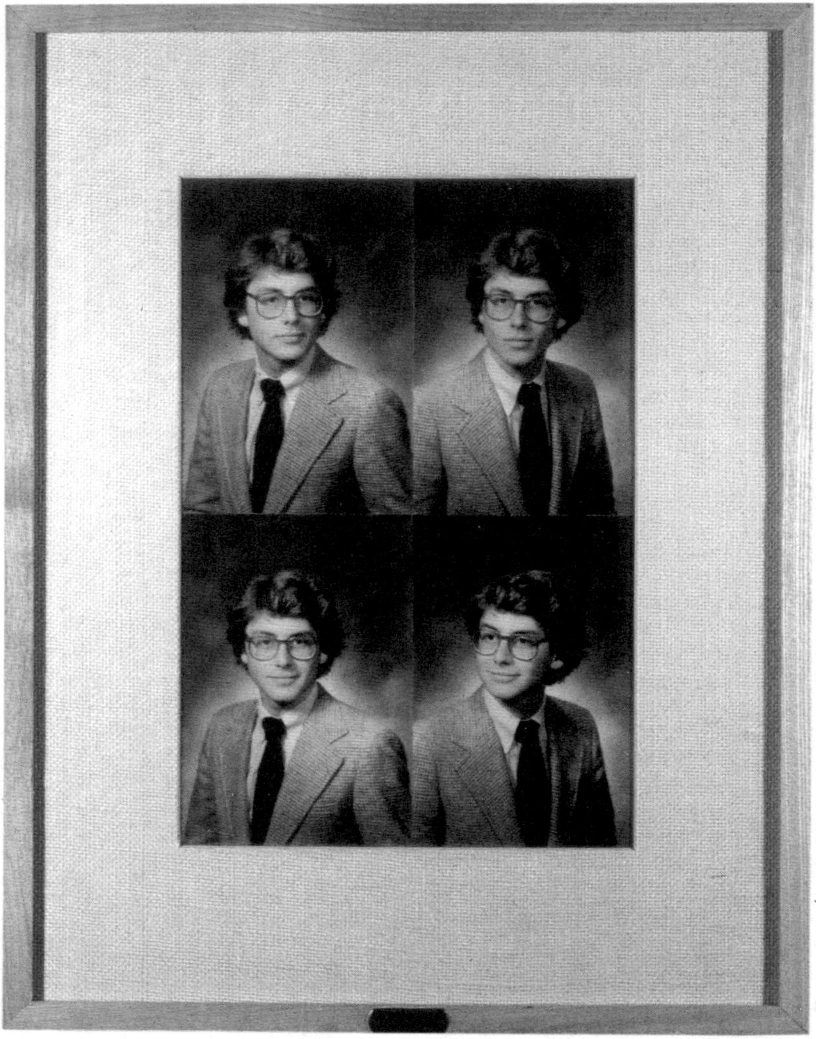

Untitled (from The David Robbins Show), 1986
color photographs, blank bronze plaque, 25" x 19"

On Talent

This text was originally published in <u>Likeness: Artists' Portraits of Artists</u>, exhibition catalogue, CCAC/Wattis Institute, San Francisco 2004.

FROM WATTEAU'S <u>FÊTES GALANTES</u> TO THE IMPRESSIONISTS' DEPICTIONS OF DANCE HALL PERFORMERS, FROM PICASSO'S HARLEQUINS TO WARHOL'S MARILYNS AND CINDY SHERMAN'S <u>FILM STILLS</u>, VISUAL ARTISTS HAVE LONG CREATED REPRESENTATIONS OF THE ENTERTAINERS AND ENTERTAINMENTS THAT DELIGHT, DISTRACT, AND SCANDALIZE SOCIETY. However, artists have generally kept the world of entertainment at arm's length, using its forms and content while preserving art's aura of superiority over the less refined character of mass culture.

I wanted to challenge—and perhaps destabilize—this tradition with <u>Talent</u>, an editioned work that I created in 1986. Composed of 18 black-and-white headshot portraits of artists who were then based in New York and Los Angeles, <u>Talent</u> offered up an image of the artist for our times. When the work was first exhibited at Metro Pictures in New York, Roberta Smith, writing in <u>The New York Times</u>, deemed it "too au courant for its own good." And yet, <u>Talent</u> struck a chord. It has since entered nearly one hundred public and private collections.

REWIND

I had multiple aims in making <u>Talent</u>.

I wanted to depict artists from the perspective of the larger business culture. Contemporary artists operate in two worlds: on the one hand, they're involved with ambitious aesthetic, intellectual, political, and moral stances; on the other hand, they're public figures who function as entertainers. Contemporary art is a kind of intellectual show business.

I wanted to depict artists in a way that was consistent with my own experience of the art world. By and large, the artists of my acquaintance were, and remain, cheerful, funny, generous, and reasonable people. I resented the image of them—of us—as mad, romantic dreamers hopelessly out of touch with reality, and I sought to make a different image, to suggest that these were good people and that art was a reasonable pursuit.

I was also interested in making portraiture. I'd always liked the clean black-and-white look of Man Ray's portraits of artists, but I wanted to inject more contemporary content into the genre.

The photographic convention of the talent headshot satisfied these requirements, integrating them seamlessly.

It was imperative that the pictures taken be actual headshots, not just look like them; they were not to be mere representation but <u>fact</u>, embodied. To more completely avoid the dreaded taint of parody, I hired a professional entertainment photographer, James Kriegsmann Jr. At the time, the Kriegsmann studio had been in operation in the same building near Times Square since the 1940s; I passed it daily on the way to and from my apartment in Hell's Kitchen. Kriegsmann took all the pictures for my project, 36 shots of each artist. I functioned as the artists' agent, booking the sessions, seeing to it that the subjects arrived at the studio at their appointed hour, and paying the bill.

I started out wanting to picture artists who acknowledged the role of entertainment in their own work: Robert Longo, Cindy Sherman, Jeff Koons. But then I realized that, to the business world, an artist's subject doesn't really matter. The business world views all artists in the same way, without regard for the subtle distinctions of media or meaning. My selection process then widened to include friends and acquaintances. <u>Talent</u> wasn't a portrait of <u>the</u> art world, it was a portrait of <u>my</u> art world.

I told the artists that I wanted to make a respectful portrait of them. I relied on their trust. That's an important part of _Talent_—that the artists trusted me enough to subject themselves to being interpreted through this work.

I selected the final picture of each artist. Consistent with the formal look of headshots, which present people as amenable and easy to work with, the mood of each photograph is upbeat and optimistic. These are images of artists who hope to get more work, who are looking forward to the future, who _have_ futures. "Hope to be working with you soon!"

Once the photographs were printed, I chose to title the work with the single word "talent." Generally talent is perceived as a positive trait. Yet some people have considered _Talent_ a cynical work. Not long ago, a friend reported overhearing a viewer comment, "I _think_ it's some sort of joke." But to me it's a sincere expression of optimism, hope, and good things to come.

THE IMAGE OF THE ARTIST

Most of our images of artists come from photographs. Old man Picasso, the super-fertile genius, fiercely studying a painting-in-progress while standing before it in his underwear. Scary Warhol, the black-leather-clad equal of the camera's lens, supremely cool and unflappable. O'Keeffe, the earth mother. In each case it's the camera that enabled these artists to concoct and promote a mythic self-image. In order for that image to reach the masses, each artist engaged in collusion, not just with a photographer but also with a mass publication and distribution system. As professional image-creators, artists are unusually attuned to the mechanics of legend building.

Talent infused a frank acknowledgment of collusion directly into the portrait itself. Having identified a specific picturing system—the entertainer's headshot—that didn't hide its aims (couldn't, in fact: headshots have their economic life—the way they function in the economy _as photographs_—built right in), I used that picturing system to present visual artists. The result was an emblem, one with specific qualities borrowed from

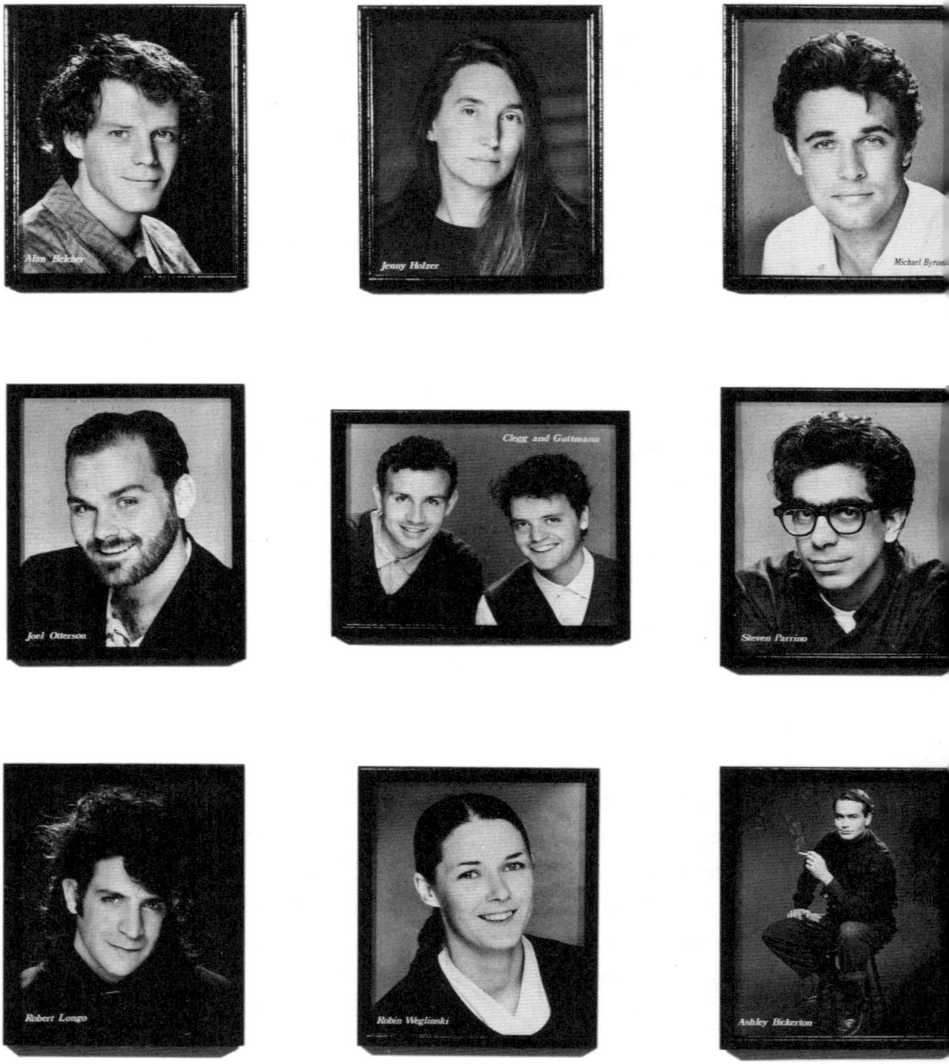

<u>Talent</u>, 1986
18 b/w photographs, each 8" x 10", edition of 100

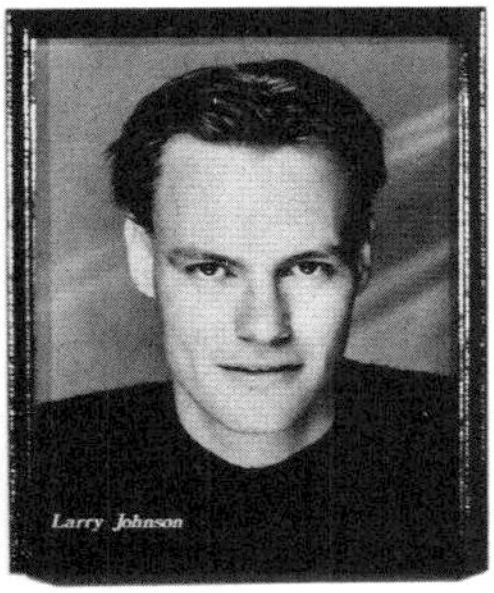
Larry Johnson

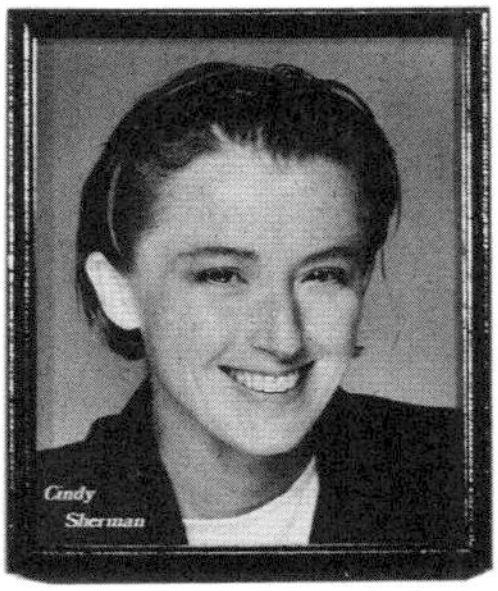
Cindy
Sherman

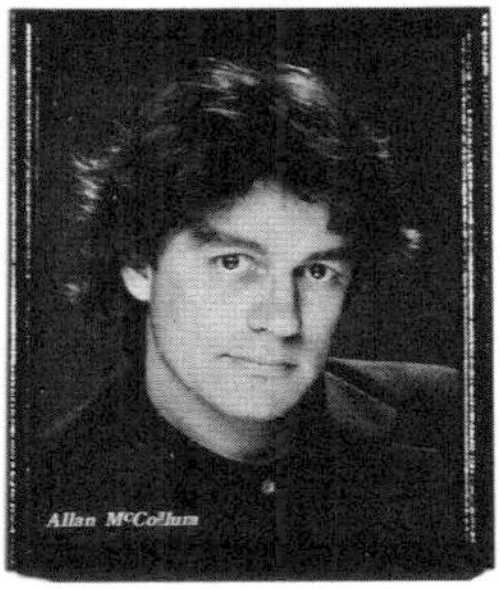
Allan McCollum

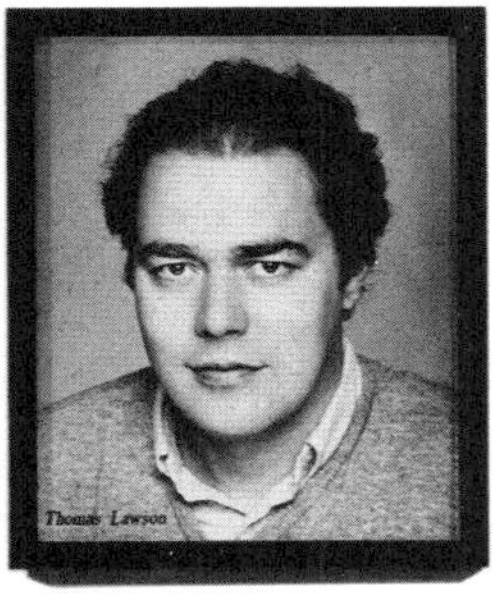
Thomas Lawson

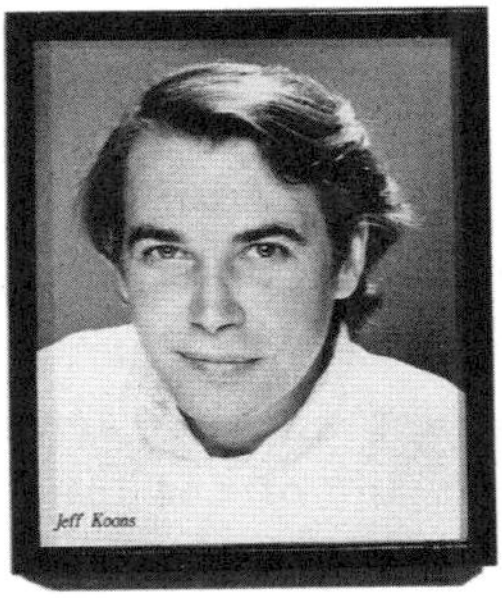
Jeff Koons

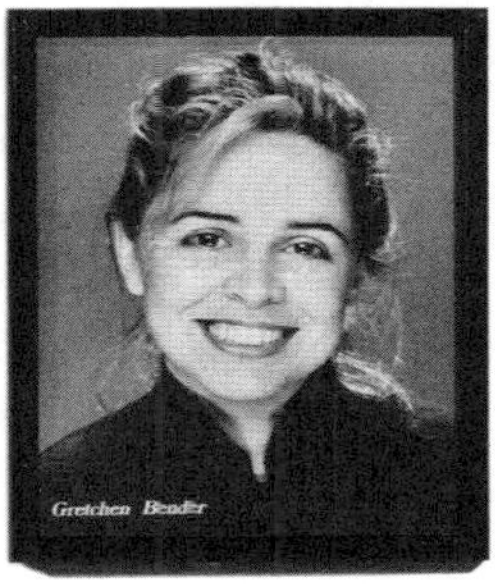
Gretchen Bender

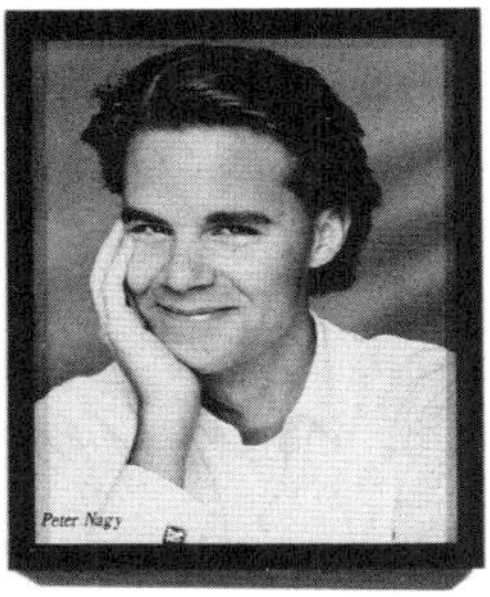
Peter Nagy

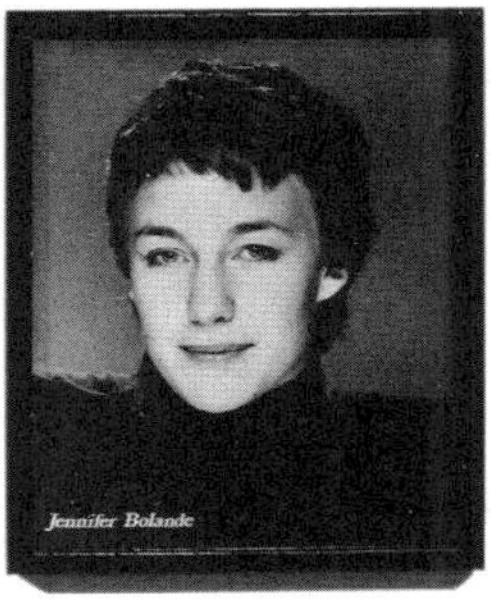
Jennifer Bolande

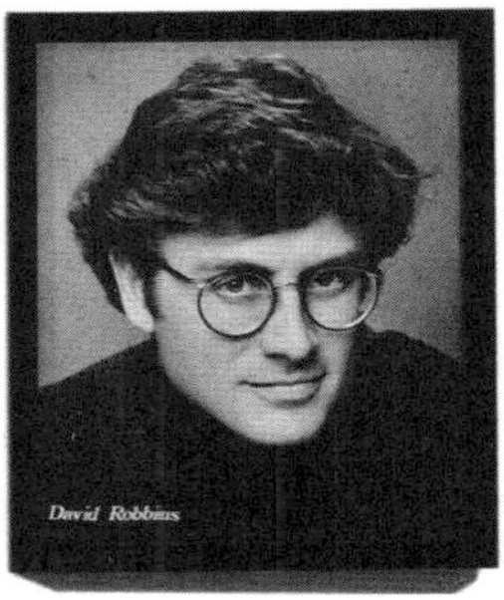
David Robbins

entertainment culture, that denied visual artists their accustomed distance from—and superiority over—that culture.

A TRIANGULATION

The headshot is an artifact designed to serve a communication system that is entirely independent of the concerns of fine art. It doesn't admit much sentiment. It replaces the image of the artist as romantic actor with another, more pragmatic image. Instead of transcendence, we get something earthbound. In the headshot, the image of the artist shifts away from the fragility and misery of a van Gogh, toward something shinier, more confident, and possibly less refined. There's also a shift away from social marginalization and toward social participation.

Talent uses a picturing system that remains separate from art, that does not seek art's blessing, and that has a different set of aspirations. Its framing of art runs counter to the art world's celebration of itself as a world apart. It expresses skepticism toward the art world's certitude that art is and ought to be the terminus point of the imagination, the pinnacle. If *Talent* is a critique of anything, it's a critique of this certitude.

That something might stand outside art and report on it, comment on it, editorialize about it *in an iconic language of its own*—this was, and apparently still is, disorienting. The reason, I submit, is that it instantiates a complication of the modernist dialogue between life and art. *Talent* suggests that the old binary model has been superseded by a triangulated model whose points are life, art, and entertainment—a competing communication system no less madly self-sustaining, self-referential, and self-celebratory than art. "Showbiz" adds another category that's neither Art nor Life.

MAYBE THE NEW, STUPID AMERICA ISN'T REALLY THAT STUPID

The insight that artists are a species of entertainer isn't especially profound. What made *Talent* stand out was the fact that the work conveying the news was aggressively contemporary in its form and unapologetic in its attitude.

Talent was made by an affluent suburban American who'd watched a lot of television, listened to a great deal of pop music, and hadn't had much exposure to or feel for classical culture. Civilization's self-appointed defenders like to assert that a pop-defined background will never yield imaginations as substantive as those formed under more refined conditions. They may be right. The jury is still out. Yet for any whose formative years coincided with the pop era, the assertion has about it a certain arrogance.

In reducing or erasing the gap between artist and entertainer, *Talent* cheerfully represents another step in American culture's gradual movement away from its European inheritance. To Americans, that earlier cultural model, with its hierarchical ranking of one pleasure over another, has come increasingly to seem at odds with this country's homegrown culture. Predicated on the concept that beer and champagne may be compared as *symbols*, but that the *pleasures* these produce in two different individuals may not be ranked, American culture is adamantly horizontal.

A work such as *Talent* merely acknowledges our understanding that no one part of communication culture, no one form of expression, has a lock on truth. A viewer of *The Sopranos* may derive pleasures from it which, while different in kind, are just as real and just as satisfying as the pleasures derived by a viewer of the paintings of Gerhard Richter. Television communicates something that paintings can't, and vice versa. To those of us who have been raised in a democracy of pleasures, any hierarchical ranking that places Richter above *The Sopranos* just isn't as convincing as it once was. For better or worse, much of the world is evolving in this direction. And the United States started this particular ball rolling.

Creating a work that acknowledges this social fact didn't make me feel cynical. On the contrary, I felt sincere and honest. As far as I was concerned, it was the classical hierarchy—artist above, entertainer below—that felt untrue and inauthentic. We needed another paradigm.

THE SUBURBANIZATION OF THE IMAGINATION

Every generation of artists configures culture to match its own experience. The conditions of our upbringing imprint us, and when we come to maturity we return the favor, imprinting our sensibilities upon the culture and bending it to our wills. The organism receives stimuli; the organism eventually responds.

Let me identify two factors that have distinguished our experience of landscape—our experiential landscape—from that of preceding generations.

First, much of our experiential landscape has been of a synthetic, fabricated nature. Actually, for us the synthetic approximates the natural; TV is nature with money. Films, TV, radio, magazines, advertising, computers—media is now indivisible from our experience. Once upon a time, movies, TV, radio, etc., merely <u>commented upon or reflected</u> our experience. Now, however, our exposure to them is so constant—partly because their role in our economy is so integral—that, rather than merely commenting upon or reflecting our experience, these communication forms <u>comprise</u> much of our experience. (My imagination was formed during this latter phase. So, perhaps, was your own.)

The second, more invisible but just as consequent experience of landscape that has imprinted on us our notions of truth and falsity is also, in a way, synthetic. Here, I intend the term to mean not "plastic," but rather, a "synthesis," a blend. This synthesis is manifested in an actual, physical landscape, the suburb—neither city nor country but instead an amalgam of the two: trees 'n' traffic. I and most young Americans grew up in such a landscape. The mass, middle-class suburbs, like the synthetic landscape of pop culture, are a fairly recent phenomenon. Until World War II, suburbs were primarily for the well-to-do. Most people lived in cities, small towns, or rural areas. The idea that vast numbers of people would live in neither city nor country is, in the United States, not much more than 50 years old. When you consider that it takes 20 or so years for a generation to mature and make an impact upon the culture, it becomes clear that imaginations informed by suburban experience are a recent addition to our cultural life. Since an enormous slice of the demographic pie was raised in the suburbs, the imagination conditioned by the suburban landscape is starting to have a significant impact on the direction of our culture.

What is truth to a mind so conditioned? The planned naturalism, the managed, neurotic landscape, the awkward "in-between" condition of the suburbs—this feels "right" to many of us. States that reconcile two states, things that are two things at once, that are resolutely, calmly, insouciantly impure—to us, these places feel like home. We are drawn to them.

And we also create them. As the suburb blurs or negates the distinction between city and country, imaginations imprinted with suburban experience want to blur, ignore, deny, or transcend distinctions between other categories. To such imaginations, the classical distinction between contexts—between, say, the context of art and the context of entertainment—feels less than accurate, because its purity fails to correspond with the hybrid landscape we have experienced. For such imaginations, neither the experience of art nor the experience of entertainment seems by itself sufficiently complex or sufficiently true to their experience, and therefore neither context is sufficiently satisfying. They can't look at art anymore without awareness of the dominant presence of entertainment culture, and they can't look at the powerful and pervasive entertainment culture without aching to refine it and to demand more from it than it is usually willing to give us.

In place of the classical either/or—city or country—the suburbanized imagination prefers the creation of cultural product—activity, gesture, and artifact—that is both/and, or that is "in-between." It looks for, demands, and creates hybrids, blends, and mongrels. Any one context by itself isn't rich enough. This kind of mind seeks satisfaction in contextual genetics, a gene splice. We are, all of us, post-collage. (Adobe Photoshop is the right tool for our time.) By identifying and framing the overlap between artist and entertainer, <u>Talent</u> indicates a position outside both models. <u>Talent</u> is frankly and unashamedly suburban.

FORWARD

If it only represented the way our world worked, Talent would be a work of journalism, not a work of art. But its equating of artist and entertainer isn't entirely true. The two roles are not exactly congruent—yet. Talent thus represents both a dry-eyed social reality and a fantasy. On a personal level, it was wishful, an expression of its author's desire to participate in showbiz. In a less personal sense, though, Talent was prophetic. The hybridized role that it imagined is indeed coming to fruition. A convergence of the roles of "artist" and "entertainer," suggested initially by the career of Andy Warhol and accelerating in his wake, is progressively blurring some of the essential particulars—media, venue, distribution systems—that previously separated the two fields.

Are artists appearing with regularity on David Letterman? Is there a TV show called Art World Tonight? Is art fame just as big and just as consequential as mass media fame? No. But the future is never merely a projection of present conditions. In a tentative, trial-and-error way—the slow, experimental way we ought to have anticipated—the change is happening. The process is evolutionary rather than revolutionary. The painter Julian Schnabel makes films for mainstream theatrical release, and the lead in Before Night Falls, his most recent film, is nominated for an Academy Award. The artist Alex Bag makes videos that play like art world sketch comedy. "Showman" artists such as Damien Hirst or Maurizio Cattelan make highly public, highly accessible work. Matthew Barney does whatever the heck he does, and 300,000 people trek to the Guggenheim to try to figure it out. Your parents may have heard of Cindy Sherman.

But that's mentioning only the stars. The more profound and lasting evolution is structural. It's taking place among countless young artists whose names we don't know yet. Thanks to the computer, kids are evolving away from the version of culture that maintained those tired divisions between contexts. With the computer, the active imagination can now create a wide variety of communication products, efficiently. On my laptop I'm developing texts for magazines, a book, several screenplays, Photoshop pieces for galleries and museums, videos that think of themselves as television, and audio pieces that think of themselves as, well, amusing trifles. Using this single, compact tool, an individual may produce in the "entertainment" formats of the mainstream mass media—the TV set, movie theater, boombox, video game, and website—and, equally authentically, in formats appropriate to gallery and museum. In short, we are becoming contextually ambidextrous. The change in the artist's self-perception that is emblematized in Talent precedes the computer, but it's the computer that is accelerating the exploration of that change, naturalizing it, allowing for its articulation, and reinforcing it.

To the contextually ambidextrous, the pertinent question is no longer "what infinite variety of materials, strategies, concerns might we include in the context of art?" It isn't "what might we map onto the coordinates of art?" These were the questions of modernism. The more contemporary question—tomorrow's question—is "who are we when we pursue a larger field of production, some of which is art?"

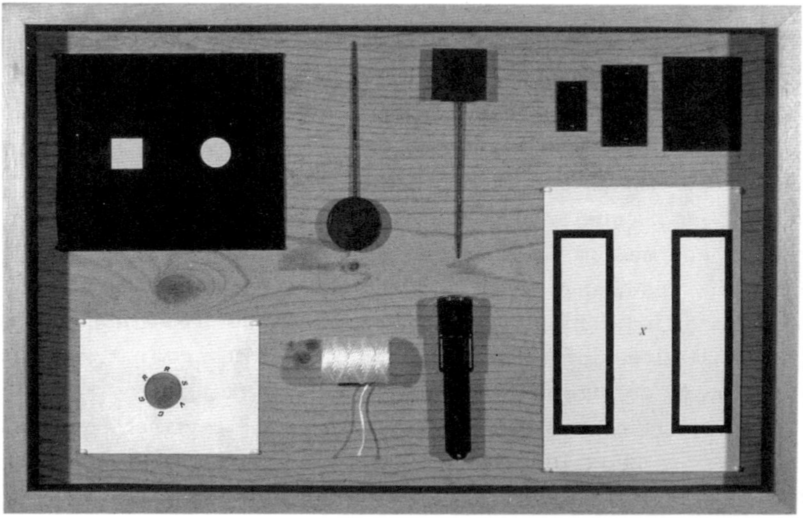

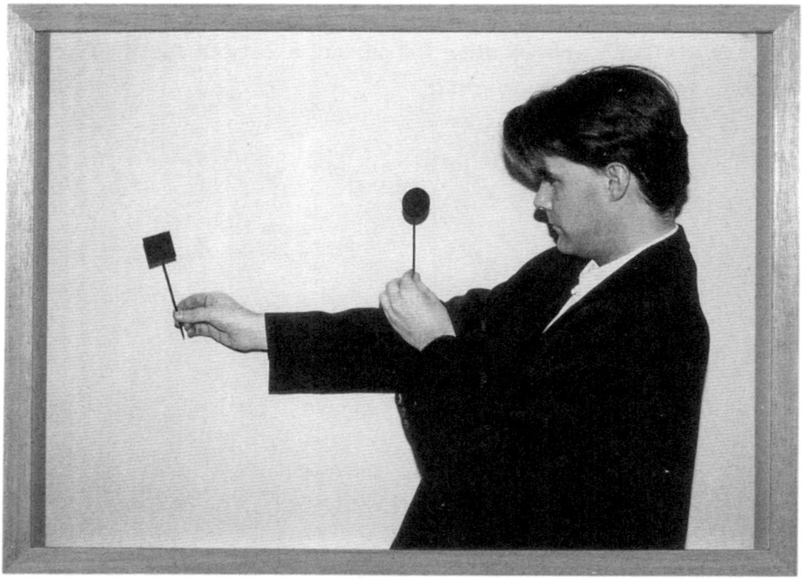

Device Box (above) with When Peter Nagy of Gallery Nature Morte looks at the square, the near circle appears doubled. The reverse is true when the circle is fixated, one of seven photographs from The Art Dealers Optical Tests, 1987
Device Box: wood, paper, metal, paint, 17" x 25"; b/w photograph, 12 1/2" x 17"; the suite of photographs is an edition of two.

Brie Popcorn

Subtitled, "An interview with the directors of Nature Morte Gallery by Rex Reason,"* this text was published in Real Life Magazine 11/12, Winter 1983.

PETER NAGY Wouldn't it be great if Leo Castelli were like Burger King, and you had a Leo Castelli[1] in every town across America?

REX REASON Franchises … well, it's like that now with him.

PETER NAGY Yeah, and then we need a farm system. It could be so big! One in Indianapolis, one in Cape Cod. The farm system would be set up so that young artists could get experience in other parts of the country and then slowly feed into New York …

ALAN BELCHER The only problem at this point is that there is a lot of work being shown, written about, and sold that is very quickly appreciated; it's either very graphic or aggressive or colorful or pleasing, illustrational, and it just pops off of the wall instantly and people say, "Oh, yeah, this is a really nice painting," without thinking about it twice. But maybe this is just the first step.

REX REASON Toward what: the grand democratization of art?

ALAN BELCHER Perhaps.

PETER NAGY Often the seed of art comes out of the lower

class or middle class, and an intellectual elite approves it. The elite fabricates the career. At this point, the New York Art World in 1983 is the ultimate cliché of the American dream. Keith Haring is the Henry Ford of the '80s.

REX REASON But that is evidence of a profound change, of what kind of success an artist wants to have or what kind of artist to be. All these middle-class kids going to art school and learning about art in universities are then shot out into a world in which they simply graft their art aspirations onto their middle-class aspirations. It's the diminution of the adversarial culture. They reject nothing. This happened almost without art knowing it.

PETER NAGY Hopefully, the dogma of art will rise above the dogma of business.

REX REASON I'm not sure it does. Art gains much of its meaning from the tension caused by its "otherness" and opposition to prevailing conditions.

PETER NAGY The need for opposition changes, and I'm not sure that's art's role anyway. I've always thought if there were a utopia it would be when everyone is an artist and everyone is looking at every aspect of life as art … a total work of art, which many artists have done—Beuys, Warhol. Maybe the only really concrete way of achieving utopia is if everyone's a Joseph Beuys!

REX REASON Who's going to clean the streets? The people who naturally love doing that?

ALAN BELCHER *We* have jobs during the day.

PETER NAGY Due to massive hype and exposure, the art world is on the verge of becoming something it's never been before. More in the vein of popular culture, movies, television, fashion.

It's competing for that segment of Newsweek magazine, that four-page color spread.

REX REASON There's a statement attributed to you guys, "In the '50s everyone wanted to have a car, in the '60s and '70s everyone wanted to be a rock star, and in the '80s everyone wants to be an artist."

PETER NAGY Yeah, or a gallery owner.

ALAN BELCHER A painter.

PETER NAGY In '78 you open a nightclub, in '82 you open a gallery, a day club. The whole change in atmosphere can be attributed to Mary Boone-ism and Julian Schnabelism. It's the mass movement of popular youth culture from music into art. The whole music thing coalesced in the late '70s, and now our stars aren't Debbie Harry and Joey Ramone, they're Keith Haring and Futura 2000. Music flopped into art. Mary Boone gave confidence to a lot of young artists. Artists were taken more seriously, getting more press, so at least it seemed like the market, the whole environment, was much more open to younger artists, to unknown people, because of the success of the biggies. The general excitement in the art world overall ...

ALAN BELCHER Of course you get a lot of schlocky work because you have more people looking at and thinking about art that had never previously done it. But it also means that soon in the future we'll be able to have art everywhere.

REX REASON How do you feel about trademark-ism in art: objects that are instantly recognizable as made by a certain artist?

PETER NAGY It's very important. It's the way our whole society functions.

ALAN BELCHER I think it's great. Especially now with such a large population.

PETER NAGY It's certainly necessary for survival. We're both artists, and we have a gallery, but we tell every artist we handle, "Look, you're going to have to be as much your own dealer as we're going to be. You've got to hype your career just as much."

ALAN BELCHER If not more.

PETER NAGY We don't want you just sitting home making paintings.

REX REASON Not to be gloomy, but what is that attitude's effect on art? Trademark-ism indicates to me that an artist constrains creative development to the issues raised by the last series of pieces, conceptual serialism … further variations on the last theme in order to support its place in the market.

PETER NAGY My background is in media, and I've always seen that as a necessary part of it—so you could get that necessary feedback so you could go out and make more. It's just economics.

REX REASON The trademark is so you can <u>sell</u> it so you can make more. To say, "Oh, it's just economics," is to sweep it under the rug—and definitely relegate the content and quality of what is made to economic concerns, which I think is newish, certainly "after-Warhol."

PETER NAGY You're advocating a quicker turnover of the product?

REX REASON I'm saying I'd rather make William Wegman's drawings than Robert Longo's: there's an infinitely greater area of play that one gives oneself access to.

PETER NAGY You feel the artists' desires should be the bottom line.

REX REASON Yes, as far as the content and range of art is concerned.

PETER NAGY I don't see trademark as being that limited. Beuys has a trademark, but it's more of a material or an essence. There's always been a lot of trademark in art: Duchamp, Man Ray had a lot of it.

REX REASON No! They were completely not about that. The variation in the look and content of the object was for them much broader.

PETER NAGY I disagree. And Sherrie Levine introduced a further confusion, she took on this sort of martyr position: when you don't have to worry about being original, you're completely liberated. Copies of copies of copies is generative, and regenerative. And most of those artists who are strongly trademarked are doing other things that you never see, like Twombly's 3-D collages.

ALAN BELCHER Warhol's "Piss Paintings."

REX REASON Are people "expressing" themselves all over the map?

PETER NAGY People don't have anything to express, except the trademark. The void is inside us. We hardly have original thoughts all the time. We're fed information all the time.

ALAN BELCHER We're filters.

PETER NAGY We're hardly ourselves. You make an object to fill the void. You're nothing inside so you make a concrete object to see yourself. It's the concrete self.

ALAN BELCHER Especially if you die tomorrow. But you're not just filling it, you're saying something about it as well. And a gallerist just picks out of the atmosphere bits one relates to.

PETER NAGY You look for things that remind you of what you never remembered before.

REX REASON You're known as having a policy of no-policy, as far as aesthetics are concerned.

PETER NAGY That harmed us during our first year because the media didn't have a label they could pin on us. We knew that we didn't want to show what was being seen in most galleries, which was neo-expressionist figurative paintings. The 90% of that that you see is pretty useless. So from the beginning that was our only direction—we knew we weren't showing neo-expressionism. We were going to concentrate on other media and other imagery, and mix things up. Pluralism certainly didn't die with the '70s.

ALAN BELCHER Our policy of no-policy is one of survival: we feel that if we become known for a certain type of work, then people will only come to see us for a few months, and then never come again. We want a long shelf life.

PETER NAGY But we are getting more focused—it takes a gallery a few years, especially when you've started out really fast like us, it takes a few years to coalesce into a style. We're on our way to having a definite outlook.

ALAN BELCHER It's becoming more apparent: we tend to go for either the primitive or the slick, the hard-edged.

PETER NAGY Serious, intelligent work: those are our artful requirements. We never wanted to show clichéd East Village art—kitschy religious art or punky aggressive paintings. Even though 90% of our artists are working in the East Village, they're certainly not making that kind of stuff.

REX REASON How do you find your artists?

ALAN BELCHER They find us, mostly. Friends of friends.

PETER NAGY We still look at slides, and it's getting a little out of hand, but we feel it's something we have to do, to at least let people know there's an outlet. FUN^2 won't look at anything.

ALAN BELCHER Our shows are planned through April, and we've got most of the people we want to work with, so even though we're looking at slides, it's a little futile.

PETER NAGY Even if we liked the work we couldn't deal with it for a year.

REX REASON Do you see yourselves functioning as filters for the gallery system?

ALAN BELCHER That's one of our motives: one of our principles is to show new people previously unshown, and then having them get shows in other galleries afterwards. Also having dealers, collectors, writers, coming here and knowing they're going to be competing with each other.

PETER NAGY We don't have a stable. We don't sign people.

ALAN BELCHER Basically we always want to have fun showing work—if we had to keep showing the same people we'd just hire someone to run the place.

PETER NAGY We're not threatened by people stealing our artists.

ALAN BELCHER We're all for it—if they steal it just makes us valid, it proves we're showing what people respond to.

REX REASON	But of course this completely plugs into the extant gallery system. It' s the food chain—artists are plankton, you guys are minnows, and so on.

ALAN BELCHER	But it's working.

PETER NAGY	We didn't feel revolt against that system. Basically that system has a lot of good in it, and it takes care of a lot of artists.

REX REASON	In order to draw meaning from the incredible variety of objects, styles, and aims that constitutes pluralism, doesn't pluralism presuppose such an intense and constant involvement with the art world that it continues and accentuates the ghettoization of artists? Kosuth said the only people who pay attention to art are artists, anyway, so let's just admit it and make art for artists, and that spirals upward to esoterica.

PETER NAGY	I live breathe think sleep art.

ALAN BELCHER	There's nothing else to do now.

PETER NAGY	It's been ghetto-ized but it's self-preservation.

ALAN BELCHER	Everybody has their ghetto.

PETER NAGY	Golf, whatever. The only way in which pluralism works against us is with the collectors—they may see two things they like next to four things they don't like. That doesn't make them shell out the money too fast.

ALAN BELCHER	The product really needs packaging and promotion to sell it. And if it's not shown a lot and written about, then it's not packaged.

PETER NAGY	As far as ads go, the art world is the pits right now.

ALAN BELCHER It's all just type.

PETER NAGY Mary Boone, Sperone Westwater … it's the same little format every month. We have lots of art magazines from the '60s and the ads were art in themselves.

REX REASON What's the difference between art and any other product?

PETER NAGY In the marketplace, nothing. Art is something different when you're making it and when you're admiring it—the difference is in the quality of the consumption.

REX REASON So in the marketplace the art object is without pretensions to meaning?

PETER NAGY Pretty much.

REX REASON Maybe there's not enough time anymore for the deep stuff—things keep moving faster and faster.

PETER NAGY That's the natural flow of society—things get more and more complex, weirder and weirder, faster and faster. You have to learn to just groove on it.

REX REASON Do you invest less and less of yourself with each micro-revolution?

PETER NAGY Yeah. The key to survival is staying on top of the wave.

REX REASON Surfing.

ALAN BELCHER Stay on the board.

REX REASON You guys are so modern. What do you look for in an object? What qualities?

ALAN BELCHER Right now we like either black, white, and gray, or generic color.

PETER NAGY We're pretty anti-color.

REX REASON By generic you mean red as "red" rather than modulations of it?

ALAN BELCHER Yeah.

PETER NAGY So many people bring us slides that are just like Salle, Basquiat, or Roberto Juarez. These poor kids are out there going to the galleries and they say, "This is what I have to do to have a show." So they run home and paint them. We don't want that. We want stuff we've never seen in a gallery before.

REX REASON And what do you think is the best art? What influenced the shaping of your taste?

ALAN BELCHER Right now, we like pretty classic late modern stuff: Pop art, Paolozzi, Indiana for logos, Duchamp, Manzoni, Beuys, Klein. Scarpitta's a favorite of mine.

PETER NAGY We think Op art is highly underrated, Bridget Riley. That's corporate psychedelia, the orgasm of modernism.

ALAN BELCHER We started the gallery because we really just wanted to get our voices in.

PETER NAGY And chose the name "Nature Morte" for its '50s-jazz, pseudo-continental appeal. Ersatz European. Franco-American Chef Boy-ar-dee.

ALAN BELCHER We wanted to be the Leper Gallery.

PETER NAGY But then I thought of the Wallet Gallery.

REX REASON Great!

ALAN BELCHER We gotta get MasterCharge. I want to see the stickers in the window.

PETER NAGY We'd love to build a sliver.

ALAN BELCHER Coop Nature Morte, Cafe Nature Morte, Cinema Nature Morte Quad.

PETER NAGY Brie popcorn. See, that's what I mean about trademarks: the image is succinct but the meaning can't be battened down.

NOTES

* Rex Reason was a pseudonym occasionally used by Robbins early in his publication history. The name refers to an actor featured in <u>This Island Earth</u>, 1955, a B-grade science-fiction film.

1. Leo Castelli (1907-1999) was one of the most influential gallerists of the 20th century. The New York-based art dealer launched the careers of Jasper Johns, Robert Rauschenberg, Andy Warhol, Roy Lichtenstein, Frank Stella, and many others.

2. A reference to Fun Gallery, run by Patti Astor. It was the hottest, hypest East Village gallery at the time.

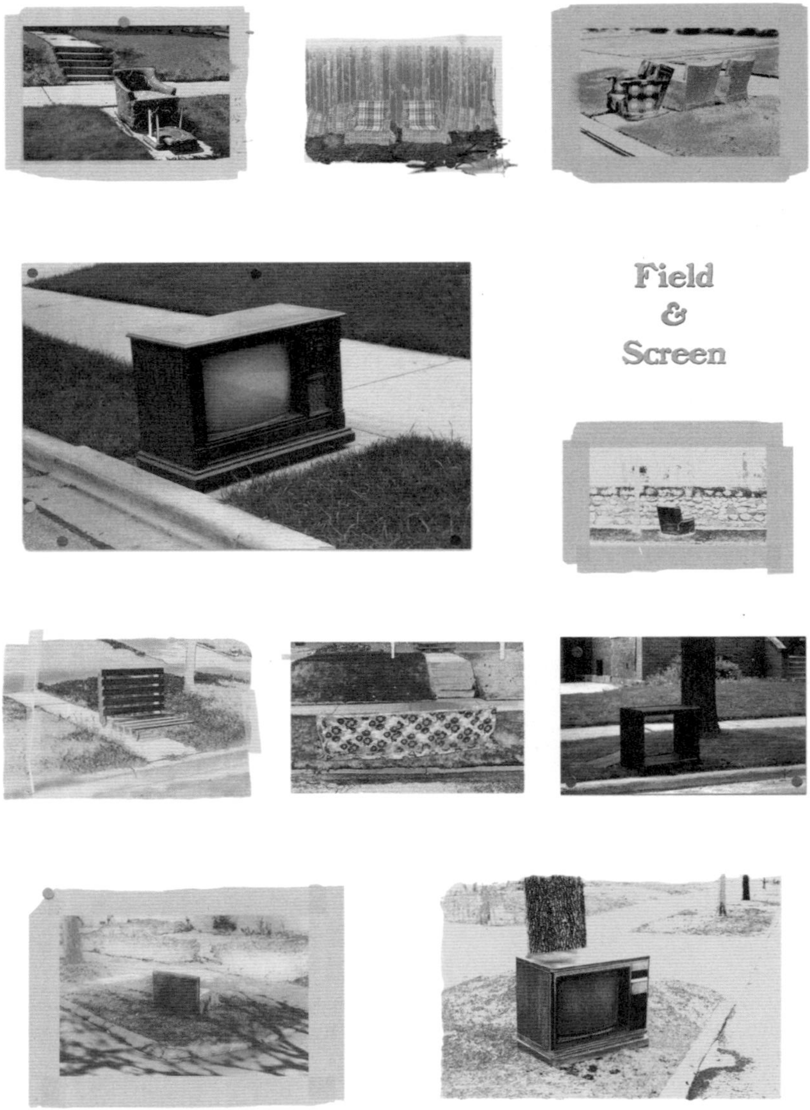

Field and Screen 2, 2003
digital print, 33" x 46 1/4"

The House of Deadpan

The author was employed by Andy Warhol Enterprises between November 1979 and February 1981. This text is previously unpublished.

THE UNITED STATES IS MAN-MADE, AN INVENTION—A CONCEPT OF PLACE, REALIZED. The structure of this new world has echoed down, generation after generation, through and into citizens for whom the freedom to create a personal world of satisfaction—the pursuit of happiness—is written into the code that organizes the nation. That pursuit of happiness clause inclines some American souls to invent their <u>own</u> new world—their own context. Or at least to <u>try</u>: not everyone can meet the challenge. Context has some impersonality about it; it's larger than any person and thus, if it's context you're inventing, your wild and free and ungovernable subjectivity will have necessarily to intersect with some sort of system, whether found or invented. When an invented context allows for the presentation of other people, events, objects, or information, that's a <u>platform</u>.

Impresario Phineas Taylor Barnum, the great 19th-century showman, was a <u>platformist</u>: an inventor of venues or of strategies for the public presentation of people, events, objects, or information—in short, an artist at presenting others. Barnum's first foray into platforming occurred in the 1830s with his purchase of one Joice Heth, an elderly black woman who claimed to be the infant George Washington's nursemaid. Sensing the theatrical value of her claims while suspending judgement about their veracity (he could neither prove nor disprove them), Barnum paid three thousand dollars for Heth and promoted her in what proved to be an exceedingly successful road show. His next big discovery was midget "General" Tom Thumb. Midgets and dwarves had enjoyed a long history at court but Tom Thumb of Connecticut added an American angle. He was independent, educated, a wit—and, for Barnum, another success: the General was even received by the English queen, Victoria. Following Tom Thumb, Barnum scored another success with singer Jenny Lind, "the Swedish nightingale," brought over from Europe and toured before American audiences to near-riotous acclaim. And for decades on went Barnum's presentations.

An old black woman whose place in history could neither be proved nor disproved, a pint-sized bon vivant, a Swedish songstress celebrated, in part, for her lack of artifice—what did these and other "acts" have in common? Why, P.T. Barnum, of course. Impresario Barnum was the reliable constant in the ever-changing show he offered his fellow Americans. He effectively made his taste a validating context: audiences never paid to see Barnum himself but to see what Barnum had found, or discovered, or just thought worth their while ... Eventually, his reputation became such that people bought tickets because a certain performer, he or she or it (Jumbo the elephant comes to mind), was being presented by Barnum. They trusted him to put on a good show, and he delivered. An eye for talent? Sure, but Barnum's impresario instincts were far more sophisticated than that. He saw that talent wasn't essential to an act's potential success. Properly presented, the natural—people just being themselves, provided they were the right people—could be just as good a draw as a unique or rare ability. And why? The species had an innate curiosity about itself; people were interested in other people. This insight of Barnum's, a simple idea but profound when implemented, argued on behalf of the fullest possible variety of human experience. And, ever desiring to be of service, he complied. The rationale for his eclectic selections became part of the audience's experience of his shows, of course—their subtext. Wittingly or not, his audiences shelled out for contact with or exposure to an abstraction: Barnum's enterprise.

It all added up to a powerful presentational aesthetic that was transparent, modern—and distinctly American. The egalitarian DNA that had been encoded in the US Constitution, and which in turn the Constitution encoded into the culture, seeks and finds implementation through the American platformist. Benjamin Franklin, with his invention of the public library, is one example. P.T. Barnum is another. Toward the end of the 19th century and over the course of the 20th, other, equally ambitious and innovative platformists would create the telephone, the movie studio, radio and TV networks, finally culminating in a World Wide Web, which transcended national boundaries entirely. Always, the most fundamental, lasting platforms allowed the display of a mind-boggling amount and variety of human ability; at the same time, they centered tremendous power among the individuals who owned and operated them. In an era of media empires and communication moguls, vast platforms, chiefly based, as it happened, on electronics and chemicals, were controlled by a few. (Some, such as William Randolph Hearst and William Paley, were individuals who, like Barnum, were closely identified with their platforms; other ownership arrangements were more corporate and anonymous.) The era of the Systems Man had begun.

The first person to identify the <u>comic</u> potential of the essential nation-building activity of platform-creation, and to implement it in concrete terms, was Andy Warhol. It's one thing to be a Systems Man; to take being one as your <u>subject</u> is something else. It's a fundamentally ironical position. Warhol understood that. He also recognized the kernel of comedy embedded at the center of the platformist's personal location—specifically, the simultaneous passivity and power of The One Who Presents—and then proceeded to push it about as hard as it could be pushed. Aggressively forging a profound confusion of Presenter and Presented, Warhol remains the most extreme and influential comedian of this, the Systems era.

Technological innovation—machinery—made Warhol's comedy possible. Whereas Barnum put ancient Joice Heth on stages from Boston to Charleston, Warhol filmed 1960s socialite Baby Jane Holzer with a Bolex for the duration of a single three-minute 16mm film reel, then projected it. Though he shares Barnum's democratic, collection-and-presentation obsession, he aggressively modernizes it by shifting it onto recordable, reproducible media. The leap is enormous, and its implications radiate outward in every direction. And this transpositional strategy is hardly limited to the Screen Test reels; Warhol's other early movies echo Barnum, too. The Screen Tests (someone just looking into, and being looked at by, a lens), and films like _Sleep_, _Kiss_, and _Eat_ (film records of, respectively, sleeping, kissing, eating) present basic human acts as subjects worthy of an audience's time and consideration. Exploring recordable media's capacity to collapse stage time and literal time, and presenting performance in an everyday manner while elevating the everyday to the level of a performance, Warhol pioneers a strategic naturalism. Never a fantasist, ever a re-presenter of the actual, like any good comedian the Pope of Pop required only two elements: the real, and an attitude toward it.

Thus, as Barnum had, Warhol established a context for the presentation of things that already existed. What made Warhol's activity _comedy_ was his understanding that none of it _needed_ to be presented again. It was already real; showing it again didn't make it more real. Something about the act of presenting it again was, had to be, a form of theater, a sort of joke on the real. Everything produced by his Factory—its films; its fabrication of film "superstars"; its re-presenting in objects and paintings the potent images circulating through and via mass media and consumer society; its magazine, _Interview_—worked some angle on this comic insight.

Warhol wasn't just interested in being a successful, independent platformist, of course. He was interested in _platforming_, as an activity, a social transaction, and a condition of mind; he extended the Barnumian model of public presence by thematizing it. Consistently aligning his psychology and his aesthetic sensibility with the machinery and media by which he engineered his presentation strategies, namely the absolute neutrality of the camera or tape-recorder, Warhol transformed himself into an emblem of his presentational strategy. He sought to become, and succeeded in becoming, a figure who never judged and endlessly presented—and endlessly permitted, too, for to withhold judgment is to permit. The world had never seen anyone choose to turn themselves into an emblem of the machine's penetration of human experience. No wonder he made people nervous. For a great many people Andy's game was, and still is, a little too modern.

The showman is part of the show. Barnum knew it, and applied the knowledge. Warhol knew it, too, and obsessively foregrounded the platformist's process—observing, selecting, engaging the technologies of presenting—as part of the comedy. In P.T. Barnum's day the confusion of background and foreground had only been implicit; Andy Warhol, by contrast, used it actively and aggressively—he concretized the confusion, made it the point. Distilling the abstractions of passivity and power implicit in the platformist's work, he lay bare yet more pure abstraction: the abstraction of "people," the abstraction of "presenting."

From the vantage of his theatrical sensibility, any and every form of reproduction was regarded as, in essence, a parodic version of its source, a parodic version of the original—a parodic version of life. Such a formulation is neither incorrect nor an exaggeration. Significantly, it also came with an equally true corollary: Any system that exists to reproduce aspects of the experience of reality is, in essence, a parodic system. "The movies," say, or "television," or "publishing," or "art"—all of these are parodic systems. That we respond to them, that they make us feel or think, that they enhance life, doesn't alter the fact that they are parodic systems.

When Warhol applied these insights at his Factory, he hit upon a truly astonishing paradox. The paradox went something like this: if you parody a system of production without emburdening the parody with additional editorial (i.e. in a deadpan manner), whatever artifact that is produced through that parody—Brillo boxes or movie stars—will be, within the context of that parody, authentic. Genuine, somehow. For real, somehow. The Brillo Boxes (1964) are a parody of form, yes, and a parody of packaging. More profoundly, they also parody a system of production. Within the logic-system of the parody, *which is perfectly consistent unto itself*, they do lay claim to authenticity. (Theirs may be the integrity of plastic, but plastic *does* possess an integrity.) Warhol, a very smart man, recognized these artifacts' curious claim on authenticity. (Just as significantly, he also knew that authenticity to be *enough*. He knew when to stop. He knew that to add any other information to something that had already arrived at authenticity was mere aestheticization or decoration or editorial, and thus *gesture-obscuring*, and thus unnecessary.)

This powerful deadpan attitude was integral to Warhol's operation, and appeared everywhere throughout it. Warhol's Factory was the world's first house of deadpan. Everything turned out by the Factory became, in effect, a prop in an elaborate, cottage-industry parody of the communication wing of the industrial revolution. Andy signed his name to parodies of systems of production. He may have talked all the time about stars and glamour, but he did so, at least in part, because he didn't want to give the game away. By directing our attention to the shiny surface he was able to distract us from the fact that *his* eye was actually on William Randolph Hearst, Louis B. Mayer, William S. Paley, and other 20th-century moguls of mass presentation. Like Paley and Hearst and the rest, Warhol ran a communications empire of his own invention. As they had, in his movies and his magazine—even in his system for making static visual art—he'd created a platform that allowed him to present the talents of other people. To Warhol, Hearst and Mayer were stars in the way he, Andy, was a star.

That Andy's empire was smaller than those run by the men he modeled himself after is entirely beside the point; like their empires, his was global in reach and responsive to the boss's personal whim. Hearst, Paley, Warhol … each could get to just about anyone they wanted. Not only that, but, as Warhol intuited at an early stage of the Factory's operations, his position actually came with certain distinct advantages. At the Factory, there were no stockholders to please, no board of directors who could remove him. A free and independent mogul who could run his business as he liked, he could pursue, grow infatuated with, present, parade, hype, grow bored with and discard whatever and whomever he liked. He was the first independent cultural figure to implement the knowledge that in the decentralized reality brought about by the distribution of cameras, tape recorders, and printing presses, what counts is not seizing the means of production but instead seizing the means of <u>rep</u>roduction. He was—uniquely—free to pursue his self-invented position in the purest possible way, namely, for its own sake, as an idea, just to see what kind of world the full-throttle pursuit of the idea might create. It was a position that was free enough, even, to make fun of itself.

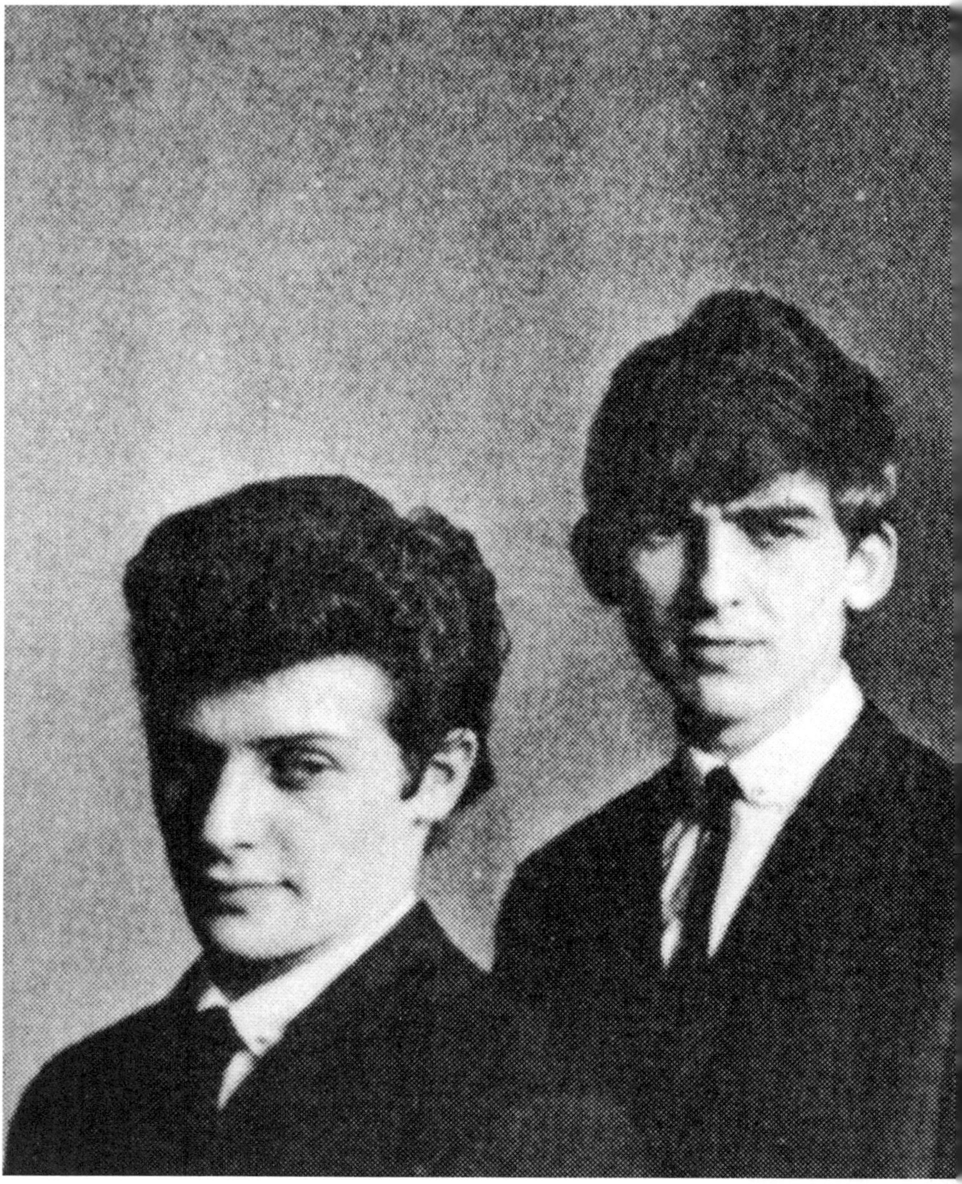

Richard Prince and David Robbins, Fifth Beatle #2, 1985
Cibachrome photograph, 6 1/2" x 9 1/2"

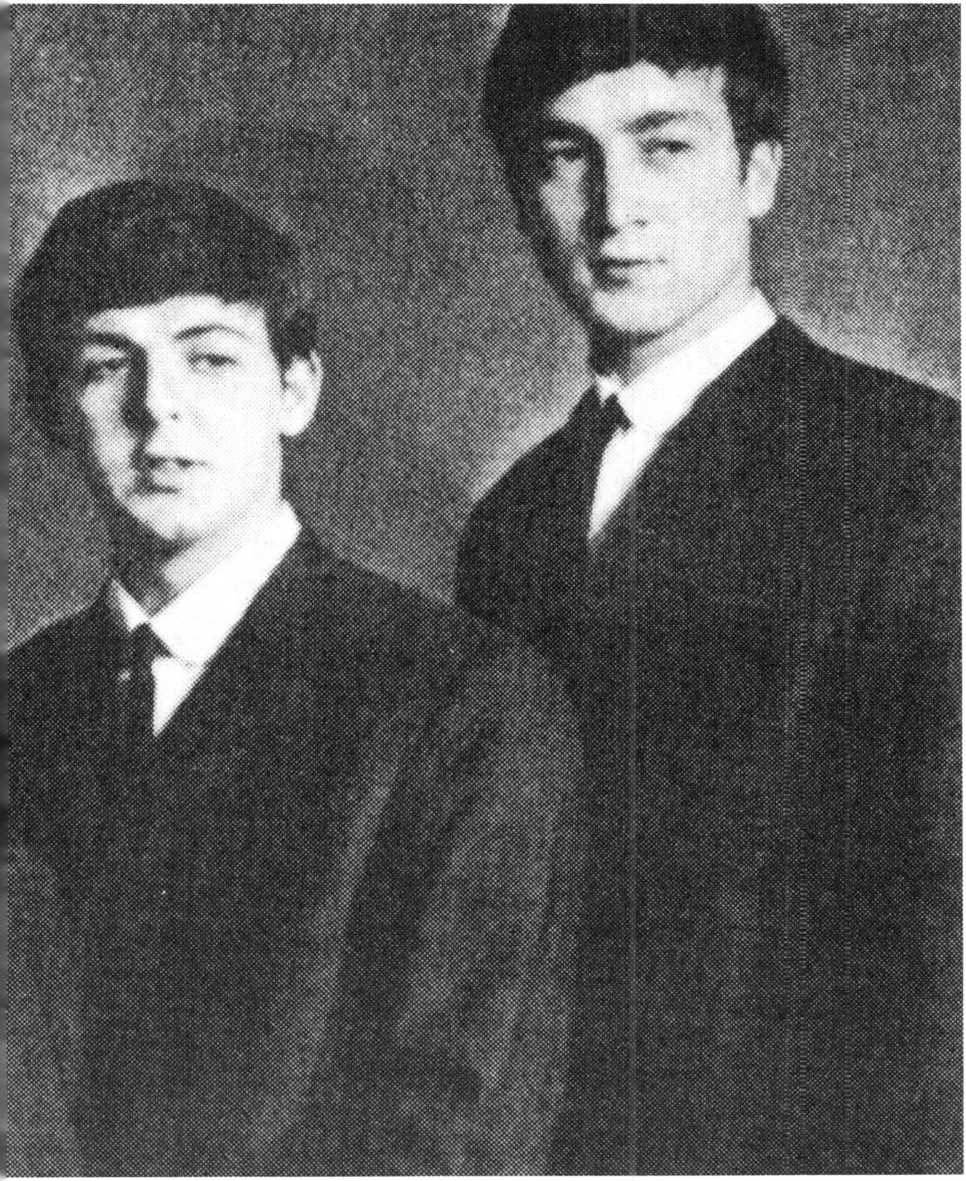

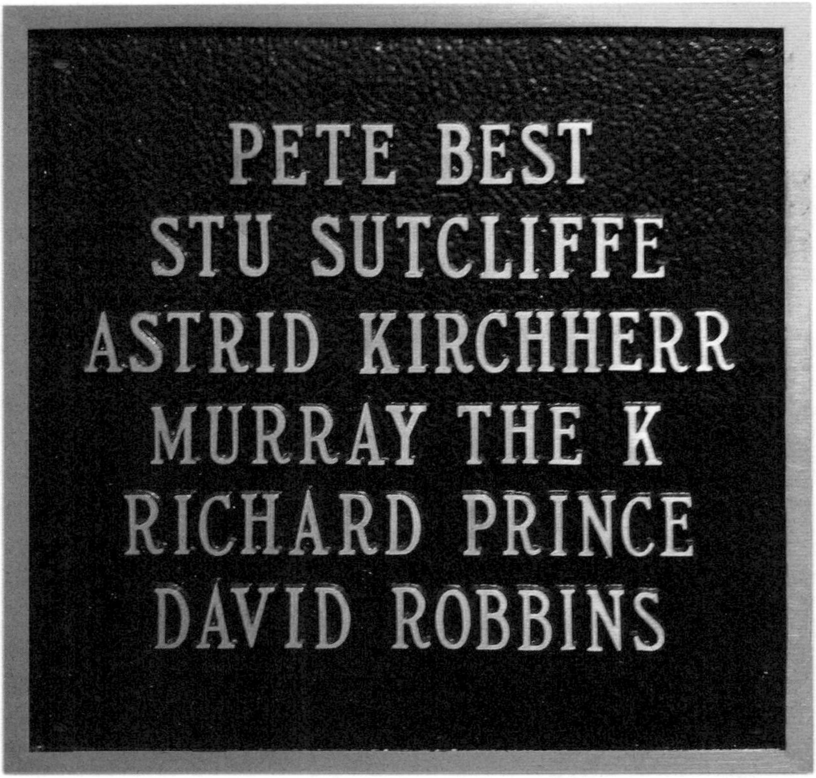

Richard Prince and David Robbins, Fifth Beatle #3, 1986
bronze plaque, 8" x 8"

Interview with Richard Prince

Originally published in Aperture magazine, #100, Fall 1985.

DAVID ROBBINS We've become proficient at interpreting the subtle subtexts of mass-culture images, like a generation of social phrenologists, so much so that whereas Godard used to speak in the '60s of his films being concerned with "the children of Marx and Coca-Cola," the popularization of semiotics in the '70s and '80s has spawned a generation we might aptly term "the children of Barthes and Coca-Cola."

A lot of the critical support that your work has received has been for its alleged "deconstruction of the advertising image." Do you see your work as being engaged with this?

RICHARD PRINCE To some extent I'm interested in what we produce and what we consume. What we think we own and what we think we control. Do we own and control our TV sets, that kind of thing. I'm interested in the assumptions we make in relation to those interests. I have read where my work is a deconstruction of the advertising image, but that's an extremely narrow reading of the work, if you ask me. Madison Avenue's decisions don't particularly interest me. My work is not about illustration, allegory, irony. I'm interested in what some of these images, which happen to appear in the advertising sections of magazines, imagine. I like the presumptuousness and the shame usually associated with these images. I like how unbelievable these images appear to be.
How psychologically hopped-up a watch can look! I've never felt

threatened by these images and certainly never felt compelled to buy what's represented in the advertisements. Sometimes, most of the time, what's represented is just wishful thinking. I'm interested in wishful thinking.

DAVID ROBBINS How do you locate your images?

RICHARD PRINCE My art supply store is a magazine store. I look at magazines in stores, in friends' houses, on planes … I just went to Burbank, California. They have one of the biggest magazines stores in the world. Sometimes it takes a long time to give my pictures the that's-the-way-they're-supposed-to-look look. You have to look at a lot of magazines to find four images, for example, that appear to be normal and work together.

DAVID ROBBINS I like your work because it zooms in on the dreamy unrealities that are constantly directed toward us by television, the movies, advertising, magazines: the public fictions in which we are steeped, images that other people want us to consume. If I turn on my TV, I get hundreds of "personalities" floating toward me, and it's hard after 25 years of viewing to know where they stop and I start. Surely most art just adds more fiction—personal fictions—without in any way clarifying our relationship to such images.

RICHARD PRINCE Sometimes I think all my work got sent away for. You know, like I saved up my box tops, sent them off to Battle Creek, Michigan, and this is what I got back in the mail. "Baking soda makes the submarine go under water and propels it!" But I'm not just making another fiction. That wouldn't interest me at all. I'm interested in the fiction becoming true. You know what I mean? It wouldn't surprise me if the day came when the earth really did stand still. I'm interested in the idea of making nonfiction art. In other words, I'm interested in making a fiction look true. It seems to me that trying to present something believable might be about asking too much. I'm interested in my photographs asking too much.

DAVID ROBBINS Certainly the fictions are out there, thriving away. But how does one go about making nonfiction art?

RICHARD PRINCE The fact that my pictures already exist in public helps to establish their reality. I obviously don't make the images up. My style is hopefully a convincing style. Rephotography is photographing what's already been determined, so obviously rephotography is about over-determination. Basically, I'm not interested in impressions, and I like to think I'm in the habit of telling the truth. I always liked the TV shows To Tell the Truth, Truth or Consequences, and Who Do You Trust? Okay, panelists, let's turn all the cards over.

DAVID ROBBINS The speculative image has been central to the art of this century: the artist's feelings about a given image as the image. You seem disinclined to operate this way. Why are you so suspicious of the speculative?

RICHARD PRINCE This is the scenario: The Perry Mason Show, right? And I have to appear before the court. The court doesn't admit impressions or an expression about something. The judge says, "Okay, mister, what makes your picture so real? Back it up!" The jury pipes up and says, "We already have our own nightmares and dreams, we don't need yours … we don't want what's you, ya schmuck. What have you been doing all your life, living in the Black Forest in a castle? What do you think you are: special? Show us evidence!" Perry Mason throws my photographs on the mercy of the court, and the court takes one look at them and lets me off scot-free. My family breaks down and cries. Reporters shake my hand and take my picture. And I get a proposal for marriage three days later from one of the members of the jury. How do you like it? I'm going to call it I'm So Excited. Simply put, I'm not interested in people having to take my word for anything.

DAVID ROBBINS Your work departs from much of what came before it—and is distinct certainly from all expressionisms—in that it is not based on the objective correlative. That is, the traditional artist manipulates inanimate material of one kind or another to communicate an experience he/she has already had, or to recreate in the viewer an experience that the viewer has already had. That's something that has always bothered me about art, that fundamentally nostalgic impulse. The wish for childhood, the curatorial wish. Such work may look really wild, may be all frothy and rabid with paint, but with such work our understanding of the nature of art stays just where it "belongs," it doesn't question either its social position or psychological use. In contradistinction, your work doesn't seem to be about recreating an experience the viewer has already had.

RICHARD PRINCE Or that I've already had. I tend to take pictures that I've never seen, pictured, or observed in my own day-to-day routine. I like to try to figure out where I fit in, my relation to an image that I have no memory of. Just what is part of my experience? My relationship turns out to be more about my personality than my personal feelings or experiences. You know, sometimes I think I wouldn't even dream of the pictures I take.

DAVID ROBBINS Right, pop memory: Is it Ella or is it Memorex* and what the hell has either to do with me?

RICHARD PRINCE Yes. So it's a species of discovery, surely, but it's not a rediscovery. It's not nostalgia, even if the pictures can be associated with particular pop histories. I have something to do with that picture, personally, because of that picture's personality, because of my personality—I wouldn't want to say otherwise. But it's not a personal reaction. I'm not knee-jerking against the picture. I'm not trying to put any kind of distance between myself and the subject matter. On the contrary: I'm trying to get as close to that picture as possible.

DAVID ROBBINS The art historian Svetlana Alpers writes about 17th-century Dutch painting in a similar way. She says that the Dutch "side-step the issue of style or manner almost completely to put nature seen before personal style or self … "

RICHARD PRINCE I like to take an unbelievable picture and present it as normally as possible. I like to present it with a sensation of normalcy. I like to think of normality as the next special effect.

DAVID ROBBINS How did you arrive at the decision to rephotograph magazine reproductions?

RICHARD PRINCE Well, certain social facts helped to point the way. The '60s had created an atmosphere whereby the manipulation and control of consumption, of the flow of products and images, became quite accessible, quite understandable by the average guy. I always liked the <u>promises</u> that went along with some of these products. You know, like "Relief in just two hours." The awakening of desire. These authorless images are very good at living it up. I mean, I wouldn't even mind being relieved <u>for</u> two hours.

DAVID ROBBINS And on top of the '60s came the one-two punch of Vietnam/Watergate, which really rattled people's belief in the authority of institutions—what intellectuals refer to as the "crisis of legitimation."

RICHARD PRINCE Yeah, and in this instance, the result of that sweeping skepticism was, for me, to stop getting my information from history. What's been presented as "history" of course has turned out to be the real fiction.

DAVID ROBBINS The official fiction. The deinstitutionalization, if we can use the word, of history is a pretty unsettling realization, from which we've seen half the nation freak out and seek an antidote in the nostalgia trip of Reagan. In any case, a different breed of art was bound to emerge from these social explosions.

RICHARD PRINCE Personally, I started practicing without a license. Not waiting for permission. I don't want to trivialize this realization. It takes a certain ability to perceive the fictiveness of history, and to proceed from there. To just decide one day, History is Fiction—it wasn't really that it was a shock, because it certainly makes sense, but once you realize it you have to come to terms with it, and begin to see the degree to which things have to do with representation. The tough part is, a lot of the time you're on your own.

DAVID ROBBINS When you began rephotographing in the late '70s, was it clear to you that your particular use of the camera—as a selector of already created images—paralleled another significant cultural change: namely, the tremendous increase in the unauthorized reproduction of music? A lot of music got transmitted and wound up in people's homes via cassettes, taping off the radio. The proliferation of New Wave and experimental music in the late '70s, with the attendant tiny independent labels, drew people's interest away from the corporate rock that had dominated the decade. Culture was becoming decentralized. I bring this up to show that ideas about "property" were in the air, as aestheticized politics.

RICHARD PRINCE I think the term at that time was "pirating." It was a business term. To me it was just stealing. "Appropriation" was a more sanitized version of the word. I'm interested when something offensive becomes respected. Taken for granted. I'm interested in being taken for granted. You know, marrying the sheriff's daughter.

DAVID ROBBINS How does one come to the decision to put a photograph or reproduction—in your case a magazine reproduction—in front of a camera? And how does one make the break whereby one goes from tearing the picture out of a magazine and pasting it so there is still an element of collage, to literally sticking the picture in front of the camera, photographing the picture, and presenting the result as a real photograph?

RICHARD PRINCE Frankly, part of what drew me to the idea of rephotography was the fact that I'd never really liked my work.

I'd sold paintings since the early '70s, had solo shows, was successful. But I never liked my work. Ever. Because I did it. Obviously, if you don't like your work, a logical alternative is to take someone else's—and call it yours. The activity of taking seemed reasonable. I started to think of the camera as a pair of electronic scissors. The public images I would take didn't need to be silkscreened or painted on or collaged. The photograph that I presented had to resemble, as much as possible, the photograph that had initially attracted me. It was a matter of being as presumptuous as the original picture. I was interested in the camera as a technological device rather than as a mechanical one. I'm interested in sitting at my desk with my hands folded neatly in my lap.

My notion of rephotography came about because I didn't want to aestheticize the picture and I didn't want to deal with collage. I didn't want to deal with a seam because, in fact, I wanted my picture to be believed by the audience.

DAVID ROBBINS The seamless real.

RICHARD PRINCE It's another ingredient that helps to suspend the disbelief that normally accompanies the viewing of unbelievable pictures. As far as I'm concerned, Freud was Montgomery Clift.

DAVID ROBBINS What does it feel like when you look through the camera at a two-dimensional image, essentially a "landscape"?

RICHARD PRINCE It's strange. It's as if I can suddenly distinguish between its manifest content and its latent content. It's like the picture starts to behave simply because I'm looking at it.

DAVID ROBBINS Much of what you've said points to a major shift in the conception of the camera. The modernist conception of the camera was at base a belief that the camera by its nature told the truth: the nature of the device, mechanically, was such that it was obligated to record accurately that which occurred before its lens. It's essentially a passive conception, with Warhol as the apotheosis of this presupposition. But by the beginning of the '70s, artists knew there was no particular reason to believe in the institutionalized truth-telling characteristics attributed to the camera: all other "governing bodies" were cast in doubtful light, and the camera's reportorial abilities came to be included. So, in the work of people like Robert Cumming and William Wegman, you start to see the concocting of overt lies that they would get the camera to believe. (In a way, it was what Avedon was doing in fashion photography in the '50s, photographing scenarios. It's also connected to what motion pictures have been involved with for years: seamless special effects.) Almost all of Wegman's work with Man Ray can be read this way. Our thinking changed from believing the camera told the truth to an understanding that the camera believes what it's told. Our current conception is that it is a dumb beast obligated by its very nature to do so. The camera will "believe" visual lies and report them as truths. So artists started to turn the camera's obligation to record accurately that which occurred before its lens against itself, and, I think, by extension, against the audience's prior willingness to believe the photographic truth. There is perhaps a sadism-in-the-service-of-truth here. In the late '70s and early '80s, artists started to make the lies less obvious, to remove the seams: Cindy Sherman, yourself, Sherrie Levine, Laurie Simmons, James Casabere, Jim Welling …

RICHARD PRINCE When I saw Cindy Sherman's pictures for the first time, I died. There's a picture she did of herself with a diver's mask on, swimming. That picture is really it. I love that picture. That's one picture I'd be prepared to brag on.

Your description seems pretty accurate, though I'm not sure whether one makes the "lying" more or less obvious by hiding the seam.

When I first started exhibiting these photographs, the reaction was not very … welcoming. Very few people liked them. But it's funny if I think about it now. People would say, "What do you mean it's a photograph of a photograph? What are you talking about?" What gave them a problem, I think, was that they couldn't understand what the actual object was. It wasn't like a collage. The literalness of the actual, physical object was disorienting. And the thing was, it looked like a photograph because it _was_ a photograph. They'd say things like, "What do you mean it's not your photograph?" Also, what I was rephotographing was a disaster. Four men looking in the same direction. Advertisements, models, accessories, pens, watches, cigarettes. Not very accommodating images. It was hard to locate _where_ the author was. Anyway, a lot of the reaction was defensive and silly. I was taking photographs; it wasn't like I was kidnapping the neighbors' ten-year-old boy.

DAVID ROBBINS As for your own use of the camera as electronic scissors: is there really such a tool?

RICHARD PRINCE Sure. It's used by art directors. You sit down at a terminal and _type_ a picture on the screen. Instead of pressing the shutter, you press a letter on a key. Any information you want in your picture has already been stored in the machine. It's just a question of entering a command. Aesthetically, I suppose, there's another kind of freedom involved in producing an image this way. I have a feeling that artists are becoming obsolete.

DAVID ROBBINS Do you think of your images as dead images?

RICHARD PRINCE No. I think my images are too good to be true.

DAVID ROBBINS If you are thinking of the camera as an electronic scissors which obviates physical collaging, what now is being collaged, juxtapositioned, against what?

RICHARD PRINCE My personality. "Who do I do."

When I was growing up, I liked buying what they used to call "personality posters." These things came out in the mid-'60s: large black-and-white posters of your favorite film stars. I'd go into Harvard Square on Saturday afternoon with my friends and we'd each pick one out and buy one. They only cost a dollar. I picked Steve McQueen. I always thought the choosing of a personality was in itself some kind of expression. It was enough. All my friends did it. We put them on our walls, in our bedrooms. I've just kept doing it.

DAVID ROBBINS You've just made your own, personalized the technology …

RICHARD PRINCE Yes. I guess you additionalize your own personality onto the image. The other things I had on my walls (this is when I was about 15 years old) were pictures of Jackson Pollock and Franz Kline. Not, you understand, pictures of their paintings but pictures of them. I was interested in the portrait of Pollock, not the paintings he did. His portrait looked it. Unbelievable. Posed. Self-conscious. Complete. Classic. Extreme. Just what an artist was supposed to look like.

DAVID ROBBINS So you're involved to some degree with mapping the contours of pop star fan identification. Like a pop scientist locating identity extenders.

RICHARD PRINCE I like to think that I make "hit" pictures. I try to put "I Heard It Through the Grapevine" in my pictures.

DAVID ROBBINS A hit means reciprocity, somehow. George Trow describes the hit as "it loves you because you love it because it's a hit."

RICHARD PRINCE My photographic "gangs" are about making hit pictures. Psychologically hopped up. "The best of." Instamatic ambience.

DAVID ROBBINS Do you ever think of the "gangs" as portraits of sub-cults, a locating of sub-cults? I ask this because I'm thinking that your work corresponds quite logically to a number of social facts. The decentralization of an institutionalized, dominant view of history coincides with or is responsible for both the rise of the special-interest lobbies in Washington and the incredible proliferation of magazines that occurred in the '70s—magazines specialized for every taste, every group ... So history becomes demography, the significant expression of preferences by large groups of people. If history is perceived as the official fiction, <u>if authority isn't believed</u>, then the concept of marginality, of the fringe or sub-cult, is obviated, because history is fragmented into lifestyle histories, with none predominating.

RICHARD PRINCE Specifically, the <u>Girlfriends</u> came from biker magazines. The <u>Girlfriends</u> is a new type of picture for me. The biker boys take pictures of their girlfriends and then send these pictures to a biker magazine, get them published, and then go out and buy the magazine. Strange. The consumer becomes the consumed. I don't think that's about being in a sub-cult. I imagine it's about wanting to be recognized by yourself.

DAVID ROBBINS It's the Fifth Beatle syndrome: wanting to be included in recorded, i.e. media, history.

RICHARD PRINCE Yes. We're interested in Stu Sutcliff and Pete Best. We're interested not just in "what happened," but in what <u>actually</u> happened. I'm interested in people who were almost Beatles.

DAVID ROBBINS That's one of the primary anxieties in New York: being left out of history.

RICHARD PRINCE "What becomes a legend most." I assume things like the Blackglama campaign** are about power and history. Lifestyles of the rich and famous. I'm kind of interested in the lifestyles of the poor and unknown. I don't know, I can't take power and history that seriously. Second banana is interesting to me. I'm not that stupid, to want to be top dog.

DAVID ROBBINS As your work has progressed, it's become more difficult to determine your sources. The early ones are pretty straightforward about their ad-image source, but around 1980 it opens up a lot more. Do you search for images that work together or do you just wait until they appear in publications?

RICHARD PRINCE Well, obviously I can only go after certain images, those without copyright or logo that fit within the 35mm frame. There was repetition, optically, in the early commodity photographs that I liked: four living-room interiors that look the same somehow but are all very different, very detailed. This similarity, this sameness within the difference, this *equivalence* was something I hoped would produce an official fiction. You know, a "look" that *appeared* to be reasonable. A look without question. It was when you turned around and went out the door that you got run over, hit from behind, flattened, floored, four on the floor, fuel injected. The boost comes in *after* you look at it. I'm interested in exactly when and where you're going to go out of control. I'm interested in delayed density.

Then in 1980 I made a series which appeared to be an obvious extension of the other work but which was a big change: three women, each looking to the left. The change is that I simply realized you could photograph black-and-white images with color film and it would give them a more even quality. It would create an equivalence that made them look even more real.

DAVID ROBBINS So in 1980 you began a discreet manipulation of the image.

RICHARD PRINCE I want to keep up or *in* … I wanted to keep *in* the habit of telling the truth. I started to try to simulate the technology of how the picture originally was presented in the magazine. Hopefully my pictures would look as up to date as the latest picture in the latest magazine. You know, it was like setting up an artificial reality to deal with what was already artificial. That's what I like about Jack Goldstein's work. Anyway, the pictures I was taking were *already* directed, managed, manipulated, retouched, and so on … I just thought mine had to be the same … just like theirs. I'm interested in the closest thing to the real thing.

DAVID ROBBINS Do you think of each series being your own campaign?

RICHARD PRINCE Sure. Sometimes they're like the Sunsets and sometimes they're like the Cowboys. It's sort of how 20th Century Fox could put out a comedy film one month, a horror film the next, and a Western after that. It's more like a movie than a campaign. I mean the Sunsets were an attempt to put on a show. I wanted the audience who came to the gallery to be entertained.

DAVID ROBBINS Did this interest in "putting on a show" lead somehow to the Entertainers series?

RICHARD PRINCE The "Entertainment Pictures" were similar to the "Sunsets" in that I wanted to, on one hand, produce a "look" that looked "bought," "produced," "managed." I started to collect actors' and actresses' publicity photos. It was like I was casting the next "show." I'd go to places where they worked. Nightclubs here in New York. I'd go backstage and watch them make up in the mirrors. Usually I got the pics from theater and nightclub managers. The movie Sweet Smell of Success, a film about the manipulation of small histories à la Walter Winchell, is in those pictures. Let's see, what else … I liked that a lot of these performers would appear in the newspaper columns with one name, usually their first and always re-spelled. Like Laoura or Nikki. The identity was so specific they each became a John Doe. I'm not sure who said it, Barbara Kruger or Kate Linker: "You are not yourself." That's pretty good. You know, it's like, what do you mean I'm not myself?

DAVID ROBBINS What accounts for the jazzed-up backgrounds in the Entertainers? Were you parodying the feel of those places?

RICHARD PRINCE What surrounds the entertainer—the visual jazz, the graphics, the colors—is an environment that originally surrounded the picture when I first saw it. I would see these picture in windows at the theaters and nightclubs and the windows would always be blacked out around the publicity picture and the colors would be fluorescent and there'd be a lot of blinking lights about. I don't make this stuff up. I want to be faithful to the content of what the original photograph imagined.

DAVID ROBBINS I think there is a very interesting development in the isolation of kinds of identity in your work, in the function of the people actually pictured. You begin with anonymous models, normalized in normal environments. The _Sunsets_ introduced normal human activities—a day at the beach—to photographically manipulated environments. The _Cowboys_ are people portraying cowboys, American exotics, actors hiding their acting in real landscapes which read as settings. They are participating in their artificialized landscape quite actively. The _Generics_ series picture the models associated with some product, acting out, simulating their enjoyment. The _Entertainers_ then move to portraits of actual actors, whose product is clearly themselves, but they are marginal actors at the bottom end of things, what remains of the nightclub circuit, waiting to crack the big time. Then the pictures of sub-cult stars: rock stars and artists. Now a portrait of Phyllis Diller, an actual actress, or demi-actress, whose function is entertainment but who exists outside the central spotlight, in some way, at this point—the tense that exists when one speaks of "has been" or "never was." All allow their images to jump, in one way or another, through the hoops of commerce.

In sum I think you are portraying various levels of image power: in effect, levels of franchisement.

RICHARD PRINCE The kinds of identity I picture are pretty much identities that are out of character. The Phyllis Diller portrait was about being out of character. It was a portrait of _her_, not her as an entertainer. It was about herself. To be yourself and still be out of character was what that portrait was about. I'm interested in being yourself and being out of character at the same time.

DAVID ROBBINS It's a kind of multiplication or layering of identity that media culture promotes. Ronald Reagan the president-actor/actor-president is the height of that confusion. "One never knows whether to believe politicians"—and here is the concrete embodiment of that uncertainty.

RICHARD PRINCE I think presidential candidates should list their likes and dislikes. I think it would make it easier for people to cast a vote. Like the Dewar's profile. Favorite book. Favorite movie. What kind of sex they like. If candidate A chose Rocky and Bullwinkle and candidate B chose The Jetsons I think you'd have a pretty clear choice of who to vote for.

I think it's pretty interesting that some of the people who run for the presidency are actors, astronauts, football players, and basketball players. Personally, I'd like to be a Supreme Court Justice. I'm pretty serious about that. I don't think the appointment would be that unreasonable.

DAVID ROBBINS Jefferson was an architect and Ben Franklin an inventor, an artist.

RICHARD PRINCE Yeah. It's not so outrageous.

DAVID ROBBINS And what do you imagine to be your own relationship to the imaging of power, of history?

RICHARD PRINCE I'd like to be remembered in a movie. I know that sounds preposterous. But having someone else play me is pretty much what I think I'm already doing.

NOTES

* A reference to a popular television and print advertising campaign, featuring the singer Ella Fitzgerald, that promoted Memorex audio recording tape.

** "What Becomes A Legend Most?" is the famous tagline used in the advertising campaign for the Blackglama mink coats of the American Legend fur company. The print campaign, which began in the 1960s and continues today, features glamorous photographs of such "legends" as Elizabeth Taylor, Lillian Hellman, Audrey Hepburn, and Joan Crawford wearing mink.

On the Confidence Game as a Model for Culture, or The Applause Sign in My Mind Is Always Flashing

This text was originally published as a catalogue essay for Hollywood, Hollywood: Identity Under the Guise of Celebrity, Pasadena Art Alliance, 1992.

TRUST ME, IT MAKES NO DIFFERENCE WHETHER YOU FRAME THE FOLKS OUT THERE AS AUDIENCE OR AS ELECTORATE: SOONER OR LATER THEY'LL DEMAND A DARN GOOD REASON WHY YOU DESERVE TO BE KEPT ON THE PUBLIC NIPPLE. When that delicate moment arises, I handle it the same way whether I'm performing at Madison Square Garden, MOCA, or some haunted grange hall out on the prairie, because consistency is the key to training the public. Consistency and, of course, ruthlessness. I let the assembled know that so far as yours truly is concerned their needs aren't even under consideration; that I'm unashamedly a media creation and, as such, an official of the shadow government, not only unelected but unimpeachable; that cutting off my access to public space'll violate my Constitutional rights; and that if they do try it I'll simply write up the experience in my memoirs, which'll only make the thing thicker and even more expensive. "Go ahead," I say, "spend your children's money." Then, as the pièce de résistance, I whip out a knife and slice my right pants leg open from crotch to knee, exposing the pursuit of happiness clause I've had branded into my upper thigh so near the delectables. It's gratuitous nonsense, of course, because by that point the crowd's begging me to say anything I like, anything at all: there's nothing like the threat of litigation—so personal! so endless!—to get a crowd lapping up every word as if it were mother's milk. Sometimes, if the audience has recovered its composure before

I've left the stage, one of the bolder men may ask how I developed such uncompromising passion for public life, and then I tell them. I always begin my story in the same way, and this is how I begin.

For many years, I never dreamed. At least, such was the evidence; if dreams there were, no traces remained in the morning. Then, one Sunday morning following a marathon of Saturday TV (an experiment in dosage and tolerance)—after cartoons and wrestling, sports and sports bloopers, film reviews and interviews with celebrity offspring, after the week in rock, infomercials and edutainment, after news and commentary, cheesy prime-time sitcoms and queasy horror flicks and easy stand-up comedy, all of it laced with hundreds of commercials—I awakened certain that, yes, indeed, I had dreamed. Recalling specific plots or specific images remained outside my capacity, naturally, because of the drug years, but I did have a distinct impression of the dreams' structure—their sequencing and duration, pacing and editing.

Here's what I remembered: some kind of narrative, perhaps 15 minutes in length, though whether in real time or a proportional "dream time" I couldn't determine. Then, an interruption: four or five shorter dreams, clustered together, each one a burst perhaps a minute in length, or what seemed a minute. Echoing commercial breaks, these shorter dreams weren't, however, surreal parodies of television commercials. <u>They were commercials for other dreams</u>. These were followed in turn by another long narrative, conceivably but not necessarily a resumption of the first. This basic pattern, alternating between rambling narratives and clumps of rapid-fire promo spots, had repeated itself, with variations, throughout the night.

Okay. Then came the part of the story where I lay sprawled under the bedcovers in a happy daze, drunk with the knowledge of something unnamable, blissed out on the vanilla glow suffusing the window shade, savoring the rich results of an experiment in self-programming ... Television had penetrated all the way to my unconscious mind's organization of its response to conscious experience.

Move over, Columbus, I'd discovered America. On that glorious morning, at long last, I saw through myself, saw that the excruciating psychosexual 3-D chess tourney-without-end I'd called my interior life was really just another, slightly more complex video game, programmed and programmable. Finally I understood what was meant by the phrase "let yourself go," and I did just that. From that day forward, the permanent out-of-body experience became my preferred means of transport. Simply put, I took myself public.

I also took action:

Dialed my analyst—at home, on a weekend—and fired him.

Fair is fair, so called my family—on Christmas—and fired them.

Stopped being an artist, and dammit, started acting like one: Why struggle to add to the great sea of images when I'd my own to maintain?

Right away, things began looking up. Acquired an agent—the notorious Faxine du Montage, from Third Person Management, way, way, way out on Wilshire. Inked a lifetime contract with a deep-pockets sponsor, General Pronouns. Endorsed the output of the right stars, and was endorsed in turn. It worked like a charm; within what seemed like minutes, I knew everybody who was anybody.

A very special someone helped me land a position with the Feds after the White House re-located to Hollywood. Not just any post, either. A culture job, cooked up by the back room cigarheads in response to mounting pressure to support the arts. Naturally, the Feds had opted for the route of least commitment, choosing to fashion a role for a National Artist which fell somewhere between artist laureate and house band. Responsibility for inventing the artist's work fell to the Secretary of Media, and though initially jittery about the danger of generating any sort of content which, later on, might have thrown a wrench into the President's re-election machine, the Secretary'd eventually found a clever way 'round the horn: the national artist wouldn't actually produce any physical work at all. No, their artist's work would consist solely and entirely of convincing top gallerists, roving curators, and museum heavies to include his name on exhibition announcement cards and in magazine ads. Et voilà: the first totally mag-lev career. Just smoke and mylar stuff? Perhaps—but perhaps an oeuvre of "merciless purity" (Clementine Standish, The New York Times), with "the artist's only real product his participation in the official version of art history" (Sugar Ray Kerwin, ArtMoment).

The Secretary had auditioned dozens of hungry unknowns eager to take on the long-term responsibilities of an artist's public life before I came along and grabbed the brass ring—with a little help from my friends, granted, though Mr. Secretary also admired my genuinely hard-won lack of depth. He certainly made the right choice, because I was totally believable—poll anybody you like. In fact, during my years as National Artist I not only pulled off every aspect of the career my superiors had envisioned, I actually upped the ante, managing to convince several prestigious auction houses to include my name occasionally in their catalogues!

So began my career in the public eye. Okay, I may have been just a speck, but even so those heady, social days and nights taught me a lot. So many functions to attend, so many appearances to make, not just at the mandatory vernissage, but at film premieres, beauty contests, embassy dinners, PAC fundraisers, pansexual orgies … Those evenings taught me much of what I needed to know about appearances—how to spot them, why they count, how to keep them up. God, it was great to be young and artificial! Of course, I still carry the scars; sometimes, around 4 am, if I've had enough Punt e Mes, I'll scrub away a layer of pancake to reveal some of the less off-putting. If I'm feeling really generous, I might even confess to that evening's companion the really dark knowledge I'd acquired from that period—how truth is only truth according to whom it is revealed. Truth must be recognized as truth in order to be truth, which means that truth'll only rise as high as the audience'll let it. Scary thought.

Where was I? Oh yeah: at me. Well, the government takes care of its own, rewarding by promotion, so up the ladder I went, out of High Culture into Popular. Named chief of Canceled TV-Family Services, working out of the Office of Retouching and Airbrush. That was some stretch, believe me, because actually showing an interest in other people was not, customarily, my strong suit. But still I wanted to serve. Dear old Faxine, agent, best friend, co-producer of Hope Is For the Young, saved the day by putting me through a crash-course in acknowledging the reality of others. Not a few tears were shed out at the beach house that weekend.

The position was a mean red challenge. Canceled TV-Family Syndrome had just been identified, and not a lot was known about it, but it was having devastating effects on the entertainment industry's morale. When movies and plays were the principal dramatic fare, actors had pretended to be families for relatively short periods—the weeks it commonly took to complete a movie, the months of a hit play's successful run. But television required actors to continue for years to imagine themselves related to a group of people with whom they shared no real blood kinship. Had those genealogical pretenses continued for a lifetime, the television actor's ability to draw from two separate sources of familial care and affection would have been enviable. Unfortunately, the ruthless commercial realities of the broadcasting marketplace propelled every televised family toward another, less sanguine fate; sooner or later, declining ratings, executive caprice, or attacks by vicious, roving packs of self-righteous consumers resulted in the cancelation of every TV show. When cancelation struck prime-time soaps and sitcoms, nationally broadcast "homes" were broken overnight, and the actors who'd been part of them were forced to re-adjust to dimly remembered uni-family lives with meddlesome biological kin. Suddenly cut off from professional portrayals of nurturing support, many actors faced fragile, confusing and unhappy life-episodes upon rejoining the often-harrowing Freudian circus of the nuclear family.

Well, one does what one can do. I did plenty. Placed a guilt lien on TV network corporate earnings. With that dough, bought 12 acres adjacent to the Angeles National Forest and built the Jack and Connie Brooks Center for the Treatment of Canceled TV-Family Syndrome, named for the Realtors who sold us the land. In six months, the Center was ready. The rest was up to the afflicted actors.

Did it work? Let's just say I had to hire extra staff to handle the influx of autographed headshots.

After that kind of success, what choice had I but to resign and join the private sector? Together with a bunch of Ivy League smart alecks who'd been unnaturally influenced by early issues of the National Lampoon and, consequently, had been unable to kick the habit of generating ideas for the full spectrum of entertainment media, I founded Cultco, the first entertainment think tank. We produced rock bands, books, TV shows, movies, art exhibitions, computer games, toys, senatorial candidates—anything we felt might serve as a vehicle for our ideas.

Cultco held that there were no bad ideas; when people referred to a "bad" idea, they really meant an idea that had been either poorly tailored for or improperly assigned to an inappropriate medium or context. All any idea required was the right lighting. My main contribution was to reposition this attitude as evidence of the commodification of thought itself—the more information contexts there existed to serve as vehicles for ideas, the more the very activity of thinking came to equal capital—and then to systematize and professionalize this resoundingly Media Age habit of mind. Pointing to a new condition of mind is half the battle, every time.

Cultco absolutely cleaned up: served the audience in every way imaginable, formulated new extremes of profitable selflessness, defined the cutting edge of the service economy. One, two, three. Brilliant stuff. People stood in line to stand in awe. Even the genius grant people phoned, but I wasn't able to name the song playing on the radio at the time, so they passed me over.

Pas de problème, because I'd spun enough gold out of Cultco to buy lifelong independence, and I knew just what to do with it—pursue the golden fleece of the Media Age: Unaffiliated Celebrity. Attained by a handful—Warhol definitely, John and

Yoko, Madonna, Michael Jackson (though he had nothing to report), and possibly Jeff Koons (though it was much too early to tell)—unaffiliated celebrity (specifically: unhampered access to public life, and the dispassionate exploitation of its plastic nature for conceptual ends, that is, for ends other than one's own glory) was the closest that Media Man could come to pure citizenship, the nearest he was going to get to the glory days of the stars of the Enlightenment, Jefferson, and Franklin and the old boys who'd had the good fortune to have vats full of raw steaming nation as their medium. In media-soaked America, only unaffiliated celebrity approximated the old guys' ambition and scope, their chart-busting, best-selling combination of genuine intellectual independence and coast-to-coast, house-by-house, tête-by-tête head-banging effectiveness. Unalloyed with any one medium or production context, and therefore free from any single set of institutional controls—a condition which amounted, in effect, to the *absence* of control—the unaffiliated celebrity was the virus in the software of public life, the Image World maverick who might do anything, say anything, support any cause, sometimes out of nostalgia for the days when congruence of word and deed was a legible human trait, sure, but often as not for the perverse and arguably schizoid joy of probing the inhuman frontiers of the public self, that self-machine both more and less than human. Unaffiliated celebrity was wild card politics, the eroticized out-of-body experience *par excellence* and, to this reporter, the only game in town. I packed a suitcase and hit the road to stardom.

Well, that's my story. Now my time is spent crisscrossing our big juicy demographic of a country, commandeering local talk shows by day, terrorizing paying audiences in rented arenas at night and, in every venue, speaking about the issues that matter today: "Just How Important is Importance?" "Should the Bill of Rights Be Digitally Re-Mastered?" "Civil Rights: A Balkanization of America?" "On the Desirability of Minting Kennedy Half-dollars with Little Holes Drilled in Their Foreheads So As To Achieve Greater Historical Accuracy," whatever ... The topic varies daily, but the sublime ambition of my candidacy remains constant, toned, and hard. It has to: I'm running for deity.

One final thought before I recede from view, for now. As with almost every public life during the past century, mine's been constructed within the sanctioning gaze of the camera. Consequently, you can't know whether I'm talking straight or just performing for the Big Lens. And that, beloved friends or audience or electorate or whoever you decide you need to be this time, means you can't even be certain that I believe what I'm telling you. On the other hand, there's always the chance that some version of me—some fortunate, neatly integrated version I can point to but can never touch—actually does believe it. There's that chance. Make you a deal: I'll just dangle here before you, spinning slowly in the light, and you can try to photograph me from just the right angle. A dollar a shot.

Interview with Allan McCollum

Originally published in Arts Magazine, New York, October 1985.

DAVID ROBBINS The surrogates are clearly "fake paintings," imitations of paintings. I'm curious as to whether you have contempt for painting ...

ALLAN McCOLLUM I don't think that it's only my surrogates that are imitations of paintings! Aren't all paintings imitations of paintings in some way? With each one reflecting every other one?

I don't think I have contempt for painting; that would be like having contempt for culture. Paintings are everywhere you look; they're all over the place—like cars, or buildings. But there is some element of parody in the way I reduce all paintings to a single "kind," to a universal sign-for-a-painting. That gesture can be read as an ironic mimicry of modernist reduction, for instance, or as some kind of reference to the relations between modern art and modern industrial production—people can make these associations. But my interests are much more centered on discovering what kind of an object a painting is in an emotional sense, without the patriarchal noise of aesthetics intruding into the relationship. What is it we want from art that our belief in "content" works to hide from us?

DAVID ROBBINS When I visit a gallery or a museum, I am seeking out objects to meet a need. That need is fulfilled through a pseudo-event engaged in with a real, physical object.

The surrogates catch me in the act of seeking out this emotional connection with inanimate objects, and force it back onto me. They do not allow for the same kind of release that the conventional art object is made to transact.

ALLAN McCOLLUM Well, that's just what I'm trying to do, to frustrate the habitual mislocation of meaning within the objects. Yes. That's why the paintings are so "reduced," why I reduce them to simple tokens of exchange.

The other day I read a remark by the psychoanalyst and pediatrician D.W. Winnicott, which I thought was nicely put, in which he claims that there is no such thing as a "baby," because "if you set out to describe a baby you will find you are describing a baby and someone." It's the same with the art object, of course. I'm interested in locating the meaning of my work—and the emotional content of my work—somewhere within those transactions that occur between the various "someones" who are involved in the artwork's circulation. To do this, I have to try to dislocate the object's so-called content. When we speak of a content as residing somehow "within" the art object, we disregard the object's meaning as an item of exchange in the real, social world, and replace this condition with all sorts of imaginary constructs.

DAVID ROBBINS What do you think a person is really "looking for" when he or she walks over to look at a painting?

ALLAN McCOLLUM That's a big question. My theory is that one approaches an artwork to displace some anxiety, or to achieve some feeling of safety and security—freedom from fear. Through artworks people construct for themselves an imaginary sense of freedom. But of course this feeling of freedom can be constructed in lots of different ways ... On the most conscious level it can be evoked through illustrative devices, in overt ways: as pictures of "nature," nudity, leisure activity, travel, that sort of thing. Freedom from moral conflict may be suggested by images of innocent children, animals, happy peasants, righteous patriots,

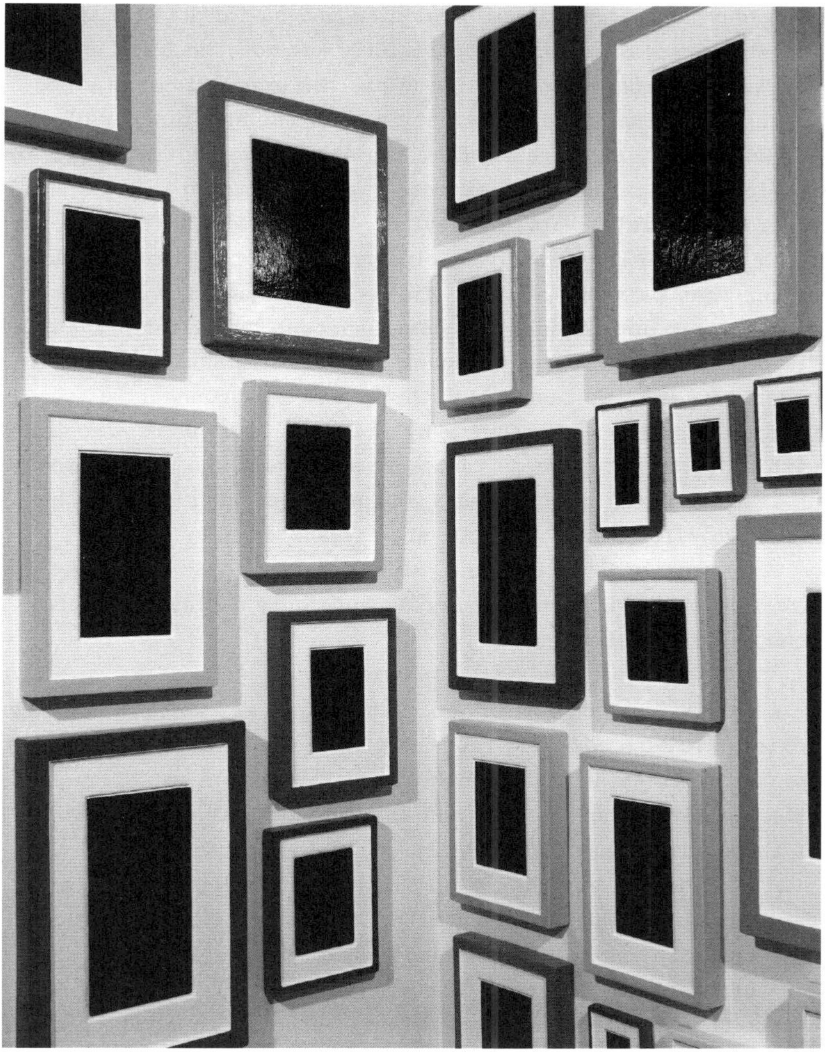

Allan McCollum, Plaster Surrogates, 1982-1983
enamel on cast Hydrostone
various sizes, from 4" x 5" to 16" x 20" (detail of installation)

religious heroes, "artistic" eroticism and so forth. We mustn't forget the moral purity of "pure form" either, the ideal space of the "non-representational." There are the expressionisms, too, which invite the viewer to identify with the spontaneity of the artist himself, his freedom from the structures of tradition, his freedom to be creative, to express rage and passion ... But I think these are all fairly obvious devices, and they don't really accomplish too much by themselves—cinema does most of this so much better than painting anyway. The sense of imaginary freedom that we seek out through art comes through our wishful identification with the forces of money and power that support and underwrite art. We identify with the art's patronage; we find a feeling of safety and security by imagining that we're associated with an elite group whose tastes we share and who will protect us from harm. If one has money and power on one's side, we believe, we will be free from all significant anxiety.

DAVID ROBBINS So art in general represents a pleasurable suspension of conflict?

ALLAN McCOLLUM Yes, I think so. But because art works to contain anxiety, it also comes to <u>represent</u> anxiety, to invoke it, to speak for it. An effective work of art can render out of us anxieties we never knew we had, and in turn, mediate the repression of these anxieties in an orderly, socially acceptable way.

It is the <u>expectancy</u> of this transformation that I'm trying to effect in a viewer, without offering its fulfillment. I'm trying to create a susceptibility, a vulnerability, to that sort of emotional deferral, but stopping short. I'm trying to create the experience of subjectivity rather than creating subjective experience.

DAVID ROBBINS How did this come to be the focus of your work?

ALLAN McCOLLUM It originally grew out of an interest in the idea of "defining" painting, the notion of reducing painting to a simple set of essential terms, and then "expressing yourself" within those terms. This was what a lot of painters seemed to be thinking about in the late '60s and early '70s. I began to see this sort of thinking as really absurd, somehow. It seemed to me that every conceivable description of a painting that one might offer to define its "essence" or its "terms" could always be found to also define some other, similar object which was not a painting—except for one: a painting always has the identity of a painting; a painting is what it is because it is a convention. It exists precisely because the culture makes a place for it. As a definition, of course, this is a lot like saying, "a painting is something often found over a couch," and yet it was exactly this sort of common sense definition that I felt was missing in all that other formalist debate. The "terms" of painting are the terms of the world-at-large!

An artwork is related to every other object and event in the cultural system, and the meaning of an artwork resides in the role the artwork plays in the culture, before anything else.

DAVID ROBBINS Art as a distinctly non-transcendent activity, in other words.

ALLAN McCOLLUM Yes. This seemed like an important truth to keep in mind. And yet I found it difficult to think of a painting as simply a term within a whole set of other terms, precisely because I couldn't picture a painting that didn't aspire to be a world-in-itself. Such paintings didn't seem to exist. So I took it upon myself to create a model, a standard sign-for-a-painting that might represent nothing more than the identity of painting in the world of other objects.

DAVID ROBBINS As if creating an advertisement for painting, or better still, for an art object.

ALLAN McCOLLUM Yes, like an advertisement or a logo. I wanted to install a useful image in my mind and in the minds of others. My first impulse was to make only one painting, and exhibit it over and over again, to create a sort of archival object—just as the government's Bureau of Standards maintains the standard "inch" in platinum. But this solution eliminated the possibility of exchange transactions. That was a problem, because how could a thing represent an art object if it couldn't be bought and sold?

Ultimately I decided to use a single but repeatable image, one that I could vary minimally in size and proportion, but which remained essentially the same: a frame, a mat, and a black center. I made many of these out of wood from 1978 until 1982, at which time I began to cast them in plaster from rubber molds. At this point I dropped the designation "painting" and began to call them "plaster surrogates."

DAVID ROBBINS So you've fabricated a sort of generic painting. Was your decision to use molds related to increasing the volume of your production?

ALLAN McCOLLUM Sure, but also because plaster as a material carries with it the connotation of artificiality, and I needed this nuance to accelerate the theatricality of my installations. Without really anticipating it, you see, I was becoming something of an installation artist. After mounting a few exhibits, I learned quickly that the surrogates worked to their best effect when they came across as "props"—like stage props—which pointed to a much larger melodrama than could ever exist merely within the paintings themselves. The surrogates, via their reduced attributes and their relentless sameness, started working to render the gallery into a quasi-theatrical space which seemed to "stand for" a gallery; and by extension, this rendered me into a sort of caricature of an artist, and the viewers became performers, and so forth. In trying to objectify the conventions of art production, I theatricalized the whole situation without exactly intending to. But, even so, there it was.

At this point, I think, I let myself become the victim of my own thesis, so to speak. The artificiality of the work functioned pretty well to displace content, as I intended, but it also gave me no outlet for the very real desperation that underlay my drive to make art in the first place. I think it was the nightmarishness of this no-exit situation that triggered the exaggerated and obsessional repetitiveness of my work as it exists now. By removing the possibility of catharsis through the work itself, I led myself into a kind of madness of production.

DAVID ROBBINS Which, given the international nature of the art world's structures, and the production demands made on artists to supply those structures with objects, seems a very appropriate "madness" to engage. You engaged your work over into psychoanalysis.

ALLAN McCOLLUM Yes, I think so. Once I began to locate the content of my work as dispersed throughout that whole behavioral complex of exchanges and meanings that is the art world, I began to discover the powerful grip of all those emotions that go into making, showing, buying, selling, and looking at art. There's a lot more at stake in these transactions than meets the eye, so to speak. You and I participate in a sect, a sect in which all the action pivots on this single token, the art object; but it's the emotional politics surrounding this token which provide the meaning and the value. The artwork is always just a substitute, a surrogate.

DAVID ROBBINS The fetishistic center of our attention.

ALLAN McCOLLUM The artwork is a kind of fetish. It's a kind of substitute for real power—or maybe I mean a kind of sign representing imaginary power. Like I said, we look at art for security, security against loss or death. I've tried to design these surrogates to invite a fetishistic attachment, the kind of attachment one might develop toward a literal sign, like maybe the old Coca Cola sign, for instance. Remember how adolescent boys liked to steal public street signs and hang them in their bedrooms? Appropriating the signs that emanate from authority?

I make my work smooth and shiny, with many coats of enamel, to humanize them. Their corners are slightly rounded, they're small, they're nice and solid. One can carry them around, one can put them in a purse, one can wash them …

DAVID ROBBINS They're user-friendly.

ALLAN McCOLLUM Not entirely. Anything that's designed to function as a fetish shouldn't be trusted. A fetish inevitably represents the fear of absence it is meant to replace, and is therefore a kind of scary object; a fetish is a function of fear. It's in this area that I try to draw parallels between the art object and the object produced for mass-consumption; both rely on fear for their circulation. Advertising works to make us insecure about what we lack, and then offers us the fetish-object designed to displace this anxiety: the product. All the while, the vast economic powers that underwrite the entire system of industrial production work to intimidate us from above, creating the insecurity and feelings of helplessness, which make us susceptible to this kind of ploy in the first place. In its fetish aspect, the mass-produced consumer product both threatens us and offers us freedom at the same time. We are seduced, of course; it's just a cheap trick.

DAVID ROBBINS Is art?

ALLAN McCOLLUM When we purchase a consumer product, we achieve an imaginary identification with the powers responsible for its production, and feel we have won the protection of these powers. With art, the viewer imagines he belongs to a select and powerful group through his sharing in their good taste. It's a really similar kind of transaction, I think.

DAVID ROBBINS The surrogates engage volume and surplus more than they do mammoth scale. The quantity and variety of them—you'd told me earlier that you've made over 2000 of them—forces the viewer into choosing favorites, that, if they want to buy some, becomes a parody of the shopping experience. You've even devised a sliding scale of discounts, which is to be applied if they're purchased in quantity. So, the theatricalization extends to commerce as well.

ALLAN McCOLLUM I hear people complaining all the time about how the world has become too commercial, but I really think that just the opposite has occurred: commerce has been completely banished from our lives as a form of social discourse. Instead, we engage in a highly controlled and sterile consumer "behavior." The pleasure of actual commerce is available only to those of privilege, those with property and power; the rest of us just stand namelessly in line in an endless series of department stores, exchanging money for what we're told we need, with a lot of nameless cashiers.

DAVID ROBBINS Credit cards remove even more of the touch.

ALLAN McCOLLUM Right. That way, no sweat is even exchanged. The marketplaces in other cultures can be hotbeds of human exchange and interaction. They can be sites of pleasure and passion, sources of anarchistic energy. In our culture, the pleasure of this anarchy is reserved for the few.

So when we set art against commerce, we distort both, I think. To define art as a "spiritual" activity, and then to deny human commerce any spiritual value—that's just ludicrous! What else does art stand for in people's minds anymore if not a symbol of wealth, a symbol of a few people's success at commerce? We see art as a kind of spiritual reward for being wealthy. When we experience the spirituality of art, we are usually only constructing a chain of fantasy identifications which lead to power—not mystical power, but just brute, human, political, and military power. The reason for this is simple: we make this association because we figure it takes money and power to own art. Even with inexpensive artworks, stylistic devices always serve to refer to the artworks owned by the privileged—the aristocracies of the past, the museums of the present.

How does art ever become "great" except through such associations? Whenever I hear the term "great art" I immediately think of this procession: great collections, great museums, great countries, great armies, great weapons. This is one of the main ways that value and meaning develop in this world. It's very human, I guess, but it's sad, too. And the mythology we construct about art and its place in the world works to disguise this simple fact, because recognizing the implications of power leads us right back to our anxiety over our powerlessness and it is exactly this anxiety that the arts are designed to alleviate. So instead of creating artifacts to carry meaning among us through social exchange, we create artifacts to facilitate our imaginary identifications with those who dominate us.

By being involved in this activity of "creating culture" by making artworks, I believe we are often simply averting our eyes from those powerful people who frighten and threaten us. We make signals to them with our artworks that we are engaged in a harmless activity, that we are not rebels.

DAVID ROBBINS Our popular notion of artists as being childlike is already perverse, but what's stranger is the number of artists who agree to this assigned behavior.

ALLAN McCOLLUM It's very important to us that our artists be powerless, like children. The artist is elected to articulate subjectivity for the culture at large, and we require that that subjectivity be passive, and without effect. All passions that might feed into any desires to disrupt order are displaced into "artistic" expression.

The way we characterize the "artist" in our culture is a clue to how we construct our emotional lives with regard to the social whole, I think. While we attribute many "positive" features to the artist, we also attribute a whole set of complementary "negative" ones. An artist may be spontaneous, expressive, idealistic, sensitive, creative, sensual, and brilliant, but he or she is also neurotic, infantile, self-centered, sexually obsessed, impractical, parasitical, and so forth. It's easy to see how the popular mind imagines that the positive traits necessarily imply the negative ones! Sensuality leads to hypersexuality, idealism to ineffectiveness, expressivity to infantilism, and so on. The artist's character is like an object lesson to most people, a walking argument for moderation in all things. I think people sometimes choose to be artists because they desperately need to play this privileged, doomed role. It's kind of like being a human sacrifice, but without any such cathartic reward!

DAVID ROBBINS The artist assumes the role so that the rest of society doesn't need to. But why does the artist, or perhaps more accurately, "the artistic," conform to this well-worn patch of personality between Peter Pan and Joan of Arc?

ALLAN McCOLLUM Well, when I say that the action of the art world pivots on the art object as a token of exchange, it is this quality of being privileged which forms the actual signified, I think. What we seem to be exchanging are our mutual illusions of being special, which I read as meaning protected or safe and secure. Certain people can't feel that they even exist unless they feel special and privileged in a really broad and exaggerated way. Artists spend their entire lives developing circumstances for themselves in which their signature becomes a valued object, one that is actually worth money.

DAVID ROBBINS Picasso's signed dinner napkin.

ALLAN McCOLLUM For example, yes. The collector of art consumes not only the art but the artist too, in a way. He acquires the fruits of the artist's moral instability from a safe distance, without having to also assume the artist's politically inferior position. The collector decides that a particular artist represents his innermost self, his unrealized or deferred self. When he acquires the art object, the collector is in a sense rewarding himself both for his success at repressing his infantile nature and for his superior socialization. The collector thinks he has the best of both worlds—he buys back the part of himself he has lost, so to speak. The artist recognizes himself to exist only when he is recognized by the collector, and the collector recognizes himself only when he recognizes the artist.

DAVID ROBBINS It's a mutual con.

ALLAN McCOLLUM Exactly. A narcissistic dyad. Who's kidding who? We use art in our culture to construct imaginary relations to others.

Now, I don't mean to say that I think that this is the ultimate and irreversible destiny of art, that it should continually reproduce this model of human relations. But I do think that our artworks and our relationships to them are just shadows of what they might be, if we didn't constantly pursue an imaginary mystical union with the powers of industry, only discovering ourselves through perpetually repeated acts of _buying_ things.

DAVID ROBBINS We tend to say to ourselves that the art object is _above_ the commodity, above the pair of shoes that I buy, because art isn't tied to a utilitarian basis.

ALLAN McCOLLUM And yet the absolute utility of art is rather clear: we are meant to discover our subjectivity in these objects—objects that are owned or controlled by the wealthy, the privileged, the powerful. Artworks function to regulate not only the way objects _mean_, the way they are valued, but also the consciousness that structures these operations. To describe art as "useless" is to reproduce a really insidious falsification. The world of artworks makes up an extremely useful and monstrous totemic system through which we all trace our imaginary lineage to power. Do you know about the Nelson Rockefeller Collection Gallery up on 57th Street? Where you can buy handmade copies of art objects in the Nelson Rockefeller collection? We think this is really funny, of course, because we think we are above all that. But isn't this just a gallery which is just a little more honest than usual? To see this gallery as an aberration only normalizes those other institutions—like the Museum of Modern Art, for instance—that work to accomplish very similar ends, really. The museum's acquisitions board collects artworks from a certain very narrow spectrum of art activity (most of which might never even have been created if it weren't for the possibility of such an institution collecting it), and is therefore very handily involved in what comes to be considered "art" in our culture. In this way, a really influential institution effects the very subjectivity we experience as our own. Our so-called "unconscious" is conventionalized, and artists reproduce museum-type art all over the country, if not all over the world. We produce our own handmade copies.

DAVID ROBBINS And official culture is established.

ALLAN McCOLLUM Yes—unofficially, of course. We do it ourselves, through our mimicry of those with power. It's an identification-with-the-aggressor kind of thing, or an identification with the object-of-envy. The privileged exclude us, but offer us an imaginary relation to their exclusivity as a substitute. Thus we exclude ourselves even from one another. The class boundaries that separate the privileged from the powerless are very real, but their representation in the consciousness of the powerless is made to be really vague and obscure, and so they can only take the form of phobias and obsessions, repetitions and rituals: boundaries of false difference.

DAVID ROBBINS Is the multiplication of effect afforded by exhibiting more than 700 imitation paintings in one location designed as a mockery of that authoritarian aspect?

ALLAN McCOLLUM I see repetition as being one of those devices used a lot in the maintaining of power relations. It is a device used by religions everywhere, and by the military, too, to construct a hypnotic spectacle. Repetition is a kind of meaning in itself. Possibly it is the language of power *par excellence*.

DAVID ROBBINS Inventing an event or an object is a wonderful thing, but inventing it *again* has more to do with power than it does with invention: you are proving that you are powerful enough to arrange the same conditions and make it happen again.

ALLAN McCOLLUM Look at the way AT&T invented a new logo just a couple of years ago, and now it's absolutely everywhere you look. It's truly magical. We love this vast spectacle of repetition that arises out of industrial power because of the safety it seems to offer, the security of a predictable authority. We are protected from loss in the glow of a perpetual industrial fecundity!

But I think this is a very fragile security we're speaking of, and this gets into one of the main reasons I produce my work in such vast quantities and install so many in one exhibit. As I said before, I think the artwork and the consumer good are both a kind of intentionally designed fetish; I believe that you can only reduplicate the fetish so many times before the accumulation begins to turn on you, and the fetish becomes your persecutor: this is why all mass-produced objects have a certain ominous presence. I might like to have a Sony video recorder, but to come face-to-face with _all_ the Sony video recorders in the world would be a truly terrifying experience. Of this I'm sure. There's a certain point, like a critical mass, where the fear that animates the fetish-object submerges the safety it offers and works against it. I think "The Sorcerer's Apprentice" sequence of Disney's _Fantasia_ depicted this sort of transformation from the helpful object to the object that threatens death. From the nurturing object to the persecuting object ...

When I was a child, both of my parents worked on the assembly line of a large aircraft factory in Southern California. At Christmas, the company invited all the employees of this huge industrial complex to bring their children to an enormous party in one of their larger warehouses, and all of us were given exactly identical Christmas gifts. There were giant stacks upon stacks of these gifts, all in identical wrappings, stacked very high. There must have been hundreds and hundreds of them, maybe thousands, and we all had to stand in line for maybe half an hour to get one handed to us by a Santa Claus, of course. What is a corporation trying to communicate at a moment like that?

Generosity? Power? Threat? I found the whole experience really frightening, as I recall, but, naturally, I wanted the gift. This is the sort of nightmarishly ambiguous atmosphere I try to create with my installations, not just in order to be nasty but to try to free up some of the desperation and anxiety that I believe is inherent in the showing and viewing of art, and which a smaller amount of artworks would only work to defer and to contain. As I've said, so much of art is about fear-in-the-face-of-power.

DAVID ROBBINS So you are demonstrating your mastery over that fear.

ALLAN McCOLLUM My <u>attempts</u> to master it. Through my own personal imaginary identification with the processes of mass production, probably!

DAVID ROBBINS What led you to take pictures of the television?

ALLAN McCOLLUM I wanted my surrogates to represent all paintings, all artworks. I wanted to show that all artworks, everywhere, are just a kind of prop—a prop that has meaning only in relation to the action that takes place around it. A stage prop seemed like a perfect metaphor for this, of course, and I was surprised to see how often images that looked exactly like my surrogates appeared in the backgrounds of television dramas, old movies, and so forth. I started taking these pictures as a kind of facetious "proof" that my works were an accurate rendering of a real-life phenomenon. Maybe I was offering a kind of pseudo-argument for my project's right to exist. A fictitious <u>provenance</u>, as one friend put it.

But to be completely honest, I'm just really fascinated at finding my work on TV. It makes me feel important, in a really infantile way; I sort of <u>display</u> this omnipotence fantasy as a part of my work, to make a point, one that I've been trying to make in this interview: through art we construct imaginary relations to power. Also, I use these pictures to ephemeralize the

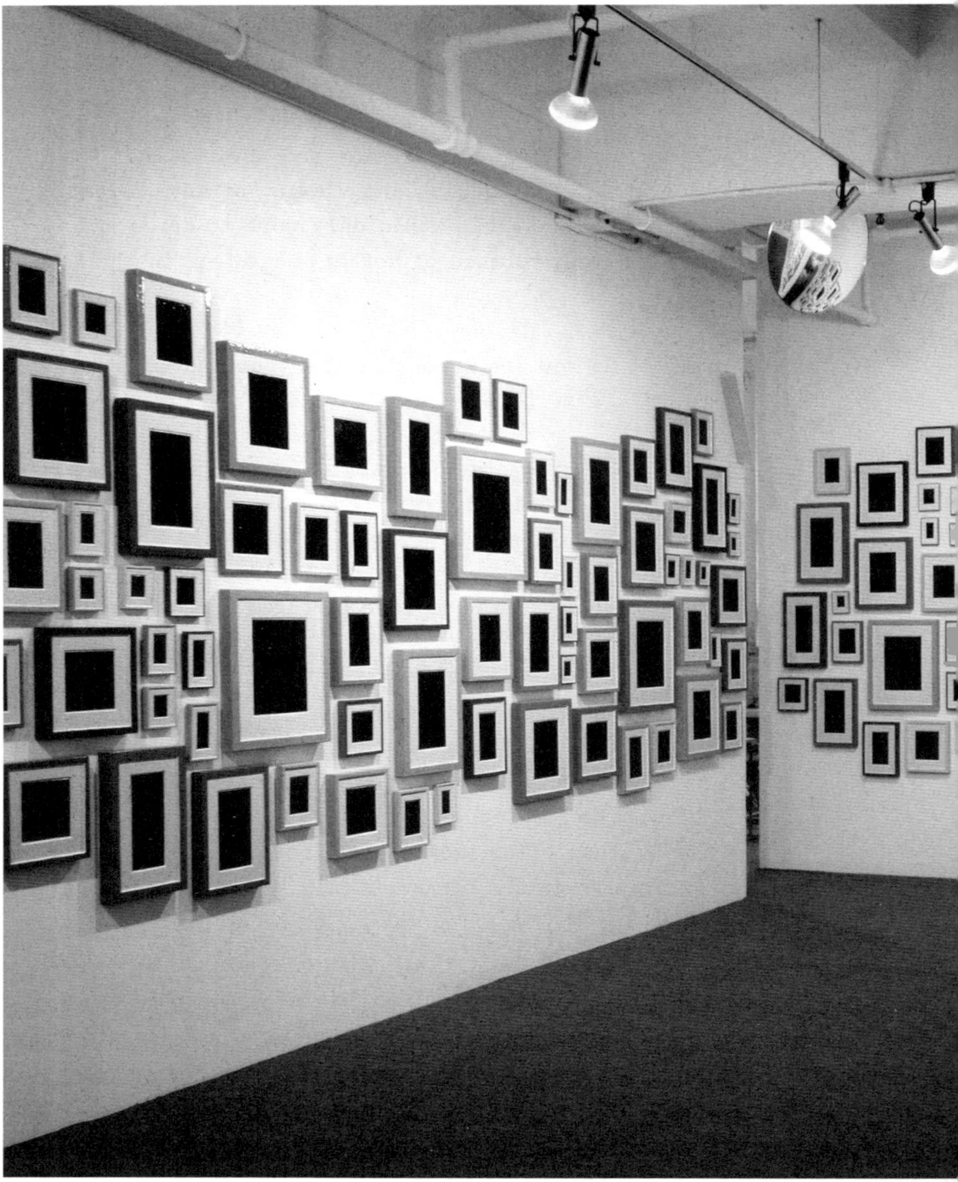

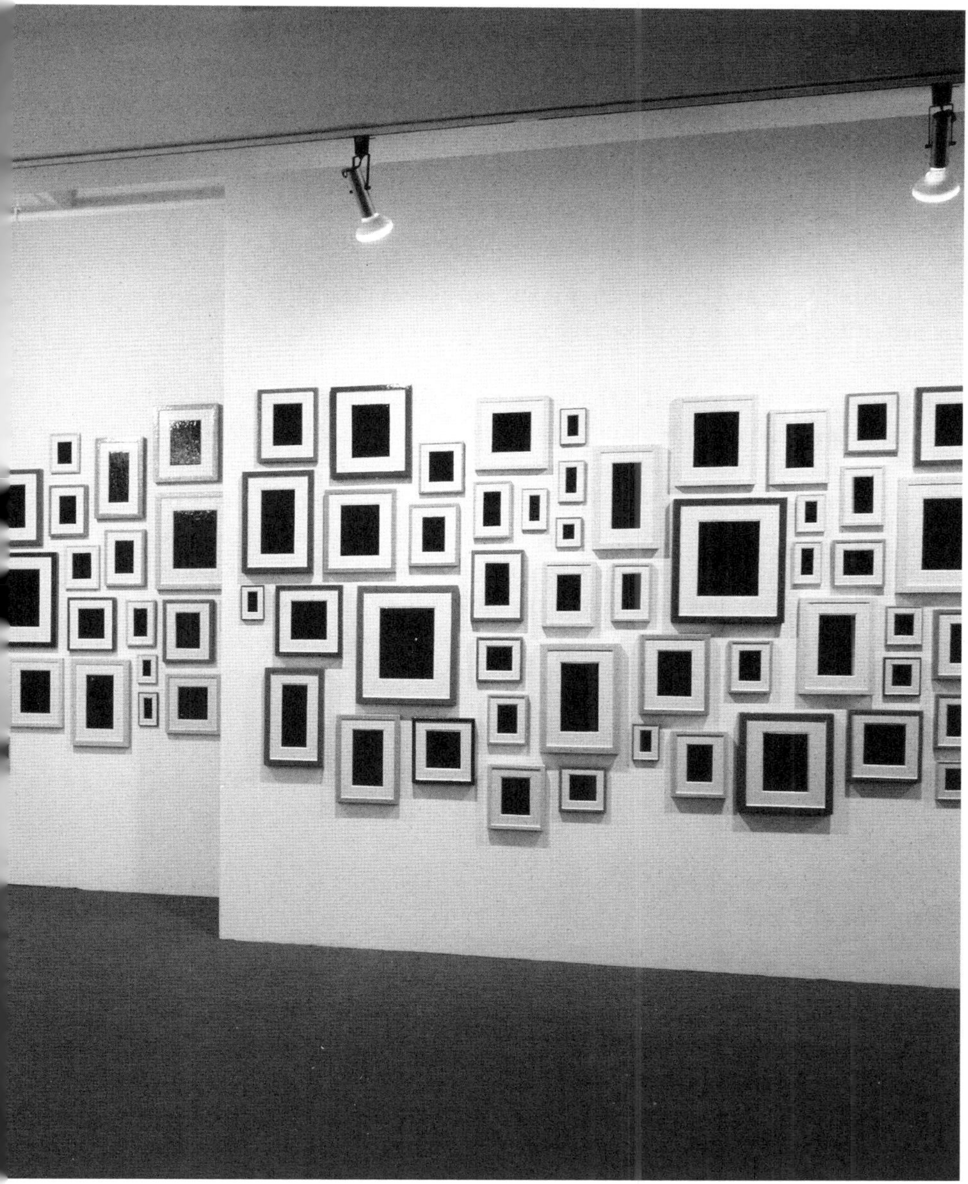

Allan McCollum, Plaster Surrogates, 1982-1983
enamel on cast Hydrostone
installation view at Marian Goodman Gallery, New York, 1983

actual plaster objects, to enhance their <u>sign</u> qualities. I'm reproducing a certain kind of strategy where photographs are used to manipulate the meaning and the value of an object—a strategy we're all familiar with: it's the strategy that the world of advertising shares with the world of selling art. There's a certain way I like to look at my surrogates, sometimes: that they exist solely to be photographed.

DAVID ROBBINS And in the TV pictures, the art is photographed in order to show its prior existence, to naturalize it.

ALLAN McCOLLUM Usually I find them only in the fantasy-world of the televised melodrama. But I do make a special attempt to discover my surrogates on walls behind politically powerful men, too. I've found "my work" in the same rooms with John F. Kennedy, Harry Truman, and Gerald Ford, among others. On a certain level I'm making a parody of a sales technique, the technique of celebrity endorsement; but in a more important way, I'm using my own infantile wishes as a metaphor for the way we relate to art in general, for that very basic wish we all share: <u>the wish to be in the picture</u>.

DAVID ROBBINS The wish to participate in history, where one's existence has been shown to count for something. <u>Recorded</u> ...

ALLAN McCOLLUM To be in on things at the source, to be involved in the Primal Scene, not out in the hall looking through the keyhole. To be present with those who have the power, to be under their gaze, and to be protected by them. We want to be somewhere within the circle of power, but safely preoccupied with something harmless at the same time, maybe. To be absorbed with something sublime and beautiful which is contiguous with something powerful and threatening. These wishes operate all the time while we look at art, but we do not experience them as part of the "content." It is only within the context of this wishing, however, that content is sought out.

DAVID ROBBINS While the plaster surrogates themselves are about locating where art is in the cultural hierarchy as commodity, in the emotional hierarchy as mediator, in the political hierarchy as class sieve, the TV pictures are about locating the place of art in the representation of life by the mass media. George Trow says that TV represents the scale of national life. It's the national home we all share. If that is so, then the TV surrogates represent that national life's use for and placement of art.

ALLAN McCOLLUM Sure, I guess so. On the wall, out of the way, incidental to the action. We have to remember that as artists, critics, art dealers, and so forth, we see art in a grossly distorted way.

DAVID ROBBINS As a hugely important thing.

ALLAN McCOLLUM Absolutely vital to life! I'm always especially happy to find an image with either a violent, or melodramatic, or historically important activity going on in the foreground, with the inactive painting on the wall in the background mutely signaling. This is the ultimate location of art, in the background—as it should be, I suppose.

DAVID ROBBINS In the second phase of the TV pictures, the ones you call Perpetual Photos, you've isolated the tiny images from framed paintings that you've discovered in the backgrounds of TV scenes of domestic life, and blown them up. You show us what that broadcast interpretation and placement of art really looks like.

ALLAN McCOLLUM Sometimes I'll find a picture that has a tiny framed picture on the wall in the background, and the image within that frame is indecipherable, just a blur. When I enlarge these little meaningless smudges up to life-size—the size of a picture we might hang in our own home—there's nothing there, just the ghost of an artwork, the ghost of content. There's something parodic in this gesture of mine, I think, and something pathetic. Looking for the limits of representation; seeking to discover those limits at which the binding of a picture gives way; releasing those emotions the representation sought to contain. This is a kind of synthetic expressionism I'm doing here …

DAVID ROBBINS But it's also an important retrieval. The first TV pictures are placed surrogates, while the second—the Perpetual Photos—are displaced images of art, grotesque abstractions, which represent the bourgeois recognition of art. You have retrieved them in order to bring them back to art so that we might understand art's mediated image, its place in the world.

ALLAN McCOLLUM Well, I think that through this "retrieval," as you call it, I'm also trying to mimic one's quest for the sublime and the transcendent, one's quest for one's own unconscious and so forth.

DAVID ROBBINS You've been very critical of the art machine as it's currently constructed. How do you answer those who criticize as self-righteous or moralistic those artists who espouse this point of view?

ALLAN McCOLLUM I'm interested to encourage an analysis of art, but through the pleasure of looking, that's all. I would like to see us be a little more anthropological in the way we assess our own cultural production. I feel that art now functions to keep people apart, to reinforce and maintain class, boundaries, and to encourage exclusion and inequality through the cult of "taste." I think this is wrong; yes, I am moralistic about this. I hope that my work might play some role in the analysis of this situation, and I hope it does so by bringing some pleasure into the discovery that the problem does not necessarily lie with art but with those forces that work to legislate its meaning.

Artificial Intelligence

First published in Rooted Rhetoric, exhibition catalogue, Castell dell'Ovo, Naples, Italy, 1986.

THE CONTEXT "UNITED STATES" ORGANIZES ITSELF AROUND THE RADICAL FORCE OF DEMOCRATISM, HUGE AND SLOW AND AS INEVITABLE AS A GLACIER. The most powerful and extreme proponent of democratic discourse—television—teaches that there are many practices, simultaneously evolving; television teaches artists that art is but one discourse among many. This has helped to encourage in art a shift from investigating the fact of the object (the task of modernism) to an investigation of the relations between contexts. Awash in a sea of broadcast images, artists are beginning to shift attention away from image-production toward a critique of artist-behavior.

In the post-industrial information society, the imagination of the artist is airborne, like electronics and radioactivity, and must negotiate with landing bases controlled by three Image Superpowers:

1. The objects and events of reality (the opaque "ism" of the real)

2. Genius Culture (art and literature: critiques of the real that are themselves real)

3. Media-reality (the display of the lifelike: movies, television, advertising, radio, records, computers, magazines ...), sovereign of the global airwaves. Together with the nuclear glow, the projected light of media-reality illuminates the obsolescence of the nation-state.

Whereas the first wave of information-society art (Conceptualism) was marked by purity of discourse (art bounded by science), the practitioners of a new conceptualism (which will not parrot the old in form or style, just as the next Duchamp will not be Duchampian) must negotiate, interminably, with media-reality (art bounded by entertainment). The job of the artist, now, is to articulate how art is <u>not</u> entertainment.

The artist is the first principle of art, and he or she is, in large measure, independent of art. Styles, techniques, and processes come and go (History atomized into many parallel histories, all presided over by the mass media, doorman to the nightclub called History) and the artist is free to publicly cultivate all manner of personal obsession and whim, but the way in which society integrates these misrepresents art as a kind of intellectual showbiz where artists are entertainers and dealers book acts.

The artist is emerging as a new kind of information aristocrat, but for the artist to behave as an aristocrat is redundant and contributes only to the History of Damage and Revenge.

The second principle of art is inutility: art's use begins with its uselessness. (This is why the readymade continues to generate power: the recontextualization which defines the readymade generates no conversion of mass, only a conversion of energy.)

To be an artist, then, is to index one's practice (one's life) to the condition of objects/images/gestures useful because without use. The production of such objects infects the artist's life with the same kind of hyperarticulate inutility.

The term "artist" represents the widest cultural aperture, because art is the only cultural practice that can construct meaning without swearing fealty to any particular medium. A writer must use words but an artist <u>may</u> use them, a filmmaker must use celluloid or videotape but an artist <u>may</u>, and so on through the list of Reflective Occupations. Because it is tethered to no specific procedure, the practice of art enables the artist to invent not products but <u>behavior</u>.

Free to live a meaningless life (that is, because the artist's life is public, free to engage meaninglessness <u>professionally</u>), the artist discovers in his uselessness-by-association the seeds of a critique of the useful (that is, all endeavors which are not-art). The artist's life, therefore, has the capacity to function as an active ongoing critique of labor.

The artist's insight into Strategic Uselessness, whether so articulated or not, casts him into a hypercritique of all behavior, so that life comes to appear a still life. The artist comes to behave as if his life is a politicized still life, an accretion of gestures yielding objects or images offered to other people for decoding and interpretation. The artist spends his life polishing his still life, preparing it for lifetimes of interpretation.

The configuration of Civilization takes priority over the configuration of Me. Artists have instructed themselves in fidelity to the configuration of Culture, a configuration that is but a symptom. (Artists have taught themselves to parody forms appearing in nature or in culture, as if the first incarnation of these forms somehow fell short!) Culture-bound art relegates the artist to a life of <u>responding</u>, reflecting upon the achievements of men and women of action, and refining a whine of criticism. (For example, the national imagination of America is obsessed with the production and distribution of images and property. The task of fixing the coordinates of Property within this civilization has inclined the artist to act as a psychiatrist of commodities.)

A new question the artist may begin to ask becomes: Is there a way to lead?

The artist's fidelity is not to tradition, institution, or state. The artist's sole responsibility is to locate the endeavor of art in relation to other endeavors, but as art's meaning must be constructed, the artist here discovers two subsidiary and inescapable responsibilities:

1. A responsibility to the legibility of his or her still life.

2. A responsibility to the context in which that still life is constructed. The context of the artist's still life is: other lives. The arena wherein the artist transforms his uselessness is: others' eyes.

The artist's life is a radical congruence of private and public selves, and art the site where these selves unite to reflect on their union.

The artist's life, which professionally engages meaninglessness so as to construct meaning for others, has the capacity to frame a kind of pure citizenship.

(Untitled) The Sublime Was Now

Originally published in Arts Magazine, New York, March 1986.

IN A PERIOD INTENT ON RECYCLING ALL MANNER OF MARGINAL, DISCARDED, OR DISCREDITED STYLES, IT IS TO BE EXPECTED THAT "THE SUBLIME" SHOULD ALSO RETURN AS A SUBJECT OF INTEREST AMONG ARTISTS. The extraordinary vigor with which any consideration of God had been thrust away makes it supreme in the hierarchy of the neglected, and its return—however temporary—appropriate and charming.

The sublime can't hang around very long precisely because it's about absolutes. For instance, in that art is a personalized device for measuring the distance from Utopia, the sublime is the ultimate, in the sense of final, subject of art. (It is this that makes art "about" the sublime seem redundant.) The irony is that our conception of the sublime is predicated on a contextlessness, a transcendence, which we do not believe possible. We know with a curiously numbing certitude that no thing exists apart from the context in which it appears. And as we are convinced that the world consists of details and systems of details, any habitual contemplation of the sublime, in one's life or one's work, becomes nihilistic, murderous, because it obliterates the foaming wake of the sublime: that galaxy of details—the plot, as it were—in which the ragged transactions of human history are located.

So for our purposes the sublime is less about belief in an Absolute than it is about desire, the interminable negotiation with a succession of elusive seductions, which remain forever outside the grasp of each individual's consciousness. Desire freed of the object of desire: desire to the nth. The sublime addresses the inability of consciousness to be whole and yet stand outside of itself: the mind's inability to turn itself in.

Art is involved with objects, so the relationship between the sublime and art may be stated (as brutally as any theory) as that between Sasquatch and a shoehorn, between the Loch Ness Monster and a fishing lure.

In America we have the habit of industriousness, so even a sublime has been pieced together—television—though it's a counterfeit sublime, and I doubt it's one Barnett Newman would have cheered. Television's endless display of the Lifelike—a display that no one either controls or accepts responsibility for—achieves a critical mass and lifts off into the condition of a (fake) Absolute which (though its sound is thinner and color harsher than we'd expect of a sublime) reproduces quite accurately the terms of the transaction traditionally effected between humans and the Unnamable. Having established its own rules of sensation, behavior, and logic, television proceeds with the ruthless purity available through electronics to form a self-reflexive universe. As the rules of actual life do not approach a logic anything like television's, and as the inheritance of our civilization prominently features a desperate, pathetic, and honorable Wish for the solace of Certainty which a system of celestial logic would confer upon us, we have embraced the counterfeit sublime. Better a perverse whole, we figure, than none at all.

Student to Rabbi: "I don't believe in God."
Rabbi to Student: "Do you think God cares?"

ABC TV

Originally published in *Artforum*, New York, October 1999.

AS NEITHER THOROUGHBRED BOOMERS NOR GEN-XERS, THE MEMBERS OF THE DEMI-GENERATION BORN IN THE LATE '50S AND EARLY '60S—MY OWN—HAVE ALWAYS FELT LIKE HISTORY'S MUTTS. Proximity to, and thus osmotic knowledge of, the utopian '60s fantasies entertained by older siblings wasn't the same as participation in them: we were too young. Too young as well, though only just, to claim as our own the funny, sour, dystopian response to the failed premises of the Revolution—punk (which response, of course, had also "failed"). Fittingly—and comically—the period of our own delivery into maturity coincided with a slippery transitional passage in the wider culture. We hit adulthood just as the quasi-socialist, welfare model of American society, put in place by FDR, suffered eviction and replacement by the Reagan era's roaringly vigorous model of Darwinian competitiveness and self-interest *über alles*. Whereupon another irony: my peers, forever "too young," were now too *old* to claim as their own the clear-eyed gaze of the Reaganite hatchlings then flocking to Wall Street and flooding the nightclubs. Much as some among us might have wished it, the ruthless cultivation of self-interest so natural to Reagan Youth was not to be our birthright. Although only a few years our junior, those kids were unblemished by memories of the Vietnam era, much less the Weathermen, and thus enjoyed—and I mean *enjoyed*—a very different relation to government and especially to capitalism.

As for a transitional generation, so for its artists. Of course, good artists will play whatever hand they're dealt, and even win chips with it. The conceptual artists of my generation who exhibited during the '80s East Village fever at the storefront galleries Nature Morte, International with Monument, Cash/Newhouse, and, a little later, at 303 and American Fine Arts, did just that, spinning significance out of our odd, unstable inheritance and advancing our impure status with inventiveness.

These artists—among them, Peter Nagy, Alan Belcher, Oliver Wasow, Karen Sylvester, Jennifer Bolande, Gretchen Bender, Robin Weglinski, Steven Parrino, Cady Noland, Richard Milani, Peter Halley, Kevin Larmon, Haim Steinbach, Julie Wachtel, Jessica Diamond, Joel Otterson, Tom Brazelton, Meyer Vaisman, and myself—were primarily white, college-educated suburbanites who, mostly from instinct but at least partially in reaction against the existentially overwrought art hyped in the press, offered objects and images that were intended to appeal to the emotions by way of the brain. Whatever envy we might have felt toward the oft-photographed neo-expressionists was directed at their wardrobes, not at their art. Our aesthetic sympathies lay with the mass-media/institutional-critique artists headquartered at Metro Pictures. We were on friendly terms with Cindy and Robert, Sherrie and Louise, Laurie and Richard. When we needed to publish writing or images we offered them to Tom Lawson and Susan Morgan's <u>REAL LIFE Magazine</u> or to <u>Arts</u>, at the time under Richard Martin's editorship and startlingly open to artists' ideas for articles and "pieces."

I was part of the Nature Morte crowd (the in-house writer as it were), so this essay is necessarily skewed toward that gallery's aesthetic. A travelogue narrated by a representative of another gallery might point out different flora and fauna, but describe another planet entirely? I doubt it; all of us were part of the same solar system. An additional note: while chartered as a gallery, Nature Morte also functioned as something of a think tank. There was a backroom, tiny and, toward evening, smoky; in it, lively, intelligent people regularly hung around for hours, watching the action and sharing ideas and analyzing stuff and making each other laugh. A generous spirit was loose in that place; if you're rich with ideas, you feel comfortable giving some away. So, when in this essay I write "we," please imagine a point somewhere on a continuum between an improv comedy troupe and a board of directors.

We who comprised the Nature Morte/International/Cash et al set were $\underline{n}^{th}$-generation Pop artists. As had been true of the legions of Pop artists before us, ours was fundamentally an art concerned with the vast synthetic world established by the camera—in television and movies, in advertisements and magazines, in photographs—and, more abstractly, with the conditions of visual experience to which the camera has accustomed the eye. (Even a painter's painter such as Kevin Larmon, in his handmade, Morandi-esque repetition of an imaginary still life, engaged the camera's capacity for mechanical reproduction, if perversely.)

Of course, every generation since the Second World War having offered up its own, there's nothing intrinsically distinctive about being the latest group of camera-centric Pop artists. That America is Pop, now and forever, is just a fact of life. We gosling East Village popsters were (to borrow a line from George Trow) only telling the truth about our imprinting. But no truth is arbitrary. Exact will be the coordinates of that experiential matrix which to any given generation signals Pop Truth Now. And since no artist ever again need dedicate energy to making the essential Warhol discovery—that of America's modern incarnation in its mass culture—each subsequent report is obliged to transmit news of some evolution. That obligation we fulfilled. Warhol had concentrated on the idea of Pop. Essentially a recognition of the way a new cultural infrastructure had impacted identity, the tone of his work had been impersonal, objective, speechless—stunned. Fifteen years later, the Metro Pictures artists figured out how to get emotion into Pop. What was the emotion? For some reason, anxiety. Longo's melodrama, Sherman's nausée struck not always the same note, perhaps, but a consistent chord, yes—a chord composed by Bernard Hermann. The horror, the horror. We East Village conceptualists, on the other hand, made Pop personal, playful, everyday. Logically so: with Pop become as nature, its coldness _will_ seem like warmth.

Mind you, there were limits to exactly how cold things could get: we worked in the pre-cyber age. Just prior: the personal computer had been invented, but most people still tapped away at electric typewriters. So, we weren't computer kids. The glow we sported came from prolonged exposure to another screen.

In an essay entitled "The Guiding Light" (written in 1985 to accompany _Infotainment_, the first substantial touring exhibition of works by Nature Morte artists, plus fellow travelers Peter Halley, Laurie Simmons, and Sarah Charlesworth), I remarked that "my generation is defined by its experience of peacetime (lacerated occasionally by terrorism), the atomization of history's authority, and perhaps most singularly, the cold glue of television." We were TV kids. Sure, references to film-induced sensation showed up in the work of some—in Jennifer Bolande's sculptures, in Gretchen Bender's movie-title pieces—but the motion picture didn't stand as our core experiential model. We deemed the movies' investment in illusionism too steep; it amounted to an investment in dishonesty. Too, their presumption of their own importance—and thus their importance to the audience—struck us as arrogant. Everything about the scale of movies felt wrong.

Television had our vote. Still, we were more than just American kids who had grown up with TV and had gone on to become artists. We were conscious of being the first generation of American artists not to regard TV as an enemy. We were the first generation of American artists for whom it was authentic to feel that TV wasn't the demise of civilization but instead the linchpin of a contemporary informational infrastructure, unnamed and still forming, perhaps, but by which we did not feel at all intimidated, from which we derived joy, and in which we even took pride. This stance was a contribution, because it advanced a reality of the culture. It recognized that a strange new world had done in the old—and that however strange, this new world had not managed to prevent the young from liking life.

Within the more parochial confines of the art world, our pro-TV attitude signaled an important power shift. The traditional eastern-seaboard intellectual had resisted and at every opportunity denigrated the tube. For a new generation of educated, Manhattan-based culture critters to consciously accept TV as (at least) a pleasurable condition of life meant, therefore, that the hierarchical, Euro-inflected concerns of the post-war New York School had lost serious ground to a more indigenous value system, the frank embrace of which was fast becoming a hallmark of artists working in that risen capital, Los Angeles. Even the Metro artists, much as we admired them, were still dealing with film, essentially, and still accessing, however subliminally, the respect accorded cinema. Our group, having been born a little later and thus a little farther away from where American culture had been—Europe—acted as a bridge leading into where the culture was heading: TV Land. Outside the confines of the art world, construction of said bridge was already well advanced, of course; the attitude held by the East Village conceptualists just forced the art world to adjust to the realities of the day.

Did we all make videos non-stop, then? No. The East Village galleries saw very little video, actually; the camcorder technology available produced too crude a look. Of the group considered here, only Gretchen Bender worked seriously with the medium, fashioning exhilarating multi-monitor video symphonies such as _Dumping Core_, 1984. Did we perhaps ape the look of TV in our static artworks? Not really. Some of us did adapt certain of commercial TV's visual strategies or effects—the use of insets; a fizzy, busy, op-arty surface—but the conscious, overt attempt to render the experience of gazing at a TV screen belonged, really, to painter Kenny Scharf. ("Not of our group," Scharf, but from the credit-where-credit-is-due department, this belated kudo: by combining aerosoled, soft-focus backgrounds with hard-edged, sharp-focus foreground elements, Scharf approximated the strange, four-inch-deep illusionism of TV imagery better than anyone else has managed to do, before or since.)

In what, then, did our endorsement of television consist? Here I am again, in "The Guiding Light": "To the children of

Barthes and Coca-Cola television affords the opportunity to monitor consumer civilization from our bedrooms." (Fancy talk, for a thief; the reference rips off and riffs on Godard's characterization—remember Godard?—of his films of the '60s as portraying "the children of Marx and Coca-Cola." My mid-'80s update surfed the cresting influence of semiotics—remember semioticians?—and of Roland Barthes, the most widely known of the tribe.) We, the children of Barthes and Coca-Cola, anointed TV to be our core experiential model of camera-centric Pop because television provided a window onto late capitalism's vast social and cultural infrastructure. If this attitude marked us as unromantic and worldly and dry-eyed, well, we meant it to. There'd been quite enough melodrama already, thank you. We had no use for either '60s naivete or '70s embitterment. Cynicism springs from disappointment, disappointment from naiveté; obvious, it seemed to us, that to ward off the cynicism's black flowers, naiveté had to be nipped in the bud. We wielded the shears cheerfully.

"[My] generation loves TV because it frankly admits with every absurd inch of videotape that it exists solely to commodify everything it touches, and this transformation of the imagination and spirit into Product is the heart of the American story in the 20th century." As a medium that honestly interrupted itself every 15 minutes to tell us just who brought it to us and, more importantly, why, TV effected the most radical reconciliation of contrasting and complementary realities extant. Television integrated commerce and entertainment, journalism and show biz, war and froth, sound and image, and did so with an attitude of fairly naked honesty about its intentions. That honesty accounted for much of its attractiveness. TV's habitual bean-spilling prevented viewers from sinking into illusionistic/narrative depths, mindless addiction to which had made movies so tiresome. The tube seemed to us the right kind of shallow. As we watched, we knew perfectly well that the camera was capable of lying, or at least that it believed whatever it was told, and so, making the best of an imperfect world, we opted to believe in disbelief. On that surface to which TV kept us close, we frolicked.

In a way, of course, the surface was mighty thin ice; television, the perfect medium for a generation accustomed to occupying the sidelines of history, was about to encounter in another piece of technology, the PC, a profound challenge to its authority—indeed, the only real challenge it had ever had to face. Within the art context, the confrontation between the two screen-systems was staged—and, to some degree, resolved—in the work of the East Village conceptualists. It was in their art that the dominant Pop mode, reinforced most powerfully and insistently by TV, began to dovetail with visual strategies distinctly of the Digital Age. Television, supreme repository of the signage of capitalism, and the computer, audience enabler par excellence, began to overlap and to merge.

The moment manifested itself as an obsession with visual strategies of integration (particularly at Nature Morte, where a focus on the question of how to organize visual information reflected the graphic-art backgrounds of gallery founders Alan Belcher and Peter Nagy.) While David Salle painted triple-exposed images in a manner introduced by Picabia, while Robert Longo rendered anxious 3-D versions of Rosenquist's billboard-collage, the younger infotainers, influenced by TV's radical synthesis of complement and contrast and, perhaps just as essentially, by the neither/nor, both/and condition of their native suburban landscape, pursued a radical synthesis of elements aptly described as postcollage. In Nagy's paintings, Ashley Bickerton's in-your-face combines, the sculpture of Belcher, Joel Otterson, or Jenny Bolande, discrete informational entities, whether material or imagistic, relinquished part or all of their identities toward the creation of a hybridized whole. (About the same time, as if on cue, science confirmed the postcollage strategy with a model of its own: the gene splice.) The evolution of computer technology may have perched these artists on the cusp of the predigital era, but the more precocious among them had by instinct already converted to the gospel of seamlessness that the cyberworld would soon preach. That effortless erasure of seams that Photoshop accomplishes with a click of the mouse these artists already carried out, albeit in more laborious fashion, with Xerox machine and paint or with stone, wood, and metal.

Or with a photograph and its support. Belcher and Bolande led the way in prying photography off the wall and out of the frame to let it stand upright on the floor, thrust forward into space, cascade from the ceiling. By emphasizing that photographs were physical _things_, the two artists extended the medium beyond both its pictorial hang-up and the more Conceptual practices of John Baldessari, John Knight, Richard Prince, et al, which, evolutionary intent aside, still worked a 2-D groove. In Bolande's work of the time, single photographs were incorporated into organic, determinedly tentative sculptures that flicker between abstraction and representation, landscape and body; in Belcher's, photos plural, referencing the synthetic/commercial realm, figure in playful volumetric constructions. The photo-object was flat-out _invention_—precedented perhaps in the display industry, but hardly at all in the biz of fine art. (Man Ray's oeuvre, Martial Raysse's, Marcel Broodthaers'—each of these might feature one or two examples, yes, but only incidentally, not as a focused pursuit.)

Once uncorked, the postcollage aesthetic expanded outward, engulfing, dissolving, "digitalizing" materials, images, styles, genres ... (Visual traditions, even. The monolithically integrationist, One World philosophy inherent to the Information Age disposed the East Village conceptualists toward spotlighting aesthetic similarities rather than differences. From there it was just a gene splice away to combining, say, visual expressions of the ecstatic, exampled in Baroque and Rococo art, with their contemporary Pop manifestation in rock 'n' roll, a subculture equally dedicated to sensory overload. Whether the results—Nagy's paintings, Otterson's furniture sculptures—embodied a Pop rococo or a rococo Pop, none of us knew for sure, and the confusion felt appropriate and true.) A flashy technique was no excuse for textual vacuity, however; the discrete, the intact, the separable may have become transmuted into the hybridized, the synthesized, and the temporary, but to the children of Barthes and Coca-Cola the result had still to deliver as signage, had still to reward our interpretive impulses at least as richly as had the source material prior to its transformation. Otherwise, why go to the trouble of making this stuff? By the same token, substantive intentions weren't enough either—which meant that content alone wasn't enough. The presence of "critique" or "commentary," no matter how brilliant, didn't justify an experience of visual impoverishment. Integration, integration, integration! Content and lush physicality, mind and body, were meant to flirt, seduce, cohabit, rut and finally, settle down to a union happy with tension. A balance of qualities being the condition of life, we looked to include beauty, wit, sensuality, artifice, and rigor in every object, not permitting any one quality to become more dominant than balance.

The jacuzzi's motor was a little rusty but once we'd gotten it started up, things got plenty sexy. Perhaps seduced by the bubbles, most of us opted to abandon any pretense of performing deconstructive surgery on society's ills. What, we wisely asked ourselves, was the sense of devoting our imaginations, our energies, our lives to making art about that version of the world that we <u>didn't</u> like? Whining about the demise of the classical world, carping about the world that capitalism had made—this was too easy. It was hypocritical, to boot: we'd seen artists get rich off their honed complaining. Moving decisively out of response mode, we jettisoned the discourse of unhappiness and voted instead to make art about all the things we liked—rock 'n' roll, fashion, TV, movies, architecture, sex, furniture, travel, humor, oh, abstract thinking—in order to build the world we preferred. We rejected the notion of justifying art by assigning it, a priori, some therapeutic function, and exposed it again to the risks of life.

We were right to do this, for our lives as well as our art. We shifted the young avant-garde's attitude from tragedy to comedy, from disintegration to integration, from deconstruction to construction. Truth's coordinates keep shifting—the computer gradually supersedes TV as the core experiential model of media, and cloning has already replaced the gene splice as a metaphor (all those cast resin bodies littering the galleries!).

The most lasting contribution of the East Village Conceptualists, intangible, but appearing everywhere since, may turn out to have been our restoration of a discourse of happiness—affirmation of the present and receptivity to the future—as an option for ambitious, thinking artists. Before our loosely clustered group took up its meagre winnings and dispersed—to India, Bali, Venezuela, Toronto, upstate New York, Kentucky, Chicago—we had carried out a generation's work.

Out of Camera Range

The text of a speech presented at Forum Stadtpark, Graz, Austria, in 1992, it originally appeared, in Camera Austria, nr. 41, Graz, 1993, and in a slightly different form, as "Speech for Prime Time," in Art issues magazine the same year.

TO LEAD YOU INTO UNDERSTANDING MY SPEECH I MUST START BY TELLING YOU THAT I'M MORE INTERESTED IN THE STRUCTURAL LIFE OF THE CAMERA THAN I AM IN HOW PARTICULAR CATEGORIES OF PHOTOGRAPHIC IMAGES FRAME ONE OR ANOTHER SOCIAL GROUP. In effect I prefer to talk not about flora and fauna but about shifting tectonic plates.

Specifically, I want to talk about particular ways in which the age of the camera has influenced our imagination of ourselves, of our own possibilities as human beings. This is more powerfully an American phenomenon than it occurs in the Old World. In European countries, indeed, in every Old World country, the impact of the camera-based industries of mass media—television, movies, modern advertising—has been cushioned by the continuing presence of classical culture in daily life. In the United States, however, we've had no strong tradition of classical culture to fortify us against the daily, incessant barrage of camera-culture's products, so the institutions of camera-culture—what we have all learned to call "mass media"—have come to dominate our experience of reality, functioning like a kind of shadow government, occupying exactly that matrix where the structural life of the camera intersects the way the nation imagines itself. So today I'll be speaking about some of the abstract conditions of life in a place where the camera-based industries of the mass media have effectively nationalized the complex problems inherent in pictorial representation, which for centuries had been held in the protective custody of the art world.

Conventional wisdom maintains that the camera never lies. I contend, however, that the question of whether the camera lies or tells some version of the truth is of less consequence to the life of our culture than the fact that the camera believes everything. The camera's inability to judge the truthfulness of what it is asked to record, its structural incapacity to distinguish between fact and fiction, has long been used to give fiction a weight of veracity equal to that of fact. Actually, it would be more accurate to say that the categories of fiction and fact disappear into the lens; the camera's mechanical credulity fuses fact and fiction into a distinct, third entity, neither "real" nor "unreal." The question that begs to be addressed, therefore, is not whether the camera tells us truth or lie—it's too late in the game for such a fine distinction—but rather, what does it mean for a civilization to locate at the center of its cultural life a machine that is incapable of knowing when it is being conned?

At this point in our cultural development, we have all been bullied into submitting to the belief that work taken note of by the cultural eye of the camera is important work. I say "bullied" because very few people reap the benefits of this belief. In the US, as I have said, camera culture now rules national life, and the people who benefit from this—the entertainment, news, and advertising industries—have been well positioned to redraft the nation's cultural agenda, effectively monopolizing the airwaves and excluding all challenges to the rule of the camera. As a result, in the States we now live with a curious condition of self-fulfilling prophecy: camera culture promotes continuously and without interference the belief that important cultural work is accomplished by holding the camera's attention. The promotion of this belief has been so successful that the camera's position of dominance in our cultural life goes entirely unquestioned. It no longer even occurs to us to challenge the camera's place in our lives. We have come to accept the mass media's needs and desires as entirely natural, almost as if they were some kind of punishment we'd deserved.

It is my belief that the camera's position in our lives has gradually effected a subtle and profound shift in our valuation of cultural work. Specifically, we have permitted the camera to alter our sense of what may constitute important work. It is no longer simply the case that the camera enables those who have done important work to be noticed by others (an innocent enough function). Instead, validation by the camera now so influences the American national imagination, it has come to see that the only way to do important work is to do work which is absorbable by the camera. All other currency has been devalued. The camera has evolved into a new and highly specialized kind of vampire, draining successive generations of the capacity to envision cultural contributions that do not involve being rewarded by the camera's attention. The question that naturally arises here: Do we really want to narrow the range of what we might consider important cultural work to include only those kinds of work usable by—absorbable by—the camera?

Think about the use of human energy. If the camera has come to represent the cultural eye, if culture has come to be the record of what the camera looks at, if whatever gains the camera's attention becomes official history, then those wishing to participate in a culture that is camera-based must organize their energies around gaining and holding the camera's attention. This means necessarily that we live in a time when the camera has galvanized around itself many of the reasons people have to pursue participation in culture.

We have a simple name for those who have successfully organized their energy around gaining and holding the camera's attention; we call them "stars." In a certain way, stars are the people who most efficiently use their energy in a camera-based culture; perhaps this is truly what we celebrate them for. To those who achieve it, stardom issues passports to many glittering points on the compass of professional life, a fact that persuades us to look upon stars as people who make a large contribution to our civilization. As is only to be expected, the camera-based industries encourage us in this view. I suggest, however, that despite the piles of money which may be earned from it, dedicating one's energies to holding the camera's attention is actually a small contribution to civilization, and that, furthermore, the more our civilization gives its attention to organizing cultural work around cameras, the weaker and more confused our civilization becomes. Without wishing to denigrate the sometimes extraordinary talents of stars—the question we are examining here is not whether beauty can be achieved, but by which means we achieve it—I challenge our blind habit of high regard for the privileged world of the camera.

In what weakness does the camera encourage us? I think the answer is that in the national life generated, shaped, and maintained by entertainment and advertising—the two camera-based industries which daily represent the evolving texture and configuration of, for example, American life to the populace—the camera functions fundamentally as a device used to represent behavior. Apart from its often-dubious documentary function—dubious because the camera can be made to believe anything, and because we can never see proof of what went on before or after the camera preserved a particular moment—the principal function of the camera in mass-media culture has been to lend credence to represented, as opposed to real, behavior.

What is represented behavior? It is, of course, behavior that is embedded within an imaginative field that has been generated for, organized around, and framed by the camera—still or motion picture or video. It is the infinitely elastic world of human pretense, of people pretending, living out fictive lives, whether as characters (in the entertainment industry) or as types (in the demographics-fixated field of advertising). Ask yourself this question: if the camera were removed, would these people have any reason for doing what they're doing in front of it? If the answer is "no, they would not," then you are looking at an instance of represented behavior.

In my opinion it is a dangerous misjudgment on the part of any culture to grant represented behavior such a position of centrality. Represented behavior trivializes human action by placing it entirely inside the realm of the fictive. Confined within the fictionalizing frame of the camera's presence, such behavior can only be performative, not actual, and so cannot give to humans any fundamental permission. It can only grant the comparatively minor permission of behavioral style: to talk or dress or smoke a cigarette in a certain way. It can achieve, in short, only the importance of fashion. Represented behavior reduces the potential effects of real human actions, so it can be claimed that the camera shrinks our sense of our effectiveness in the world, our ability to displace content and matter—and thus literally to make history—through our actions.

Thus it is not surprising that in the United States we are able to chart a direct relationship between the increasing centrality of the camera—the device par excellence for representing behavior—and an erosion of participatory democracy. The participation of the populace in its governance requires on the part of each citizen a clear sense of empowerment and action, a sense that one's actions have consequences in real time and space, a sense that one's actions matter because they do not occur within a landscape of fiction. But in America daily and intensive contact with the cameras of the mass media has worn away people's sense of empowerment by seducing their sense of action into a den of pretense. By elevating the camera-based mass-media industries to such levels of privilege within our civilization, we have unwittingly elevated as well the camera's reckless capacity to erode our individual sense of power. The camera's enervating effect on our national life may be accurately termed the theatricalization of franchise.

That is really the first point I would like to make: that continual immersion in camera culture theatricalizes and aestheticizes our sense of our own ability to act and thereby diminishes that ability. The second point I would like to make about the impact of camera culture also pertains to an idea about action. It has to do with the way in which I think mass media has altered our perception of ambition, specifically as it pertains to creativity.

Ever since people in the West became self-conscious about the presence of mass media in their lives—possibly this can be dated from around 40 years ago, or about the time a particular attitude became manifested in the example of Warhol, the shift in attitude measurable in the distance between Marilyn Monroe, who was consumed by mass media, and Warhol, who consumed it, and her—the goal of culturally ambitious people has been to "use" mass media for their own purposes. Widely considered to be the most sophisticated attitude to take towards mass media, those who hold it are often thought to represent the most determinedly modern take on creativity itself, perhaps because theirs has seemed the only attitude that held any promise of reconciling personal goals with the fact of mass media's occupation of the site where the symbols of reality are negotiated and managed: first, one attracts the attention of mass media, and then one manipulates and manages it for one's own benefit.

Yet at the same time, our interest in people who've so organized their energy is invariably transformed and, I believe, diminished once they are embraced by mass media. Ironically, we begin to lose interest in them at the very instant they achieve their long sought-after goal. Why should this so consistently be the case? Partly because we have always regarded participation in mass media as an ascent to a kind of heaven, so our response to those who gain that participation is not dissimilar from the response we have when someone has died. "They have been taken from us. A distance has been introduced. They are less a person now than a memory of a person." We might further account for the diminishment of interest by the fact that, in order to communicate with us, pop creatures must always allow themselves to be positioned in such a way that they are "presented by" mass media, which means necessarily that they give up any possibility of establishing a method of information production that could fundamentally challenge the mass media's self-appointed role as the presenter. In effect, pop creatures agree to behave themselves.

But neither of these seem to me the real reason why mass media stardom has lost its attraction, its edge. The real reason is that the activity of arranging one's creative life around the goal of obtaining and holding the notice of cameras no longer seems a high level of human invention. It may have been enormously inventive 70 years ago but today, as a cultural goal, that particular ambition contains little or no real invention. It has become instead a cliché of human aspiration.

I need to take this critique of mass media camera-culture one step further, because I think that considering this idea about a cliché of human aspiration can lead us to an awareness of what I regard as mass media's darkest influence on our behavior, namely the manner in which mass media has altered our ideas about why anyone might choose to dedicate their lives to creativity. What begins as pioneering behavior, the instinct to pioneer and possibly thereby to invent something fundamental, a tool that hasn't existed before, and to live a life by this invention and within this inventiveness—in short, to dedicate one's life to risking the creation of new models of human behavior, and from these the establishment of new worlds to sustain the human imagination—this glorious and honorable and very basic motivation has been transformed and trivialized in the age of mass media into a tendency to live the pioneering life only until the attention of mass media has been attracted and sufficiently secured, in order that the glamorous and easy life—the heaven—offered by mass media may become our lives, and we will no longer be required to live the difficult and earthbound life of the pioneer. <u>In effect, mass media operates according to the hypothesis that we become creative pioneers in order to be noticed by mass media</u>. Here, to be fair, we should recognize that, quite by accident, mass media has hit upon a minor truth—that the life of the pioneer is indeed difficult, and often does not at all resemble any sort of heaven—but by the same token we must also recognize that mass media has inflated that minor truth until it has become something monolithic and oppressive, something ideological and no longer recognizable as any sort of useful truth. By so grotesquely overstating this particular minor truth, mass media reveals its grave misunderstanding of the artist's life, fatuously mistaking creativity as something to do so "successfully" that <u>we won't have to do it anymore</u>. Such an attitude demeans, and has done much to erode a human tradition of commitment to pioneering—the inventions of worlds that have yet to exist and which, I might add, may challenge either incidentally or by conscious design the ordering of values put forth by mass media.

What is our future to be under the dispassionate imperialism of the camera? Will our culture continue to pour energy into the black hole of represented behavior? Will access to mass media persist as a major cultural goal? Or might people begin to secede from the camera's empire? Might they, realizing that there was a time before the camera's dominance, imagine a time after it and go about creating the conditions of such an environment? To call for the physical destruction of the technology of mass media is both reactionary and a misuse of energy—not to mention silly. Better, I think, to cultivate internal resources and develop a state of mind that de-emphasizes the importance of cultural work that depends on the camera for its existence. We can demand of ourselves a mature and sophisticated appraisal of camera-culture's contribution to civilization. In time, we can make selective abandonment of camera culture seem a natural next step. If the camera believes everything, then it's of limited usefulness to human society, unless we prefer to become a society of fools.

We need to envision alternatives to a future under the camera's rule. We must begin again to exercise our imagination of the future—a muscle that has atrophied since the invention of the atom bomb, when our educational apparatus began dedicating itself to instructing citizens in fear of the future. In a certain way, we can be grateful to mass media and camera culture, because during The Fear they have served as bomb shelters for our imaginative lives. But these days it looks increasingly as if there is indeed to be a future, so it's time to come out of those bomb shelters. We need to stop wasting time diverting our energy into camera culture and represented behavior, once again regaining memory of the effectiveness of real actions.

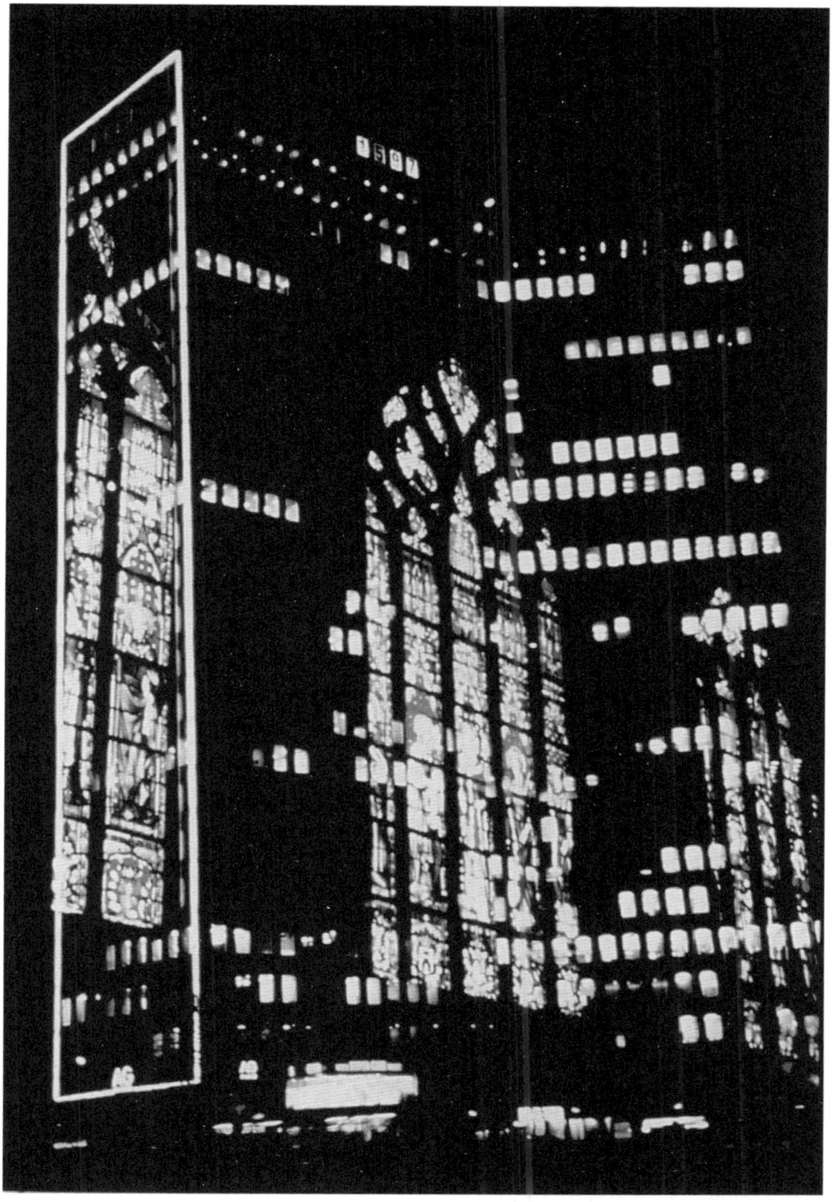

Bruxelles Lightbox #1, 1990
Cibachrome transparency and lightbox, 73" x 47 1/4"

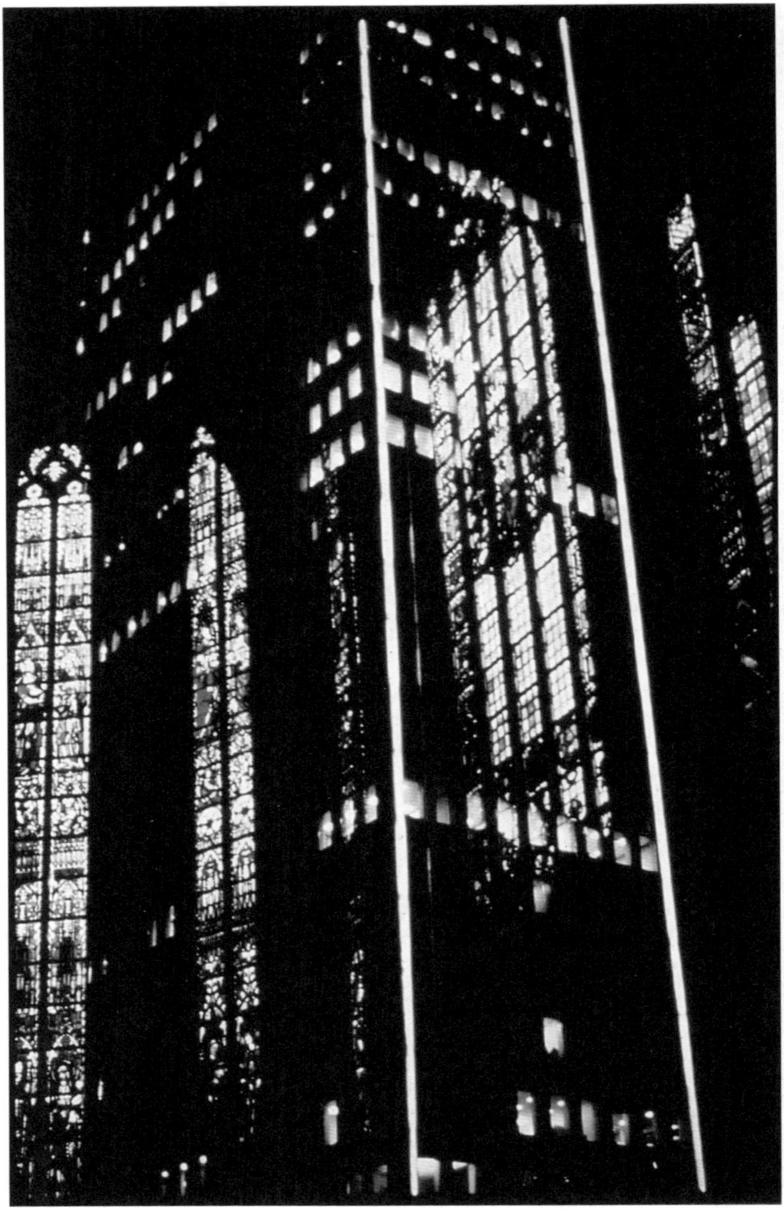

Bruxelles Lightbox #2, 1990
Cibrachrome transparency and lightbox, 73" x 47 1/4"

Entries from the Brussels Notebook

Artist's statement accompanying the exhibition at Galerie Hufkens, Brussels, 1989.

LIVING AT THE SABLON IN MONKISH ELEGANCE: NO PHONE, NO TELEVISION, NO REFRIGERATOR. Only the radio, the ticking of a borrowed watch, and the competing bells from two churches.

Investigated the church across the street, Eglise Notre-Dame au Sablon. In churches, stained glass is meant to overwhelm the eye's focusing mechanism, to dazzle the eye ... indeed, to push the eye to the limits of dazzlement in order to initiate another level of "vision": an early attempt to "blow the mind." Stained glass is psychedelic iconography.

The photographic transparency (whether a positive or a negative) may be thought of as the modern version of churchly stained glass. Apart from the simple shared fact of transparency, both are "holy" picturing systems; that is, as regards the claim to representing "truth," both are picturing systems in which we "have faith." What would result, then, were one to make and exhibit photographic transparencies of stained glass? A partial answer is that doing so would push to the breaking point of literalism the camera's unwavering faith in whatever image is presented to it. "The camera believes everything," I always say. Let's push this truth into overdrive and see what happens.

As stained glass is to photographic transparency, church is to lightbox. Downtown Brussels is filled with modernist office "lightboxes," my favorite style of architecture. The exterior is simplified and we think more about the interior. These office buildings at night display row upon neatly ordered row of green glass rectangles that frame infinite variations on the theme of the neon-lit office interior … new "stained glass" monuments raised to honor the secular deities of commerce and bureaucracy.

Church as lightbox from the inside during daylight hours. Office building as lightbox from exterior at night. Fusing the two photographically produces no-time and no-place (or rather, art-time, art-place) and, furthermore, parallels the condition of "belief" which is always, essentially, the radical confusion of exterior and interior states.

The fusion of "sacred" and "rational" architectures provides a metaphor for the psychology of the art gallery, the site that accomodates the production of both "mystery" and "analysis." Placing such fusions in a gallery, then, creates a kind of psychoanalytic stage set for the gallery. In effect, the gallery is caused to exhibit stills from a movie about its unconscious life.

Stained glass and office buildings. Break them down into constituent parts: color, light, architecture/lightbox, photography. Shuffle and recombine.

The act of re-presenting images of stained glass via photography and lightbox isolates for our consideration the question of "faith" and "belief" in art. Are you a believer? If so, where do you locate your belief? In the activity itself (whatever that may be); the social location of the artist; the result ("experiencing the object"); the result (meaning or effect)?

Reductio ad absurdum: any examination of faith reveals that what one has faith in is, finally, faith itself. Faith is the ultimate self-defining characteristic: whatever the object of our belief, whatever reasons we provide ourselves in order to maintain our belief in our enterprise, when it comes right down to it we simply and stubbornly believe in our belief. When our reasons burn away, or when we have long forgotten them, we resort to faith in our faith.

So too in art. We've not a shred of proof that art performs any of the functions with which we credit it. We simply believe "in it"—and fueled by that belief, art _does_ perform. Art, then, is the medium for belief in art. Art _houses_ our belief in art.

Question: what is produced when one "loses faith in art" but continues to make art anyway? Is it art that is made or something else?

On the strange fruit of photographically produced "impossible" stained glass (out of focus, double-exposed, etc.): What interests us, quite apart from the formal arrangement of a given picture, is a person's decision to "extend" these representations of faith via the "technological naturalism" of photography and lightbox? The _behavior_ interests us: stained-glass-as-lightbox seems to me to be comedy of the highest order … extremes of faith and skepticism made entirely congruent, one with the other. Such an enterprise is very likely _sublime comedy_.

SECTION II
INTELLECTUAL SHOWBIZ

The Today Show and The Tonight Show, 1989
two panels, each 60" x 40", denim, embroidery, bells, spotlight

Art after Entertainment

Originally published in Art issues, in February (Part 1) and April (Part 2) 1989.

PART I

CONTEMPORARY VISUAL ART IS DEVELOPING A ROLE AS A KIND OF ENTERTAINMENT. In my experience, enthusiasm for this development is limited to American artists and audiences, perhaps because the United States is generating the phenomenon. Europeans tend to consider offensive the equating of art and entertainment, as if such an equation could only be a trivialization of the noble ambitions of high culture. But to Americans, who long ago rejected the authority of the European model of civilization in order to construct a culture along more democratic lines, the reconciliation of art and popular entertainment seems a reasonable development, one stuffed with possibilities that in no way threaten "civilization."

Life in the United States is organized by the Constitution, surely a civilizing document in intent. The Constitution may be regarded as essentially a document of conceptual sculpture, in that it is addressed to the psychological organization of space: specifically, to how one is to contend with the presence of others, or The Other, in a social space determined by law to be equally accessible to all citizens. As a product of this Constitutional framework, the American mind is constructed with a peculiar lack of closure, a perpetual awareness of the presence of others. It's why we are quite naturally an audience culture. The voice of the American artist reflects this by implying "we," as in "we are like this now." By way of contrast, the voice of the European artist says "I," as in "I am the text."

The spatial organization articulated by the Constitution instills in Americans an advanced and complex sense of social space, how to live in it, move through it, think about it. In fact, the particular ordering of social space laid out by the Constitution <u>is</u> the nation. American life is constructed around the idea of shared space, the <u>concept</u> of it, and American culture is the product of our examination of this concept's ongoing negotiations with the contours of human nature and the details of daily life.

The modern United States is distinguished from other nations by its mass democracy, its radical diversity of population, and a hyper-developed mass media that unifies the populace by spinning around them an electronic web of popular culture. The citizens of the United States come from such radically diverse origins that in order to have any sense whatsoever of a unified national identity, American culture cannot encourage citizens to look back to their origins. Thus we have little feel for "the Past," for to acquire an understanding of it would require us to look back to origins that can only separate us, the Chinese-Americans from the Hispanic-Americans from the Greek-Americans. Instead, emphasis is placed on what we have in common: the eternal present of popular culture as generated and managed by mass media. Americans communicate with their neighbors by assuming a familiarity with the mass experience of entertainment culture—TV shows, pop songs, sports, bestsellers.

Andy Warhol's discovery of how this nation communicates to its citizens its sense of unity and identity made him this century's Christopher Columbus. Warhol discovered America's modern incarnation in pop culture. The considerable surprise since Warhol's discovery is that <u>pop doesn't go away</u>. Pop wasn't a phase, or the culmination of something. Pop is the raw material of the

American vernacular. Pop is what we have to work with, the clay. We are only now beginning to deal with this stubborn fact. And one of the things we need to recognize is that pop culture didn't just stay at the first level of discovery, the Warhol level. Whereas Warhol proclaimed and celebrated as the distinctly American contribution to world culture the radical idea of the egalitarian product—the idea that the Coke Liz Taylor or the President drinks is no better or worse than the Coke you or I drink—mass democracy has rolled on, further leveling our experience of reality. I think that in America we are now grappling with the next phase of egalitarian culture, which I describe as the democracy of pleasures.

Everyone is accustomed to arranging the symbols of pleasure into a hierarchy—champagne vs. beer, classical music vs. rock-and-roll, _Romeo and Juliet_ vs. _Laverne and Shirley_.* But American culture refuses systematically to rank the pleasures produced by these. It obliterates the opposition, removes the "versus." That is to say, in American culture, the pleasure derived by one individual from drinking a beer is considered no less worthy of respect than the pleasure derived from another individual from drinking champagne. Again, the symbols of pleasure may be compared (indeed, are compared endlessly by the advertising industry) but the respective pleasures themselves, the pleasures associated with two different symbols by two different people, are not to be compared or arranged in a hierarchy. This is Constitutionally sanctioned, the central cultural reality of mass democracy in America now, and it will be interesting to see whether or not we can survive it.

The American democracy of pleasures can be characterized as a _horizontal_ culture; Europe, which is dedicated to the idea that indeed some pleasures are more worthy of consideration and respect than are others, is a _vertical_ culture, instructing and encouraging people to arrange experience hierarchically. From the American viewpoint, unless it's an American whose personal need for a sense of aristocracy is threatened by the democracy of taste, Europe has got it all wrong. But here's the catch for Americans: there's some question as to whether a _civilization_ can ever be constructed from our horizontal culture, because in such a culture the institutions traditionally charged with maintaining civilization and instructing children in its tenets—schools, churches, the civilizing practices of the individual imagination (painting, literature, theater)—face the problem of being believed, for the challenge to their authority is built into the very document, the Constitution, which sanctions the social space to produce a horizontal culture. I will here take the chance of defining a civilization as a society that has the ability to pass along to succeeding generations an understanding of how that society is organized, and furthermore, that the vehicles that pass along the civilizing code in that society have an awareness of their role as civilizers. So the question arises as to how, in a horizontal culture, the idea of civilization can be constructed, let alone maintained?

I think that the evidence of contemporary American life, the sense of disintegration, leads one to conclude that, in a horizontal culture, those institutions which continue to be based on hierarchical, vertical models of civilization in fact are not believed or have failed to make themselves believable. In a democracy of tastes, the traditional civilizing forces do not communicate to citizens their ancient civilizing role. Their authority is sufficiently doubted to weaken their claims to leadership, and the civilizing force leaks out into other vehicles more appropriate to the context of horizontal culture.

I would suggest that in a radical cultural democracy such as America's, the task of passing down the information about how society is organized and maintained falls not to the inheritors of the European model of civilization, which hierarchizes cultural consumption and is therefore unreadable to the citizens of horizontal culture, but, rather, to those information forms which are specific to the development of horizontal culture. Thus, in America the pop, the responsibility to instruct in the organization and use of social space falls not to painting and literature but to the mass media. Further, the civilizing code is no longer embedded in the genes of a specific show or song, as was the case with pop's more naive manifestations of 30 years ago;

instead, the civilizing code communicating the complex responsibilities of life in mass democracy is contained in the pop distributive structures themselves, the conduits through which pop songs or TV shows are pumped to consumers. We are accustomed to thinking of these conduits as the inviolable infrastructure of our cultural life, the culmination of our struggle for national unity and identity. Why not instead think of our national pop distributive infrastructure as the first step toward building an American civilization?

I'm suggesting that there has been a fundamental shift from pop surface to pop structure. The *Billboard* "Hot 100" chart, for example, a structure that exists in order to organize and promote pop songs, is now more important to the national identity and communicates to us much more about our sense of national life than the "interior" content—lyrics, musical style—of any 45 rpm record by, say, Madonna.

With the exception of a few comedy shows (*SCTV*, *Letterman*), this shift from pop surface to pop structure has gone unrecognized or has been purposely ignored by the establishment mass media. While American mass media have done an extraordinary job of unifying the citizenry and communicating the crucial link between national identity and the egalitarian product, our media have been unable or unwilling to pass to the more complex level of civilizing now required of them. The mass media are holding the ball, but they do not know what the game is. *Masterpiece Theater* is not the answer. Neither is *Entertainment Tonight*. If the mass media which so dominate the construction of reality in this country continue to exclude from the airwaves any examination of the content they daily produce and the meaning they daily displace by their dominance, they will ensure that America will never develop as a civilization. The sense of civilization that needs to be built from the raw material of horizontal culture will never be built, will always remain at the level of a culture, if the vehicles in a position to convey the civilizing information remain incapable of accepting responsibility for the role they play in the national life. There is a sense in this country that a crucial opportunity was missed ten years ago, an opportunity for the mass media to move to the next level of civilizing. But they didn't know what to do, and as a result we've been drowning in a culture of parody, re-run, and sequel. It has retarded our sense of the future. Do we want only an endless extension of present-day cultural rituals? Are we only to look forward to watching the 650th Academy Awards Presentation, live from Dorothy Chandler Pavilion City, and then the 651st, the 652nd, the 653rd … ? If so, include me out.

Entertainment producers today exploit the audience for private gain but refuse to acknowledge in their products the impact that they have on the audience and the larger role those products play in the national life. Entertainment producers seem not to notice that the United States is an entertainment, mass-media culture, and not an art culture. The inability or unwillingness of American entertainment producers to create products which explicitly accept the civilizing role played by mass media in a horizontal culture means that someone else—the audience, the site of exploitation—has to do the job.

To get a closer look at this curious state of affairs, then, I spent time in Hollywood working in television. Apart from learning that the shadow cast by Hollywood's mountain of money blacks out subtleties, I found that entertainment culture has little capacity for, and little interest in, self-criticality (when questioned about this failure, entertainment producers absolved themselves by claiming "It's only entertainment"); that entertainment workers devote their days to recording make-believe; entertainment producers to have a habit of saying "ideas are a dime a dozen";** that, in entertainment culture, you have to get permission to do your work.

It is difficult not to conclude that the self-imagination of the mass-media communications systems of the United States, in so far as communications systems are necessary for the construction and continuation of a civilization, seems integrally flawed. The basic relation of the American mass media to the population it serves is: professed democratic content produced by corporations. In its products, the mass media addresses an abstraction of "the democratic," which it imagines to be the needs of the receiver but which in fact is invariably defined and determined by the values and needs of the sender. The sender never admits this. The basic tension, then, is this: a content of anti-hierarchy is produced and managed by hierarchical organisms (corporations). The dilemma that results—the structural misrepresentation of content—is a suffocating and dispiriting fact of adult American life, and suggests to children growing up in such an environment a fundamentally incongruent transcription of social reality.

PART II

As George Trow says, culture is our third parent. Children raised by the American entertainment monolith of movies, TV, records, and magazines feel toward it the primal, pressurized admixture of love and hatred, respect and fear, dependence and resentment felt in greater degree toward biological parents. In European countries, these powerful, conflicted feelings have traditionally been reserved for a different "third parent"—high culture. While the struggles of Modernist artists against high culture's domination of the European imagination yielded the fecund, perverse, and revolutionary attitude of anti-art, in America, where mass-media entertainment culture, not art culture, dominates our imaginative lives, the struggle of consumers against this domination is beginning to produce an "anti-entertainment" sensibility—wobbly and uncertain at first—that may in time prove to be as complex and fertile as its European counterpart.

Until recently, Americans have been unable to analyze their relation to entertainment culture <u>in the language of that culture</u>. (After all, entertainment culture's rule over daily life was cemented only in the early '50s, with television's invasion of homes from sea to shining sea. And it took a few decades for the novelty of electronic communications to wear off to the point where we began to ask certain questions about the wizard behind the curtain.) Initially, corporations alone possessed the technology needed to be able to speak in the language of entertainment culture, so that any attempt by the lay public to come to grips with entertainment culture was restricted to the language of high culture—literature and art. Thus restricted, analysis produced was at best mere commentary, water boy to the main action.

But as the technology necessary for aural and visual electronic recording became less expensive, more portable and easier to use, the tools required for speaking in the dominant cultural language of popular entertainment passed directly into the hands of the audience. Though most have chosen to employ personalized mass-media technology to extend their habits of consumption—recording music or TV broadcasts—or to chronicle private histories, a percentage regards the availability of this technology as a long awaited opportunity to research the structural life of entertainment and to decentralize entertainment production.

Technology is only half the problem, however. The stubborn problem of venue continues to challenge and confound the growth of the anti-entertainment sensibility. Attempts have been made to distribute anti-conventional entertainment products through small independent networks, but they have remained relatively weak, marginal, and short-lived compared to the extraordinary strength of those distributive networks owned and operated by the producers of status quo entertainment. In order to go forward, research into entertainment culture's impact on the national and individual imagination has been forced well outside the distributive structures of mass media. The search for a haven has led (as such searches frequently do) to the art world. With its strong traditions of tolerating oppositional culture, celebrating research and encouraging experimentation, the art world has developed into the most important and independent laboratory for identifying and calibrating entertainment culture's myriad effects.

Allusions to popular entertainment have appeared in visual art for centuries. Over the years, entertainment as a component of visual art has grown progressively concrete, materialized, a subject for consideration in its own right. Watteau's troubadours and Picasso's harlequins were pictorial renderings of entertainers, representations made with the quintessential high art material, oil paint. In the post-war period, Eduardo Paolozzi introduced specifically mass-media entertainment culture into visual art: his collages of the late '40s used science-fiction imagery from movies and comic books. The British and American Pop artists who followed in the '50s and '60s mimicked the industrial look of the artifacts of entertainment culture—movies, album covers, magazines. American artists who emerged in the late '70s and early '80s, notably Cindy Sherman, Jack Goldstein, Robert Longo, and Gretchen Bender, transferred the entertainment discourse away from the material of high culture—paint—to the vernacular materials of popular culture—photography, video, film. Their work consciously injected entertainment into art's physical substance, the vehicle of its presentation. These artists, and to a greater degree their New York peers who came to international attention in the mid-'80s—Jeff Koons, Haim Steinbach, Richard Prince, Clegg & Guttmann, Barbara Kruger—combined the crowd-pleasing strategies of entertainment with the spirit of critical investigation derived from the idea of the artist-as-scientist promoted by influential conceptual artists of the early '70s. Fusing critical content with a lush and unashamed physicality, these artists succeeded in making criticality entertaining. By so doing, they expanded the audience for serious contemporary art while educating that audience regarding the need for critical thinking about cultural production.

However much visual artists have been drawn to the dazzlements of entertainment, they have kept it at arm's length, claiming always to be "using" entertainment, whether as form or subject matter. Artists' sense of superiority over the raw populism of entertainment culture has remained inviolate.

In 1986, I produced a work, _Talent_, in which I attempted to remove the refuge of critical distance and explicitly equate artist and entertainer. _Talent_ consisted of 18 black-and-white "headshot" photographs of contemporary artists. The photographs were made by a Times Square photographer who for 40 years had taken this kind of photo for aspiring actors and actresses, singers and comedians. Thus _Talent_ was intended as neither a representation nor a parody of entertainment culture; it was instead meant to be a <u>fact</u> of that culture. It blew open a hole in the membrane separating the context of art from the context of entertainment. Through this hole, the structures, conditions, and aims of each context became for me gloriously and hopelessly polluted with the presence of the other. I hoped <u>Talent</u> would cause both avant-garde culture and entertainment culture to confess their habits of mind, thereby framing the issue of criticality itself. It was my attempt to tip the critical and the non-critical into a perpetual motion of mutual critique, simultaneously indicting art's naive, shrewish criticality and entertainment's smug, oafish complacency; art's chronic marginality and entertainment's brutal populism; art's fierce autonomy and entertainment's collaborative nature; art's addiction to disposable theory and entertainment's poverty of theory. <u>Talent</u> X-rayed two late-20th-century bureaucracies of the imagination—one an Industry, the other a World.

Art objects can freeze-frame the flow of experience. Indeed, art objects can slow sensation to such a crawl that the structural life of a sensation—even a sensation as fleeting and resistant to analysis as feeling "entertained"—enters our radar range. Entertainment's presence in our lives is so continuous and ubiquitous as to be invisible. Our relationship to the world of entertainment is at present akin to being captive at an interminable press conference where no one asks a single question of the speaker. But if isolated for consideration, entertainment qua entertainment is a babbling fount of information. Entertainment includes a complex body of suppositions about what brings pleasure to people; it implies a critique of labor because it provides relief from labor; it typifies the tyranny over cultural production exercised by the audience in a cultural democracy; it charts the interplay between masterpiece culture and mass culture, and it examines how all these things are organized within the specific context of a single national culture.

Addressing entertainment means addressing the coordinates of the aesthetic of reality in American life. This is important work at a time when the world's obsession with American culture is abating. We can no longer assume that American culture will be the focus of world attention, as it has been for more than 50 years. The global competition of cultures will have many consequences, not the least of which is that the inflated, self-congratulatory, award-bestowing popular culture we wallow in will be challenged to reverse its retreat into parody and irony. Surely this is a good thing. I am calling for the planting of the flag of a third culture that might draw upon the virtues of both contexts, art and entertainment. By processing entertainment through the sensitive faculties of art, we can discover the patterns of entertainment culture in order to determine those aspects of mass-media culture most worth preserving. And by injecting the experimentalism of art into entertainment, we can produce more satisfying models of entertainment and eventually blackmail our irresponsible entertainment culture into becoming a civilizing force.

NOTES

* A lowbrow but amusing '70s TV sitcom.

** Several television producers actually said this to me. Compare this attitude to visual art, a field in which the whole point is to come up with an idea that obviates the need for the other 11! Art is about efficiency of expression, while entertainment wants access to all 12 ideas. Entertainment, then, seems to be about employing people.

The Sphinx, 1994
four b/w photographs, each 14" x 11", edition of three, photo by Oren Slor

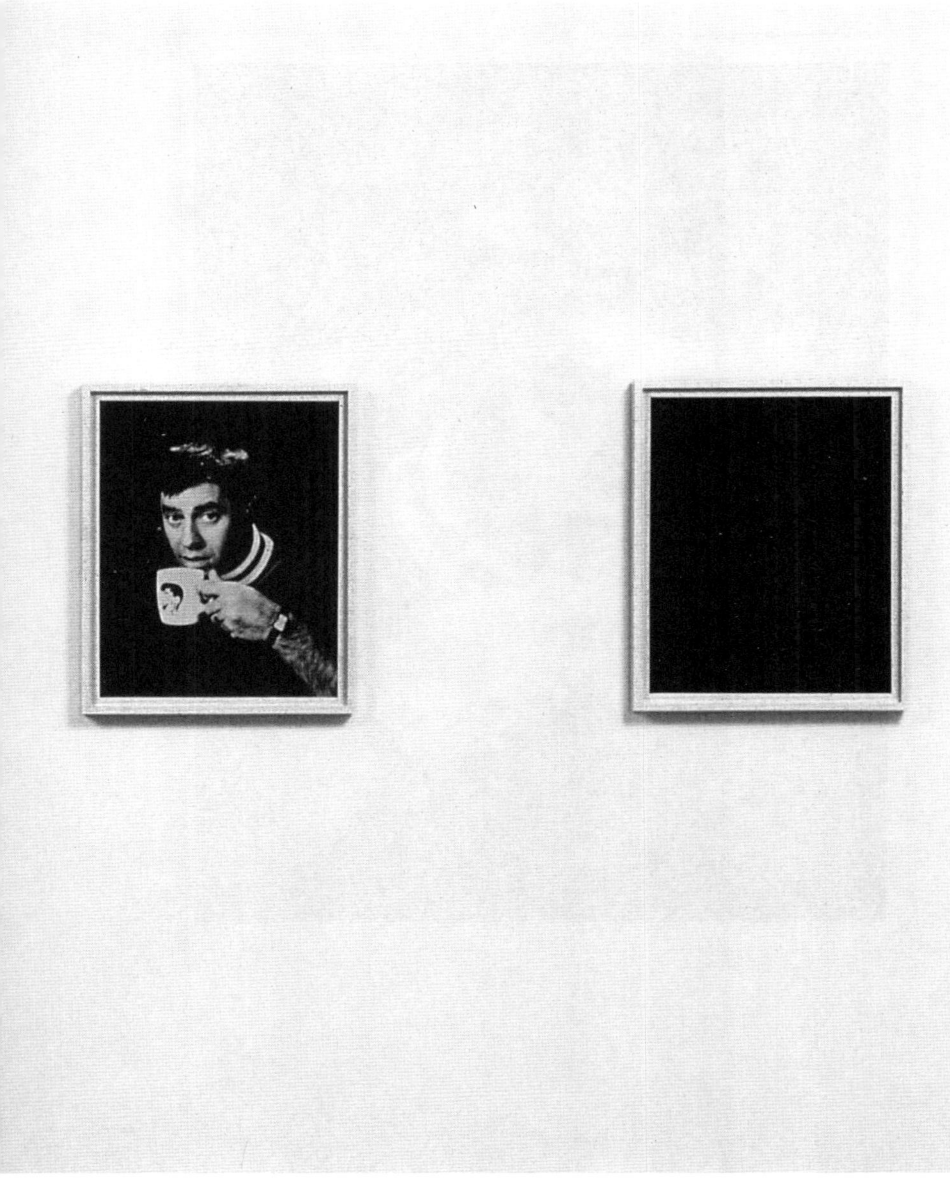

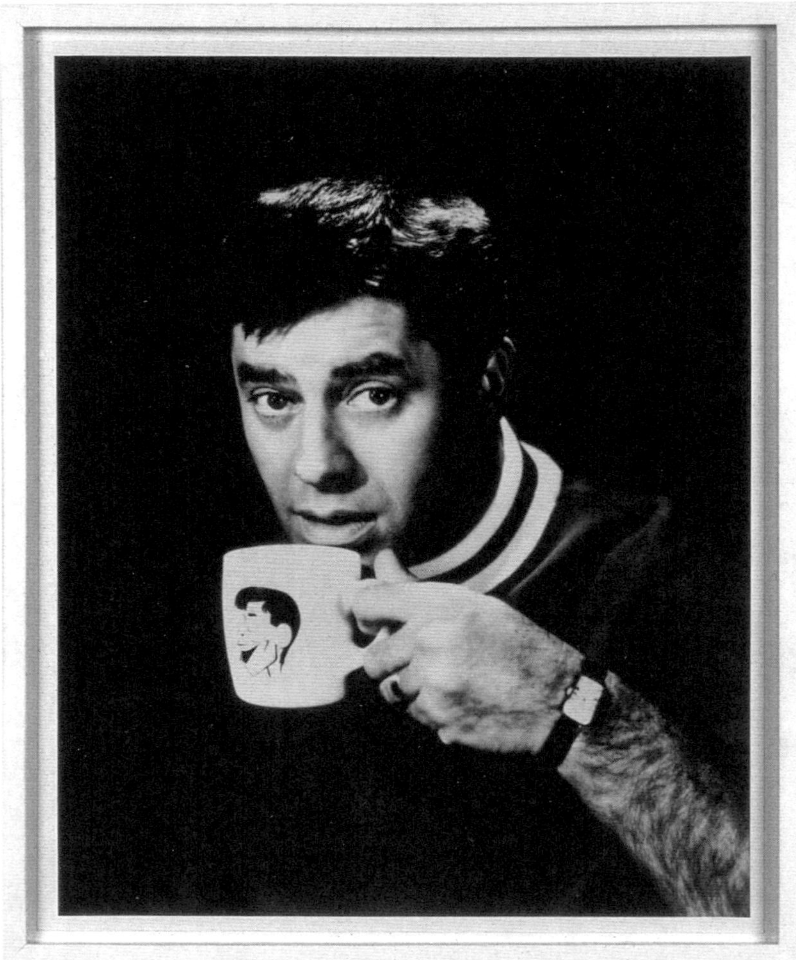

The Sphinx (detail)
one of four panels, each 14" x 11", photo by Oren Slor

Points

Originally published in Art issues, January/February 1999.

Many a movie has aimed a pinspot at the liposuction-worthy underbelly of show biz—All About Eve, The Sweet Smell of Success, The Player, The Big Knife—but none has been as frank, as unflinching, as stingingly theoretical as Points, the latest threat from Keyboard Pictures. To rehearse the Hollywood community in the trauma which is expected to follow the release of this uncompromising film, and thereby, we hope, to diminish its effects, we beseeched the screenwriter to publish a portion of the script in advance. (Academy members might remember his acquiescence when voting the Hersholt.)

The scene: A dinner party in the fashionably retro-modern dining room at Shambles, the seven-acre Holmby Hills estate of Rudy O'Selznick, legendary producer of the films Because I Said So, Is That Mine?, and You're Late. It is early evening. Seated around a walnut-root Gio Ponti table are O'Selznick's guests: long-time girlfriend Ptina, a mono-monikered contemporary artist whose chosen medium is pretentiousness; Ascot Tucker, heir to his father's endorsement empire, unapologetic elitist, and last year's Sexiest Man Alive; Lycra Duvall, Curator at the Museum of Contemporary Acquisitions; Dr. Schaeffer, director of the Center for Celebrity Control; and, visiting from Chicago, O'Selznick's cousin Marsha "Mashie" Niblick, according to her books' dustjackets The Funniest Woman in America.

A tall, athletic maid sporting an astronaut's brushcut serves the first course against a background of ethereal theremin meanderings while the table vibrates with the rhythms of conversation. Before the guests can begin their meals, all hear the faint chirp of a cellular phone. Their host reaches into his jacket and takes the call. O'Selznick quietly utters a sequence of directives while the others proceed. The maid disappears.

MASHIE During my flight in from Chicago, the 20-something Asian-American go-getter sitting next to me commandeered the airfone for the entire trip. From take-off to landing, call after call. Incredible!

ASCOT Those telemarketers never rest.

MASHIE Oh, but I've no idea what the calls were about. He was completely discreet, not at all loud or obnoxious. Even so, three hours! At no point during the flight is this guy off the phone! And of course, for three hours I positively itched with annoyance. Simply could not figure out why, until I was halfway to the hotel.

PTINA Share.

MASHIE The guy assumed I'd no need to make a call!

PTINA Ouch! That would hurt.

MASHIE What do I look like? A temp?

RUDY (his own call now completed) Speaking of personalized technology, Ptina's been trying to get herself onto talk shows again.

(An amused groan arises from many at the table as all eyes turn toward the artist. Ptina slaps Rudy's arm, not only playfully.)

MASHIE You say it the way other couples announce they're trying to get pregnant!

LYCRA Again, Ptina? Why do you do this to yourself? When are you going to accept that in America artists do not appear on television?

PTINA Never! Because, Lycra, any person who is a genuinely modern person knows that art's just one more branch of the global communication industry. We belong on TV.

ASCOT Odd, how lightly this oh-so-obvious and compelling reality appears to weigh on the shoulders of your "colleagues" at the networks …

PTINA (dismissive in a studied kind of way) It's just my version of sport, really. A hobby.

RUDY It's her golf.

ASCOT As frustrating as golf, too, I'd imagine.

MASHIE I'm new around here. Just why is it you're trying to get on television, Ptina?

PTINA To be of my time, of course. History is indistinguishable from television's coverage of it. How can I claim to be truly of my time if I'm not on the air?

MASHIE Why not just put together your own show on cable access?

PTINA Puh-leeze! I've got enough work to do. Like anyone else in show biz, I deserve to appear on the air for the work I've already done.

MASHIE Fair enough. How exactly have you been going about it?

PTINA Every other month I mail to national network talk shows—morning, mid-morning, noon, mid-afternoon, late-afternoon, late-night, late late-night, all-night—I don't know how many press kits featuring selective documentation of my most recent artistic actions. After the mailing I barrage the shows with follow-up phone calls.

RUDY Most of the receptionists can now identify her calls just by the quality of the connection.

MASHIE Persistence does pay, Rudy.

RUDY No, cousin, I pay. The phone bill. All ten pages of it.

LYCRA Be sure to save those bills, you two! We'll do an artist's book.

PTINA Good idea, Lycra. We'll get something out of all this. Because I'll tell ya, not one of the booking agents—not Gerri's, not Octago's, not Lorgnette's—has ever bothered to get back to me. No form rejection letter, nothing. I don't know which bugs me more: their arrogance, or my own lack of success in capturing the attention of people who know they're powerful enough not to give a damn how they might be perceived.

MASHIE Mightn't you do things that are a little more, I don't know, sensational? To get their attention, I mean.

PTINA Of course, but I refuse to do them. Why should I have to? Artists deserve to be on TV. We're part of the culture, too. We ought to be treated with respect.

ASCOT Artists want to be outside of society, don't they? Always have, I thought.

PTINA Do they?

MASHIE Where would that be, exactly?

PTINA Outside? Whatever for? I certainly don't!

RUDY There's no "outside" anymore, Ascot. The only route of escape, now, is to get as close to the controls as possible.

LYCRA Ptina honey, television is for performers. You're not a performer.

PTINA Dancers and poets are performers as well, Lycra, and they're not allowed on TV either. That can't be the reason I'm not getting on. I, too, have product to offer, after all. Why shouldn't I have the chance to promote _my_ product on some late-night talk show, just as actors and singers do?

RUDY Gee, hon, think it has anything to do with the fact that no one in the vast viewing audience cares to see _the esoteric and arty things you'd offer_?

PTINA Be more supportive, my patron, my love. Really, Rudy, you can't know that they wouldn't. Nobody can know in advance everything that other human beings will or will not find attractive. Period. And how many times do I have to tell you? Never use the word "arty" in the presence of an artist!

Rudy kisses Ptina's forehead. Her smile signals truce.

LYCRA It's just business, Ptina. Why let it bother you? This culture is organized around entertainment, and entertainment resists artists because they embody questions about what is and what isn't entertaining. Artists represent The Higher Entertainment. TV has correctly identified them to be, by their nature, enemies of everything it's interested to promote.

MASHIE She's got a point, Ptina. Remember: TV only _plays_ dumb.

DR. SCHAEFFER Actually, it's altogether possible to argue for the _inevitability_ of Ptina's appearance on TV. If the table doesn't mind accommodating a dissenting opinion, that is.

RUDY Requests we play. Dissent away.

DR. SCHAEFFER Suppose we transpose the problem into geometric terms. TV represents a quite devastating _horizontality_, planned and executed. The aim of television is to include as many viewers as it possibly can. Fanning out across the landscape, it enters each and every home. Art, on the other hand, is entirely a vertical discipline. Art proposes that certain experiences are, let's put it as modestly as we can, more worthy of consideration than are others. For that reason, art puts forth the somewhat-less-than-egalitarian view that human capacities both of imagination and response have never been and never will be equitably distributed—and furthermore, that to pretend otherwise is dishonest. Two lines we have, yes? Horizontal and vertical. Television and art each order experience in a way that is an anathema to the other. Yet neither can claim the last word. While art may encourage people to fly higher, television, its reach broad and aggressively inclusive, covers more ground.

PTINA Sure hasn't gotten 'round to including me yet!

RUDY Clever presentation, Doc. But I don't see anything in it to make Ptina's appearance on the tube "inevitable."

LYCRA TV is free entertainment. So are galleries. But can that be where you're headed ... ?

DR. SCHAEFFER No, no. Recall your basic geometry, Ms. Duvall. If television represents a horizontal line and art a vertical line, then the exclusion of artists' from the airwaves constitutes a violation of natural law, for is it not a fundamental principal of geometry that, assuming them to be on the same plane, vertical and horizontal axes inevitably cross?

ASCOT Aha!

MASHIE What is this, My Dinner with Professor Irwin Corey?*

RUDY "Aha" nothin'. They're not on the same plane, Schaeffer! I make films, the films make lotsa money, with some of the lotsa money I buy art. One, two, three. Not three, two, one. Never three, two, one. Who out there makes art first and produces features with the proceeds? You take your geometric laws, Doctor. I'll stick with the financial ones. Look, let's cut the crap: Ptina's just jealous because all those actors and singers are friendly with each other, and they participate in a superior reward system. Mine!'

LYCRA Anybody catch Vince Nichols last night on Another Night? Vince was there to promote his new movie.

ASCOT Another one? What's this one called?

LYCRA Wallace, the Clairvoyant Dugong. Something like that. Vince is proud of his work in it. To dispel any doubt we might have as to whether receiving 12 million dollars to star in a flick about a visionary sea cow had done anything to erode his seriousness of purpose, Vince hauled out the craft spiel.

ASCOT Which?

LYCRA You know, how acting's a craft and all. How the craft's helped him grow and learn. How humbled he feels when faced with the demands of the craft.

MASHIE The craft cheese.

RUDY What do you want the man to say? "I got paid 12 million bucks for three month's work on a Hawaiian beach and it was awful." "Wonderful, Vinny, just promise us you'll do something foolish with the money. Get in some kind of serious trouble. After all, we're paying ya to entertain us. We don't care how you do it! Vince Nichols, ladies and gentlemen!" C'mon. The guy's just being honest. What's the problem?

LYCRA It's only a craft, Rudy. That's the problem. Or my problem with it, anyway. It's a craft, and in every respect the reward given actors is way out of proportion to the contribution made by their craft. The 12 million dollars, that's just a symbol of the problem.

RUDY You should have such problems. Really, Lycra, you're

getting awfully moralistic in your advancing years. Who are you to judge anyone's contribution?

PTINA She's a curator, Rudy, remember?

LYCRA I'm at least able to measure acting against other forms of imaginative work. Do that, and acting's fundamental weakness really stands out: control. Actors can't control what's offered to them. No matter how big an actor gets he's never in a position to exercise enough control over the roles he's offered to build a coherent body of work, worth contemplating for itself.

RUDY Where'd we find you? So an actor doesn't have control? Lemme tell you, as a producer I don't want them to have control!

LYCRA But Rudy! For a creative endeavor to lack the capacity to build conceptual coherency is a pretty serious shortcoming: It means that the actor can't create what Keats called "an allegorical life," as artists who are more than craftsmen can do. Since acting lacks that extra, call it conceptual dimension, which control would deliver, craft becomes the only claim to artistry an actor can honestly make. That's why every third time an actor's interviewed he drags out the craft thing. He has to. It's all he's got.

RUDY Keats, teats. Anyone who's tried it can tell you, Madame Curator: just getting a movie made is pretty goddam heroic.

MASHIE At least it's in a world where the writing of a screenplay is looked upon as important work.

LYCRA Yes. And what kind of world's that?

RUDY Uh, the real world, I believe it's called? Christ, even the kids in the coffee and copy shops understand that. They know that writing scripts is a way out. A way up. Leave that white cube once in a while and take a look around, will ya please?

ASCOT Yes, Lycra, why such stridency? A curator makes distinctions. Surely there exists a distinction between good pretending and bad pretending …

LYCRA But qualitative distinctions no longer matter when a premise is magnified to a scale as gigantic as the entertainment industry has magnified pretending. Why do you think it is that so many kids are <u>facing</u> coffee-shop futures, Ascot? It's because of the accumulated effect of the constant overvaluation of pretending. Never before have humans been exposed to such an insistent, unavoidable river of pretending. The camera has turned out to be a Pandora's box. A monstrous unreal has been unleashed. And the more immersed we've become in the camera-based culture of pretending, the shabbier and more unruly and less likable the real's become. We've let the infrastructure of the real go downhill. We're forever celebrating actions that have been undertaken because some camera has been there to record 'em. Take away the camera, people wouldn't be doing them. They'd have no reason to. Something that's done only because the camera's there to watch it can never be as real as something that's done away from the camera.

ASCOT Except to the people who are doing it, of course.

MASHIE Touché. Hey, fella, you are sexy! Slightly less sexy than last year, of course, but still …

RUDY Sorry, Lycra, I can't agree. You're choosing to see the camera as an adversary. That's mistake number one. You ought to see it as an <u>ally</u>. A lens creates a field of possibility, right? An <u>inexhaustible</u> field. In it, you can do anything you can think of.

ASCOT Our gracious host is right. Are you certain, Lycra, that, however eloquently stated, your objection to pretending doesn't just mask a lack of imagination?

LYCRA It may, Ascot. It may. And I'm rude to criticize the source of this delightful meal, I know. Forgive me, Rudy. But don't you see that there's a price to be paid for entering your "field of possibility"? Certain terms—the camera's terms—must be agreed to. You have to agree to behave in a certain way. You have to agree to be <u>not quite real</u>. You have to <u>pretend</u>. The camera gets people to pretend, so that they can remain within the "field of possibility." That's the camera's power over us.

I'm saying we've gotten to the point where too much human energy is being expended on pretending. Away it goes, into a black hole. It's <u>disappeared energy</u>—energy that didn't go to inventing geometry or calendars or medicine or irrigation techniques or the cotton gin or the lightbulb.

MASHIE Or the camera.

<u>Close-ups of raised eyebrows of each guest in succession. Cut to medium shot of a cake shaped like a woman's head, atop a cart now wheeled in by the maid. The frosting forms elaborate curls.</u>

MASHIE Jayne Mansfield!

RUDY Mashie, enough already! Who's that supposed to be, really?

PTINA Marie Antoinette. I've been collaborating with the chef.

RUDY My clever girl. <u>(While the maid attends to the cake, he returns his attention to Lycra)</u>. Listen, kiddo, seems to me, your opposition to the camera is nothing but an <u>idea</u>. What the camera really offers is a hell of a lot bigger than any <u>idea</u>. It offers <u>experience itself</u>. You don't approve of anyone wanting to be a pretend person, but what's so great about being a real one all the time? What's more fun: selling insurance, or putting on a cowboy outfit and ambushing the stagecoach?

MASHIE How about donning a cowboy outfit to sell insurance? "If your horse is stolen ... "

ASCOT I have to side with our host on this one, Lycra. When an actor invents a character they're not just inventing the character's life, they're also inventing their own. There's a kind of freedom in that ... I've always admired actors—and not only because of their ability to memorize all those lines. They get to operate in a free zone that most the rest of us never know. Sometimes I think they're the only really free people ...

MASHIE Aside from criminals and the super-rich.

LYCRA La dolce vita. Doesn't that company tell you anything? If that's the "really free" crowd, I mean?

RUDY Tell us what, exactly?

LYCRA That "total freedom" may be over-rated, if all it amounts to is pretending to be a cowboy, and being associated with criminals and the super-rich. Freedom without any ... undertow dwindles into meaninglessness. Given enough freedom, most people try to get as close as possible to the conditions of childhood.

MASHIE Sounds good to me. My god, Lycra, you're even harder on people than I am, and it's my job to be! Still, I have to admit there's truth in what you say. As a goal, gaining the attention of some camera somewhere is hardly a high level of inventiveness. Not any longer, anyway. As a human aspiration it's become a cliché.

ASCOT If it is a cliché, it's only because it's become merged with our natures. After a lifetime of watching movies and TV you can hardly expect people to distinguish the reflection from the mirror.

LYCRA Especially if we stop asking them to try.

PTINA God, I'd thought I wanted to be on TV but now, after listening to Lycra, I'm not so sure. It'd be like, I don't know, going over to the _enemy_ or something. I'd be heading straight into the battle between the real and the pretend! Hmmm, maybe _helmets_ have possibilities …

MASHIE Perfect timing, Ptina. War movies are back. Rudy, you really oughta produce one about the Gulf War. I already have your title: _It's Saudi Duty Time!_

RUDY Dear cousin, you _are_ exhausting.

MASHIE Hey, I'm from the Midwest. We make fun of everything.

ASCOT If you can't hit a target with precision, spray it with an AK-47 …

LYCRA Don't be snobbish, Ascot. Part of being sophisticated is recognizing the virtues of places that appear to be less so.

RUDY I've read that someplace. Where … ?

MASHIE Ellis Island?

ASCOT Snobbery ain't the issue, my friends. The issue is: the appeal of assault-rifle humor is to minds basically afraid of the world.

PTINA Ascot Tucker!

MASHIE That's okay, Ptina, I can take it. You're from Manhattan, Ascot, so you're blind to the way that New York and LA impose on the rest of the country their ambitions for the culture. To you it just seems the natural state. But the vast territory in-between isn't so enthralled with the arrangement. Over time we've developed a few strategies for defending ourselves against the barrage of stuff put out by you guys in the centers.

ASCOT A little colonization never hurt anybody.

RUDY I hear the sound of restless natives.

MASHIE That mane may be thinning, Rudy, but the hearing is still good.

RUDY Sure you're not just jealous of others' success?

MASHIE Maybe. But the successful _have_ been known to overvalue success.

RUDY Baloney. Only those who haven't achieved it question the value of success.

MASHIE On which investment services brochure did you find that one? Unh uh. No value is above questioning, Rudy—including success. Success may be good for an individual, but it isn't necessarily good for the thing they're successful at. You want an example? Comedy's the perfect one. Success usually induces the successful to protect their position. In comedy, that has the effect of reducing the degree of risk taken. Reduce the degree of risk, and you weaken comedy's critique of life. You weaken comedy's potential.

DR. SCHAEFFER The visiting Ms. Niblick's observation is worth considering. The Center for Celebrity Control is about to publish a study that arrived at a similar conclusion.

You all know that the Center tracks myriad aspects of our media culture. Our man Watkins, quite thorough, quite fair, absolutely incorruptible, just completed a study of post-war American comedy. One of the things he turned up is a particularly problematic fool-king pattern among those who'd served on the staff of the Yardley University humor magazine, the _Harlequin_. Of course, we anticipated that a certain complexity would show up in these people, since they'd opted to hold the fool's position at the king of American universities, where professors are consultants to the leaders of business and government, classmates come from influential or powerful families, there's the huge Yardley endowment … Not to mention the mystique of Yardley in the national imagination.

PTINA Yardley, Yardley—one perk of exhibiting abroad is that you get to spend lots of time in places where those uptight Eastern hierarchies have no meaning.

ASCOT Ptina, the entire world understands what Yardley signifies, I assure you.

DR. SCHAEFFER Of the many things that Yardley signifies, success may be the most important. Its students are people who, all their lives, have been associated with success, whether earned or inherited.

ASCOT Well, Doctor, we can't all be so fortunate as to come from nowhere.

DR. SCHAEFFER After tracking one hundred alumni over a period of 20 years, we found Yardley graduates to have an unusually static relation to existing models of success. Trained to be insiders—it is, one might almost say, the <u>point</u> of an institution such as Yardley—the success they go on to achieve is real success, unquestionably, but it is a profoundly conservative idea of success which leaves the existing social arrangements fundamentally untouched and unaltered.

RUDY Never knew you were such a rebel, Doc. Listen, science is one thing, life's another. Why would anyone go out of their way to risk losing the power they'd gone to Yardley to acquire? That'd be idiotic.

DR. SCHAEFFER I'm only reporting what the study indicates, Rudy. Whether for reasons characterological or environmental a willingness to forego the acquisition of personal power doesn't seem to be in the makeup of those trained at Yardley. Within the American comedy industry, ex-Harlequin staffers assume positions of responsibility at television shows, at large-circulation magazines, and at movie studios, where in effect they transcribe Yardley's own privileged relation to power onto the commercial context of the media business, and thereby remain utterly consistent with the relation to power they'd been trained to have.

LYCRA Because they don't know any better.

DR. SCHAEFFER Literally. Un-success, powerlessness—such is not in their experience.

LYCRA Excuse me, but I seem to be missing something here. Where exactly is the tragedy in all this?

PTINA Right. You're asking us to feel sorry for the winners?

DR. SCHAEFFER Ah, but is it so clear that they are winners, in the long-term? The study suggests that one ought not to look to Yardley graduates to deliver the profound behavioral innovations that in turn deliver the future.

ASCOT He may be right. Most of my friends went to Yardley and, brilliant as they are, I can't say that any of them risk deep "behavioral innovation."

MASHIE My point exactly, Ascot, thank you. They're incapable of inventing at that fundamental, animal level, precisely because they're unwilling to risk failure and invisibility. Just as I'd been saying: success is a threat to comedy. Play it safe, require that comedy be "successful," and you squander its more profound intent.

ASCOT Which is?

MASHIE Liberation from the worldly. Comedy's meant to help get us beyond categories of success and failure, not to serve them.

ASCOT Those who mock power never acquire it, and so remain children.

MASHIE _(pounding the table with both fists)_

Waaah!

The butler suddenly appears at the entrance to the dining room.

BUTLER Pardon me, sir. I'm sorry to interrupt. You have visitors. The entire cast of _Hercules versus the Spiraling Cost of Health Care_.

RUDY What? Again?

Fade on Rudy's exasperated countenance. End scene.

NOTE

* "Professor" Irwin Corey (born 1914) is an American comedian and self-described "World's Foremost Authority."

Merrill Lynch, Pierce, Fenner, and ... Smithson

Originally published in Art issues, January/February 1998.

Unusual Sotheby's Deal Reflects Changing Art Market
In an unlikely pairing, the 253-year-old auction house said it has purchased a 50% stake in Deitch Projects, the art gallery in New York's Soho district that represents art world bad boy Jeff Koons.
—The Wall Street Journal, September 15, 1997

RESPONDING TO ITS CHIEF RIVAL'S INNOVATIVE STRATEGY, AUCTION POWERHOUSE CHRISTIE'S YESTERDAY PURCHASED THE REMAINING 50% OF DEITCH PROJECTS. "Ever so clever are we," an obviously relieved Christie's spokesman chuckled when contacted by telephone. Reached at his Soho office, Mr. Deitch also expressed elation, as the investment guaranteed him the money to fund large-scale works, among them bad boy Jeff Koons' stainless steel replica of Sotheby's New York headquarters.

Though flattered by the news of the artist's planned homage, the announced deal nevertheless left Sotheby's feeling insecure. In order to restore its advantage of the previous day, the venerable house snatched up 50% of Christie's.

The flurry of activity did not escape the notice of America's corporate titans, who, struck as one by the knowledge that they could no longer afford to ignore the ever-expanding market for contemporary art, pounced in unison. With shares of Deitch Projects unavailable, industrial and post-industrial giants alike obtained stakes in other gallery operations. Blue chip bet on blue chip as, among dozens of acquisitions, Abbott Laboratories merged with Sonnabend, Archer Daniels Midland absorbed Leo Castelli, Exxon agreed to buy Margo Leavin, and Rockwell International snapped up the sculpture interests of PaceWildenstein. Capping an extraordinary day, Burger King inked a contract with bad boy Jeff Koons to produce a chocolate-covered, stainless-steel-centered version of the artists' famous bunny, which is to be given away free to customers who purchase a Whopper, large fries, and a Coke.

The two independent art dealers remaining, Elaine McHenry of Trust Fund Fine Art and Hudson of Feature, expressed concern that the new corporate partners' demand for consistent earnings would further erode traditional valuations of aesthetic achievement. "It's going to become like the movie business," noted Hudson, "art by committee." But McHenry admitted (prior to departing for art world bad boy Jeff Koons' studio to take her turn conducting an interview with him about his new, nearly-ready-to-be-released body of work), "We were close to that already. The individual artist's importance already derived less from what they made than from where they exhibited. The corporate invasion is just another course in the long wake following the death of the author."

Most gallerists appear thrilled to find themselves mentioned in the will. They eagerly anticipate the stability that multinationals such as Chevron, Merck, and General Electric are sure to add to the business of marketing the unquantifiable, the uncategorizable, and the whimsical. "The hairpin turns taken by the human imagination are entertaining enough, sure," says Santa Monica gallery owner and newest Union Carbide board member Natalie Gucci-Karan, "but try basing a business on them! Things had gotten really tough. With expensive rents to pay and payrolls to meet, we art dealers could no longer afford to place our trust in something as unpredictable and undependable as inspiration. Nor, with so much competent work being made by so many more or less equally gifted artists, could we rely on our own judgement to decide which brilliant invention deserves to be elevated over another." Insists Gucci-Karan, "When art history becomes a matter of opinion, you've got to find a way to reduce your risk."

Until yesterday's tidal wave of buy-outs, the only method that had dependably done so was a practice called the fixed election: an artist is first anointed by a high-profile gallery and then exhibited at a network of satellite galleries, which strategy renders the consensus considered necessary to establish artistic reputation a fait accompli. Gucci-Karan avers that the fixed election merely acknowledged the realities of the art marketplace. "Why wait for consensus when you can fabricate it? The fixed election instantly validates an artist's work and lends it the patina of exclusivity. We needed something that could accomplish that because collectors are successful, busy people, with businesses to run, families, a wide range of interests—you've got their attention for only the briefest of moments, so you have to make their art-shopping as easy and efficient as possible if you're going to survive. The fixed election has stabilized the art scene. Do you think that these corporations would be getting into the game if we were still using the old system of just hanging the work and letting people make up their own minds?"

And how will the artist fare in this strange new land of the quarterly report? In art as in life, more will accrue to the few, most probably. The aggressive downsizing popular among corporate managers means that large numbers of artists can expect to lose cherished, long-held jobs as professional imaginers. At the same time, the demand for the most profitable inventors, such as Jeff Koons, for whom the self has always been but a congeries of interlocking directorates (a characterization copyrighted by the art world bad boy just prior to utterance) is likely to reach fever pitch.

Art industry executives like Gucci-Karan point out that there has always been an attrition rate among artists. She sees only opportunity ahead. While not deaf to the complaints of purists, she won't allow them to drown out the percussive chime of the cash register. "The old-timers keep asking, 'In a corrupt system of valuation, what does it mean to be a star?'" says she. "Kvetches! Worse: naive kvetches! They're stuck on yesterday's question. They ought to be asking one that's more illuminating, more profitable, more today, one that's arrived at by slightly reconfiguring the old question: 'Is a star in a corrupt system any less a star?'"

Mr. Entertainment's Diary

Originally published in Art issues, January/February through November/ December 1992.

MONDAY JANUARY 14 After five years of public life as a professional artist, participating in the international commercial avant-garde gallery system and supporting myself with sales from exhibitions of my work, have discovered that I wear the whole enterprise better if I think of myself as an entertainer.

It's not my intention to demote art. By choosing to foreground the fact that, inevitably, any creative work exists, or fails to exist, in the eyes of an audience, like any artist I'm simply trying to tell the truth about one person's cultural imprinting. Throughout my childhood and adolescence, popular entertainment—television, movies, pop records and show music, mass-produced toys, comic books, light periodicals, and best-seller fiction—had comprised my experience of what constituted culture, so that even after I'd reached adulthood, discovered art, and decided to become an artist, even, years later, after having gained some recognition for my work, entertainment remained the bedrock model for cultural endeavor and ambition.

THURSDAY THE 17TH Entertainment's part of me. Not ashamed of my roots. Yet the fact that entertainment has irradiated my life and molded my conception of public life does not in itself differentiate me from millions of other Americans raised into the same condition. What sets me apart is only my conscious decision to return entertainment's embrace. I'm convinced that entertainment's domination of the national imagination during this period in America's development as a civilization is a fundamental cultural truth of our time which, for history's sake, must somehow be recorded, and so am determined to document the consequences to human aspiration of a culture dedicated to generating entertainment, daily, year after year.

FRIDAY THE 18TH Entertainment has never in history had such enormous cultural power within such an enormously powerful culture. "What Saudi Arabia is to oil, the United States is to entertainment," a market analyst commented today in the Times. Exactly. The United States is a mass entertainment culture obsessed with inventing cultural forms and formats equally accessible to millions of people from radically diverse backgrounds. We're always looking for an experience of culture equivalent to the blue jean. Entertainment culture is thus the New World's most distinctive contribution to world culture, the one socio-cultural invention unforeseen by the Old World. Mass entertainment culture is indigenous to modern times, not only proposing new cultural forms, but creating new methods of mass distribution for them, and progressively defining and reinforcing both form and distribution until, finally, they've crystalized into a cultural ideology that situates entertainment as the political culture of the mass audience. As a new trajectory in history, there's no telling where entertainment culture will lead.

Therefore, it's no small or simple thing to declare oneself, within the high culture context of art, an entertainer. Both art and entertainment mirror life, but each structures that mirroring in ways that remain hostile to the ambitions of the other. True, the best entertainers are called artists in the end, and the best artists are always mindful of audience, but no entertainer is well served in the Industry by being considered "arty," and artists are invariably utterly ruthless in their determination to snuggle up to art history and elevate their work above "mere" entertainment. Identifying myself as an entertainer while functioning as an artist will cause the mirrors of art and entertainment to face each other, so it's reasonable to expect an unreasonable world of reflections to result.

MONDAY THE 21ST If entertainment represents the new, more democratic aspirations of mass culture, distinct from the art cultures of the Old World, it faces a formidable challenge in the recent economic and political recuperation of the Old World. The triumphant return of Europe and Asia to the world stage also resuscitates Old World values, certain of which, like the overveneration of "refinement," "strength," and "importance," have been the cause of a great deal of trouble in this century when they confronted the democratizing thrust of modernism. The aspirations of art-culture reside on a continuum with these values; entertainment emphasizes other qualities. Beuys said that we are all artists, or that at least we can all become artists—but experience has shown me that we don't all want to be!

From traveling and living in Europe, I know that the Old World doesn't fully recognize the dense reality, much less the validity, of New World cultural values. Indeed, more often than not, those institutions charged with polishing the carapace of the Old World are dismissive of, even hostile to the values of the New World.

FRIDAY MARCH 11 Have come out as an entertainer, publicly referring to myself as such in the company of my professional peers. Nearly a unanimously negative reaction from those interested to recognize themselves solely in the mirror of art. Curators and dealers resent what they regard as a devaluation of their sometimes hard-won cultural authority. Collectors don't like to think that they're spending their money on works in any measure ambivalent about aspiring to the conditions of art. Most of my artist friends disapprove of entertainment's disregard of the traditional artistic obsessions—medium, style, and content—and they certainly don't welcome being told that the larger intellectual, political, and moral dimensions engaged by their work might amount "only" to another form of entertainment. By and large the contemporary art world, especially its

European branch, considers my position a reckless insult to Art.

Such reactions to a simple declarative statement make it all too clear that however politically powerful the central generator of New World values, the United States, and however generous a gift to the world the idea of a democracy of tastes embedded in entertainment culture, respect for and understanding of the sophisticated social nature of that gift has yet to be won. The coexistence of contexts, cultural and political, is the only possible future, however, so a way needs to be found to respect the New World's cultural reality—the reality of the history of a place that yielded an entertainment culture.

WEDNESDAY THE 14TH I suspect that embracing art's coordinates as a species of entertainment will effect a transformation of the cultural location of the artist. Always the most interesting game in town anyway, that transformation now seems absolutely necessary. Modernism's radical experimentation with the internal conditions of art—the "fact" of art—is no longer the site of maximum invention. A full century of modernism's antics have demonstrated that however inventive artists are, their work always ends up assigned by society to the same <u>psychological framework</u>—namely, Art; when society wants some art, it simply reaches into that pocket, as if it were reaching for candy or chewing gum or cigarettes. Art is tucked in, so unless they acknowledge art's coordinates as a species of entertainment, artists risk deluding themselves with nostalgia for the glories of art's past, like Norma Desmond in <u>Sunset Boulevard</u>.

Artists whose work tries to reform the context of art through a critique of the institutions in which art circulates have the right intentions, but I doubt that "institutional critique" art will ever go far enough. Using criticality to reform the culture of criticality (high culture) is analogous to FBI efforts to police itself. Every institution has some interest to protect; artists can always be counted on, naturally enough, to protect their need or desire for, or simply habit of, making art. Reasonable enough, but it means that artists pull their punches when criticizing the institutions of art. Because they proceed from the assumption that art is indispensable, high culture analyses of high culture are doomed to a kind of timidity, almost, in the end, a cuteness. And "institutional critique" is as bound by the rules of entertainment as any other kind of art, its audience simply holds more radical political views.

The true configuration of culture now is elsewhere altogether. The maximum site of invention, now, is one that forces the culture of criticality into direct and continuous contact with its strongest and most radical cultural alternative, the culture that thrives despite art's low regard for it, the culture, ladies and gentlemen, that actually expresses respect for lives conventionally led, the culture that doesn't need art: entertainment. The only way to stand outside the incestuous superstructure of art-thought is to approach critical culture through the offices of a strong non-critical culture. This would effectively deny to art its claims to an interior life of higher ambitions—claims for which there is circumstantial evidence but no proof—and place art on a par with other kinds of cultural production. If cultural democracy is going to have to fight for its view of culture, the way to start is by denying or canceling the absolute primacy and authority of Old World values. By positioning art as the equal of entertainment, two opposing configurations of culture will be fused precisely at that point where either's claim to superior value dissolves into the denial of that claim by the other; the point where that continual dissolution and resurrection of value takes place will be separated out and magnified to become a volume. Inside that volume one can establish a settlement that bridges the opposing ways in which the Old World and the New World structure cultural experience; that reconciliation represents the true configuration of this moment—and of the foreseeable future—and I'm resolved to map my cultural practice onto it.

WEDNESDAY THE 23RD Ironically, while my cultural education predisposes me to take entertainment's role in society more seriously than it takes itself (and consequently to upgrade entertainment so that it possesses at least the weight and density, if not the specific ambitions of high culture), the art world has been busily conducting its own negotiations with entertainment culture. Even beauty, it appears, has found it necessary to abide by business civilization's cardinal rule of culture: Never Bore the Audience. As a result art has become much more like show business, albeit intellectual showbiz, the show business of intellectuals.

Most artistic revolutions are led by artists, but this particular upheaval has been initiated by art's audience. Alerted by Pop art to art's capacity to frame, absorb, record, reflect, and (on rare occasions) alter the content generated and displaced by the other contexts of modern visual culture—film, television, advertising, magazines—a large and, so far as their knowledge of art's history is concerned, largely uneducated contingent of enthusiasts has transformed the demographics of the audience. In just a few decades their stubborn presence has challenged historical discourse for top billing, and influenced a reconfiguring of art in accordance with their own needs. No longer the citadel of connoisseurship, the art world has evolved into a queasy democracy of affluence, open to anyone with funds sufficient to participate. Serving a new and insecure master, contemporary artists transformed themselves into hit makers and bestsellers to ensure and maintain their access to the microphones of public life. As a consequence, their autonomy has eroded to the point where artists no longer determine the conditions and definitions of artistic success. Just as in show business, careers in the art business are now made—and careers can be broken. Nonartists—gallerists, curators, and collectors—have forced artists to accept a coalition government. In the brief history of an artistic avant-garde which has always guarded its independence, this is news.

To survive in this unfamiliar atmosphere, the disoriented and rapidly weakening classical model for artistic achievement agreed to merge with another powerful upstart: the other and, in America at least, the dominant visual-culture industry, Hollywood. Their union has brought forth a sleek new model for artistic success in which the complexities of both an artist's style and art's content become the equivalent of an "act" subsequently booked by galleries and museum curators into their respective venues. (Some artists are fortunate enough to have long runs with their acts, while others win only short sprints across the public stage.) Each season, galleries introduce new stars for the public's amusement and consumption. Artists and rock stars are offered as the co-attractions at the opening of haute couture department stores. Press coverage features photographs of the artist almost as frequently as reproductions of their work, and the art magazines peddle artistic reputation by the quarter, half, and full page.

Fact is, there's nothing necessarily wrong with any of this. True, at times the ruinous caprices of the newly democratized market for art seem a rather ham-fisted assault on the aristocracy of sensibility represented by the artist, the rabble's revenge on the tradition of independent criticality, but not all of the changes wrought by the merger are for the worse. Artists are no longer forced to operate on the margins of society, for one thing. More importantly, the spirit of democracy ushered into the art world by the new audience allow people to like what they like, not only what they're supposed to like—much to the chagrin of the intellectual elite.

I applaud the democratization of culture, defend it (most often to Europeans, who put up plenty of resistance), and identify myself with it, in part because it's inevitable and in part because I have to: the classical, Old World model of art has no room for someone like me.

THURSDAY THE 24TH Originally, I'd been drawn to art because I'd considered "artist" to be a shorthand term for the widest aperture of cultural endeavor—art being the only cultural practice that has the capacity to construct meaning without pledging allegiance to any particular medium. A writer, in order to be a writer, has to use words, but an artist might use words in his work, once, twice, then never again. A filmmaker is required to use celluloid or videotape in order to be a filmmaker, but for an artist those materials are an option, and so on down the list of reflective occupations and media. Because it's tethered to no specific procedure, in the end the practice of art enables the artist to invent not products but behavior, concrete actions sculpted in time. Being an "artist" invites the possibility that a truly content-based endeavor—a kind of pure citizenship—might be framed.

To my way of thinking, art objects are to be valued because they point to the behavior that has produced them, but it's far more important to concentrate on creating the behavioral model itself, which others are free then to follow in future (or not). This "modeling" is the artist's real creative work, and it underlies every object and image that I choose to make.

A few years in the art world, however, have taught me that my point of view is idiosyncratic enough to guarantee a lifetime of rough going in the hardball professional environment of art making. I don't mind so much that the art world consistently celebrates the glories of the art object over the invention of behavior; mistaking the history of the art object for the history of art is understandable, given that all one has to go on, finally, is the record of what gets made. But I find tiresome and unforgivable the art world's arrogant tendency to dismiss as inferior any invented behavior that is not in the final analysis categorizable as art.

FRIDAY THE 25TH Perhaps my willingness to get art "wrong" stems from the fact that, having neither attended art school nor systematically studied art, I've never been initiated into the correct habits of thought about artistic practice that derive from an institutional education. Even now, after years of exhibiting my work and traveling the world by it, I still don't know how to behave convincingly "like an artist": I've yet to have a studio; I've informal, undefined, open-ended working relationships with a number of galleries in a number of countries; at the openings of my exhibitions, shaking hands and smiling, I feel as if I'm running for artist.

The lack of a formal art education may have reduced my arsenal of traditional artistic skills and forced me to sustain a public life on cleverness, an ability to recognize good ideas, and a free-floating commitment to invention and intellectual adventure, but it has also liberated me from the need to identify my production as art.

Schooled in the structural life of reality by the radio dial and the television channel, I see the world as a constellation of competing contexts, each of them exhibiting specific virtues and specific limitations, and none of them more important than the fact of their coexistence. Overvaluing art seems too willful and careless a disregard of the conditions of life in the mass-media age (which age doesn't look to be ending anytime soon). Art is capable of framing certain of the subtleties of human experience, but not others, and there's such a large body of sensations which art excludes; like a rich man who insists on eating only in the best restaurants, art misses out on so much. True, art is useful as a kind of philosophical game preserve: its conserving instincts can be engaged and relied upon to preserve existential gestures of the most delicate, ephemeral, abstract or seemingly nonsensical nature, thereby ensuring that one's production, no matter how obscure, stands at least a chance of being saved for future consideration. And the art world has a reasonably respectable history of valuing, celebrating, and salvaging the work of certain sensibilities which are not destined ever to be popular but which nevertheless expand the range of human possibility, whether along philosophical, scientific, political, or uncategorizably inventive lines.

Singular though they are, these virtues do not in themselves offer conclusive proof that being an artist is _a priori_ of greater value than being an entertainer, for surely it's better to be a good entertainer than a bad artist.

TUESDAY JUNE 22 Examining within myself the range, type, and degree of pleasure I've received from the two endeavors—artist and entertainer—after many years as a member of the audience for each, I've decided that entertainers are as capable as artists of manifesting radical structural changes in human behavior. There are no fatal flaws in entertainment media that preclude this possibility. Neither context corners the market on genius: If artists are to be admired for their independence and self-reliance, entertainers are to be admired for their willingness and ability to bravely mount the most modern cultural machinery and ride it to new kinds of success. Pioneering occurs in either context, and talent is talent.

TUESDAY THE 29TH However much I might regard myself as a species of entertainer, I'm not remotely useable to the entertainment industry as it's currently configured. My professional life has been formed entirely within the art world. I can't sing, dance, or act. I prefer not to tell anyone else what to do, so I can't direct or produce. I'm neither enabled by talent nor permitted by conscience to write scripts in the way the entertainment industry needs them to be written. My talents, such as they are, provide no passports to entertainment's customary venues of stage, page, or screen. In short, I'm not a natural. All I know is that somehow, without seeking to, I've crossed the wires of two endeavors, artist and entertainer, and fed into each the social and psychological structures of the other. When working on my art, I frequently have ideas appropriate to the context of entertainment. When thinking about entertainment, I have ideas for artworks. I <u>require</u> the entertainer's reward of immediate applause, but I <u>want</u> the artist's reward of the deferred applause of history. The genes of two separate and distinct cultural coordinates have become spliced in my imagination, and like an idiot I feel a responsibility to history to acknowledge this fusion in my public life.

Though I lack the usual talents of the entertainer, I've already earned what every entertainer needs most: an audience. The measure of success I've achieved in the art world supplies me with a readymade audience for my ambitions and frees me to explore entertainment with far greater independence than a conventional entertainer. I'm not required to engage the overdetermined vehicles or venues of traditional entertainment, nor to contend with the inflated, unionized commercial realities of the entertainment context, nor to obtain permission from entertainment culture's corporate owners to gain a forum for the display and distribution of my ideas. A lifetime of observing the fickle cultural spotlight controlled by mass media has made it clear that if one can't capture real and lasting power within the entertainment industry—power enough at least to guarantee one's continued participation—it's wise to retain access to a context that mass media can't control, doesn't understand, and always misinterprets. With the anarchy of the art world as both shield and smokescreen, the only person who will be able to put me out of business will be myself.

WEDNESDAY THE 30TH Within the art context I can contemplate the structural life of entertainment apart from its purveyors in the mass media. Discomfort with the powerful distortions introduced into life by mass media have served the same function for my generation that the Vietnam War had served for the 1960s generation—that is, as a ubiquitous, chronic, and unifying complaint—but so far as my own research is concerned, such heavy breathing only fogs the lens. I look at the excesses of mass media as one looks at someone who seems to have forgotten that they are a guest in one's home. For my purposes it's more useful to focus on entertainment as a consistent psychological and social coordinate separate and distinct from whichever vehicle—TV or record or movie or publication—happens to deliver the entertainment. Regardless of medium, form, or content, entertainment as a human experience has its own steady, throbbing life, as if it were an element on a periodic table of sensations, and so can be justifiably isolated as a subject for study. Want of the entertainer's usual talents simply allows me to get that much closer to entertainment's pure essence.

JULY 4 If it can be shown that a point of behavioral equilibrium exists between the two endeavor-structures, artist and entertainer, my goal is to locate that point, mine its substance, refine it, inject it into my attitude toward my artistic production, and live out its implications in my public life.

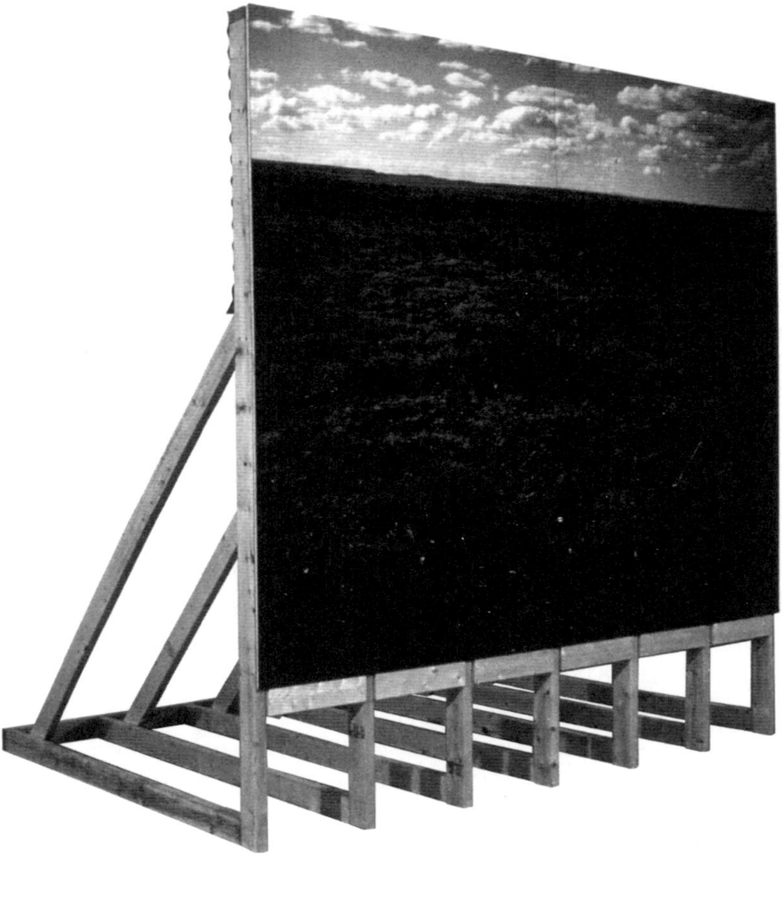

Clegg & Guttmann and David Robbins, Petrified Forest Estates Lot #296, 1987
Cibachrome photograph, billboard structure, and 1 1/8 acres of Arizona desert land;
billboard 102" x 98" x 71"

SEPTEMBER 13 For a while, behaved like a typical artist, bringing the artist's customary objectivity toward subject matter to bear on the complex social role of the entertainer, its relations to power, to production, to audience—as if, in the interests of science, it were possible to map the structural life of entertainment, its architecture, and its surface contours. In Stuttgart I'd met a German computer software whiz who'd offered to help design software capable of schematizing entertainment's structure. That generous offer had been gratefully accepted, but as our work progressed via post, I began to notice that my temperament only permitted this scientistic, scholarly approach toward entertainment to rule for brief periods before the anti-analytic, anything-for-a-laugh entertainer in me demanded satisfaction.

SEPTEMBER 17 Revelation. Sitting in the Times Square Howard Johnson's, nursing an ice coffee and staring through the window at the winking, bulb-studded theater marquees outside, it occurred to me that any attempt to isolate and analyze the structural life of entertainment is doomed to inauthenticity and inaccuracy unless the analysis itself is entertaining. Failure to communicate in my analysis the sensation of <u>being entertained</u> violates and betrays entertainment's structural integrity. Entertainment can only be shown to possess a structural life if the conditions of that structural life are allowed to penetrate to one's cultural <u>practice</u>. Rather than make artwork "about" entertainment by treating entertainment objectively as subject matter or by aping the look of artifacts from the entertainment context, it's more ambitious, more modern, and more authentic to acknowledge in one's <u>behavior</u> that one's experience has been so dominated by popular entertainment culture that one cannot separate from it the particular configuration of one's aspirations for public life.

FRIDAY NOVEMBER 28 Have continued to work like an artist, making objects and images for exhibition, but increasingly think like an entertainer, and the cross-pollination's slowly shaping my views, not only about how to proceed as an artist, what determines value in cultural production, and "meaning" in art, but about a potential role in public life. Thus whereas I'd initially thought to apply critical, analytic methods to the resolutely pleasure-principled, aggressively non-critical, wildly anti-theoretical subject matter of entertainment, that same non-critical element has begun to annex and overwhelm my attempt at a critical method. Dr. Jekyll is disappearing into Mr. Hyde—truly an entertaining development!

DECEMBER 11 Have decided to obtain prerecorded television laugh tracks in order to play them through hidden speakers in galleries during exhibitions of my work.

THURSDAY JANUARY 14 The deeper the entertainment aesthetic eats its way into my imagination of my cultural practice, the clearer becomes my vision of a species of behavior beyond the habits of visual artists. Today, while working with a video camera, searching for a "non-narrative" acting style, I realized that as a model for artistic production, entertainment positions audience—other people's pleasure—ahead of the artist's vain aspiration to glory and "importance." The audience's pleasure is the entertainer's sole consistent goal, the only king that he or she must serve. Extreme congruence of word and deed—doing what you mean, and meaning what you do—has come to be the accepted yardstick by which serious artistic purpose is measured in contemporary artistic production (with the most radical proponents of this approach—conceptual artists—transforming themselves into streamlined, nearly human packages of content), but it is not by any means a prerequisite for bringing pleasure to an audience. I'd tried to organize an analysis of the structural life of entertainment as yet another conceptual art "project," as that term has come to be valued among artists, gallerists, and curators—that is, a highly integrated art of consistent subject matter, content of a critical or theoretical nature, rigorous presentation, and systematic investigation—but the structural conditions of entertainment didn't recognize these as necessary virtues.

More importantly, merely processing entertainment through the existing intellectual filters of conceptual art fails to challenge the behavioral location of artists—the most ambitious thing you can attempt as an artist. Allowing entertainment to infect my cultural production at the behavioral level is specifically intended to generate alternatives to the prevailing model of the serious avant-garde artist, which, precisely because of its unquestioning faith in the value of totally integrating method, medium, and content, has become predictable and stale—and, as a model for behavior, anything but avant-garde. If art in the 20th century has frequently seemed bored with itself, if a configuration of the avant-garde has brought itself to a boil and slowly evaporated, it's because, regardless of artists' formal and conceptual inventiveness, this once-imaginative behavioral model has ossified.

JANUARY 27 Have jettisoned conceptual art's paradigm of the artist as a package of stable meaning, preferring to remap artistic practice on a bipolar model using the only quantitative, i.e. verifiable elements in cultural exchange: the producer, and the audience for production.

JANUARY 28 Because there are countless ways to generate pleasure for other people—the means being limited only by the imagination of the producer—modeling one's artistic practice after entertainment gives permission to the broadest possible range of production, and permits multiple, inconsistent, conflicting, even mutually canceling contents. The entertainment aesthetic provides a cagey policy of no-policy, a theoretical justification for virtually any working method; that person who shapes his production around the structural life of entertainment is freed thereby to create in any medium using any procedure (be it systematically and as the product of meticulous research, or as isolated instances of serendipitous revelation) every manner of work (political or anti-political, staunchly progressive or radically frivolous) which might conceivably bring pleasure to an audience. That person is equally free to make work which self-consciously and explicitly investigates the entertainer's psychological and social location, because at times that will be the most entertaining thing to do: the entertainment model of art not only functions as an anti-theory, arguing for the widest spectrum of artistic production by de-emphasizing the need for a consistent, stable meaning, it is _itself_ a perversely unifying theorem which, by organizing all production toward the goal of the audience's pleasure, renders consistent any and all inconsistencies of style, content, and medium.

FEBRUARY 9 Like a powerful laser, the entertainment aesthetic slices through any theory or intellectual construct that threatens to obstruct one's access to one's idea pool. It effectively guarantees me _complete access to my own mind_.

But after the laser is unleashed, how to control its intensity and duration? I've no idea how to turn it off once it has scoured from my mind the biases and intellectual encrustations of contemporary artistic practice. How does one stop the laser's disintegrative power from devastating the membranes of thought which separate ideas into specific contexts for use? And if those subtle, supple membranes are destroyed, what will be the consequences to my cultural practice when access to my idea pool continues without any intellectual means of organizing or arranging into a hierarchy the ideas found there? "Everything goes when 'anything goes' all of the time," warn The Replacements on my tape player, while I sit here fretting that my entire hypothesis about the usefulness of entertainment as a model for cultural production might only camouflage the dilettante's aversion to discipline.

MARCH 1 The child of mass media is no more able to plug the geyser that routinely brings up fragments of a collective, Pop past than he is to dam the stream of memories from a more personal and individuated history. Of the regular and reliable flow of ideas for movies, TV shows, pop songs, books, and magazines that surface in my imagination, many are sufficiently amusing to hold my attention, and some are intriguing enough to introduce into public life. It's over the manner in which these ideas should be treated, finally, that I break with the established practice of even the most radically contemporary artists.

Years of exposure to the radio dial and the television channel have taught me to recognize and respect each context in the constellation of competing contexts. Therefore it's only natural for me to resist the impulse to gather every idea into a single context and elevate it above every other. I refuse to invest in the Old World attitude, which holds that, in order for them to be worthy of consideration, ideas that have their origin in the experience of entertainment have somehow to be brought into—validated by—the cleansing context of art.

A more authentic response to the teachings of the New World is to acknowledge in one's cultural practice the integrity of the contexts from which one's ideas have derived; it's much more modern not to consign odd or dangerous ideas about popular culture into the neutering hands of art, and to try instead to return those dangerous ideas to their original contexts. It's more dangerous to try to participate in the original, source culture. Instead of making video art with my ideas about television, it's both more inventive and a fuller recognition of others' achievements in television to try to produce real television shows which negotiate the accepted conditions of broadcast for a mass audience. Rather than make artist's books for distribution via the art-world pipeline, I'll aim for the professional context of literature. Yet because objects have the capacity to "entertain" in unique and subtle ways, I seek to expand my production into these other contexts without forfeiting my access to the art world—though when working in entertainment, I will not be nor do I wish to be identified as an artist.

Indeed, am becoming increasingly convinced that I might no longer be an artist. Art is situated in the progressive refinement of an invented behavior; I accept and respect that definition. But what if the behavior that has been invented happens to be of a nature that consciously and ruthlessly treats the context of art as but one venue among many, useful for certain projects, wholly inappropriate for others?

MARCH 3 Early and constant exposure to the experiential structures of popular culture have made it impossible for me to lose myself in a full endorsement of art. Instead of encouraging a close identification with the structural life of a single context, the radio dial and the television channel condition their audience to see a context's limits and limitations, the borders where <u>this</u> configuration of endeavor stops and <u>that</u> one begins. By daily demonstrating that there are many coexisting practices simultaneously evolving, television and radio incline those who are raised by them to value <u>the relations between contexts over the conditions of any one context</u>.

Anyone who travels a great deal is familiar with the way that travel becomes a separate realm, abstract certainly, and borderless, but for the traveler no less a defined and specific context. One quickly learns to make a home in the privileged homelessness of travel, and once one has adjusted, the thought of settling comes to seem unnatural. In a similar way, the radio dial and the TV channel prime receptive members of their audience to perceive and identify another kind of travel—contextual travel, from Channel 4 to Channel 6, from Channel 6 to Channel 28, or from 98.5 FM to 920 AM and back again—and to consider it a normal, everyday experience.

In fact, radio and television not only designate contextual nomadism to be a distinct and very real modern condition, they raise their audience to understand that the relation between contexts is itself a context. In order for Channel 4 and Channel 6 to exist in a relation to each other, they must perforce be suspended in another context, not the medium of television per se (TV is only the vehicle) but rather the perceptual <u>emulsion</u> that instantly materializes in the viewer's mind with the juxtaposition of any two contexts. This imaginary emulsion, in which two or more separate contexts can be suspended, is itself a medium; in the fertile agar of the contextual emulsion, behavioral cultures grow which, properly cultivated and harvested, enable one to transgress at will the boundaries of discrete contexts. Because its own structural life is never entirely determined by the limits of any single context, the contextual emulsion represents a more complex configuration—a purer distillation—of invented behavior.

The emulsion is contextual RNA, glistening transparent viscous ropes of pure context. _Here_ is the material I've been looking to inject into my cultural practice. For if it's the case that the relation between contexts is itself a context, then by causing one's practice to include any two contexts—for example, art and entertainment—one imposes on oneself the conditions of a context. One essentially _becomes_ a context—initially described only by the letters of one's name, perhaps, but over time, assuming that a sufficiently deep structure has been envisioned, apt to attract other people's contributions. When that occurs, the model of invented behavior will fulfill its intended function as a model.

Contextual genetics—establishing a behavior that fuses, bridges, or cuts across two or more contexts—_that's_ the new frontier, the site of maximum invention. Situating one's cultural production entirely within a single information context, such as "being an artist," can still be rewarding, especially if one has been endowed (saddled?) with a capacity for virtuosity, but the behavioral terrain that virtually aches to be explored is the one that splices two or more contexts to create a third, partly because this new terrain has been shown to exist and partly because it's the true stuff of cultural democracy, open to any lacking traditional skills, but brave or desperate enough to cross into it. Contextual genetics presents the possibility of real behavioral _adventure_. The physical frontier had closed a century ago, but behavioral frontiers remain.

MARCH 8 If, by their fusion, the genes of art and entertainment have genuinely produced in me a behavioral mutation—if X equals a new kind of person—it's both my duty and my right to explore every fractal of productive, potentially audience-pleasing behavior available to me within the limits set by that mutation's particular configuration. The pure liquid essence of entertainment will become my medium, and I'll pour it into any vessel that can contain it; the creation and skillful management of pleasure in other people will be my artistry. The purity and scale of my ambition will equal that of the comic book superheroes of my childhood: Look! Up on the stage/page/screen/gallery wall! It's Entertainmentman! Able to distill the essence of the cultural life of the nation in order to unleash it generously and at will for the pleasure and satisfaction of millions!

APRIL 16 As Entertainmentman, I seem to have acquired the ability to inhabit or disinhabit, at will, the commitment to a personal content. I can stand outside of it, and watch it fold, or I can re-inflate the idea of personal content and slip it on like a perfectly tailored second skin. For the past few weeks I've thought of this newfound ability only as a kind of personal problem—that is, while it's fascinated me, I've felt guilty about both ability and fascination. This morning, however, an innocent spring morning, an incident occurred which provides exactly the intellectual ammunition needed to cover my flight from older, unicontextual configurations of sincerity.

Walking along Houston Street at the northern edge of Soho, I was stopped by a young man who seemed not only down and out but, as indicated by the slow, stumbling manner of his request for assistance, enjoying an afternoon on some drug or another. As I prepared to deliver the automatic refusal favored in New York by the league of self-important young men on the go, the bum asserted that he didn't want money. Swaying on the sidewalk, he slurred and growled that he wanted only to have a phone call made for him. He showed me an envelope with the name "Dr. Stone" and a seven-digit phone number written on it. Inside the envelope were three coins. Each coin looked both old and foreign, and each was presented in the manner of the amateur numismatist, pinched between two pieces of clear cellophane and displayed in the circular window that had been cut into two pieces of white cardboard, the entire sandwich neatly stapled together at the edges. A brief description of each coin its date, and its market value—all three in the thousands of dollars—was written in a neat, legible hand on the white cardboard.

The young man asked me to dial the number written on the envelope, and to inform Dr. Stone that three coins, presumably his and presumably lost, had been found. Though I was in a hurry to get on with my day, it seemed a simple enough favor to perform, so I popped a quarter into the pay phone, dialed the number, and when a woman's voice answered, asked for Dr. Stone. In a moment a gravelly voice identifying itself as that of Dr. Stone came on the line, and I carried out my duty, informing the doctor that three apparently rare coins had been found in an envelope bearing his name. "You found them!" Dr. Stone shouted. "Where did you find them? This is fantastic!" I explained that they'd been found by another young man who appeared in desperate need of a windfall. Dr. Stone said that there was a cash reward of $1000 for the safe return of the coins, and that whoever had found them had only to return them to to his home at 877 Park Avenue in order to claim it. Holding my hand over the phone's mouthpiece, I related to the young man the news of his good luck, whereupon, to my surprise, the guy groaned that if he couldn't even dial a phone number to reach the doctor he could hardly get up to 877 Park Avenue. While the doctor waited on the line, the young man told me that he didn't care enough about the reward to go all the way uptown to retrieve it (perhaps $1000 was enough money to force him to change his life and he had no interest in tempting the possibility), and proposed that in exchange for $75 I could take the coins and claim the reward myself. After hesitating a bit, as I had a luncheon date and errands to run, I agreed, as it seemed foolish not to seize the opportunity which had fallen into my lap. I told Dr. Stone to expect me with the coins later that afternoon. The doctor said that anytime that afternoon would be fine, he would be at home all day. I promised to call before coming uptown, signed off, and hung up the receiver.

The walk to the bank was a short one, and on the way my new partner and I made awkward conversation. I learned the young man's name, then listened to Joe's history. How he'd been thrown out of the house by his parents at 13, lived in foster homes, run away, and made the street his home. When we reached the bank, I withdrew from the cash machine the money I'd promised him. Thanking me, Joe handed me the envelope with the coins, and we said goodbye. I wished Joe good luck and watched him shuffle off towards Bleecker Street.

After lunch, I made a call to Dr. Stone to say that I was on my way, but there was no answer. I used the time to take care of errands, then returned home where I again dialed Dr. Stone's number. Still no answer. Pulled out the phone book and looked up "Stone," checking for doctors. No Dr. Stone listed on Park Avenue, either as a residence or as an office. Checked the medical listings, which confirmed that there was no Dr. Stone on Park Avenue. Knowing that certain apartment buildings are listed in the Manhattan White Pages, I looked up 877 Park Avenue. No listing for 877, but there was one for 879 Park Avenue, so dialed the number. A voice answered, and after I'd ascertained that I was speaking to the doorman, I inquired about the location of 877 Park Avenue. The doorman to 879 Park Avenue stated that there was no 877 Park Avenue.

I'd been conned.

This afternoon, I felt by turns stupid, embarrassed, and angry, until, early in the evening, I realized that "Joe" and "Dr. Stone" had conned one of the few people who could actually benefit from obtaining the objects used in the con. As a result of their ploy, three objects charged with a rare and unique valence of ambiguity had blundered into the zone of art, a context in which hard evidence of intention is always useful, sought, and celebrated. The fact that these coins have a shadowy anecdotal history gives them an eerie potential for presentation in public life that they could have acquired in no other way. (The victim of con artists, I now have the opportunity to produce genuine Con art. Ironically, if I can manage to guide these professionally insincere coins into the art context in just the right way, I'll be able to re-sell them for considerably more than the amount of the offered reward.) Even if it had occurred to me to do so, were I to have walked into a numismatist's and purchased three coins in order to assign to them the story of the con, those coins could not have had the same twisted integrity, because they would have possessed an altogether different history. They would have been mere souvenirs of a groundless fiction. Instead, I have on my hands something stranger than fiction: the embodiment of a stubbornly authentic inauthenticity.

But the value of this experience is not that it's provided me with the material for Con art; however amusing, it'd be a one-time only project. It's much more interesting to consider what the coins represent: specifically, the gap between integrity and the appearance of integrity. As an idea, this gap possesses its own integrity. What is the difference between integrity and its appearance? What are the signs by which a difference can be discerned? Indeed, can one even tell the difference? These are powerful and alluring questions, in sophistication worlds away from the minor aesthetical distinction between "real" and "fake."

<u>These coins are real coins. What was claimed for them was an invention, a pure fabrication</u>. The gap between integrity and its appearance is a serious business, a philosophical schism never entirely resolved, and an adult game with real consequences. From integrity to its appearance stretches a shadowy corridor, off which politics and religion have long had their head offices. Toward one end of the corridor, art, dedicated to the constant and extreme cultivation of integrity—the necessary, self-flattering illusion that one is actually doing what one claims to be doing; toward the opposite end, show business, requiring but the appearance of sincerity, and then only in the presence of an audience, yet entirely believable when unleashed ...

JULY 18 For some time now, have kept the little gap between integrity and its appearance under observation, turning it over in my mind and studying it the way one studies a snapshot that has caught some disturbing trick of the light. Curiously, nourished by my observation, the sliver of space has grown, little by little, until at last, today, I've discovered that it's expanded into a philosophy. Yesterday the gap had been inside me, today I'm inside the gap. There's room enough to move about freely.

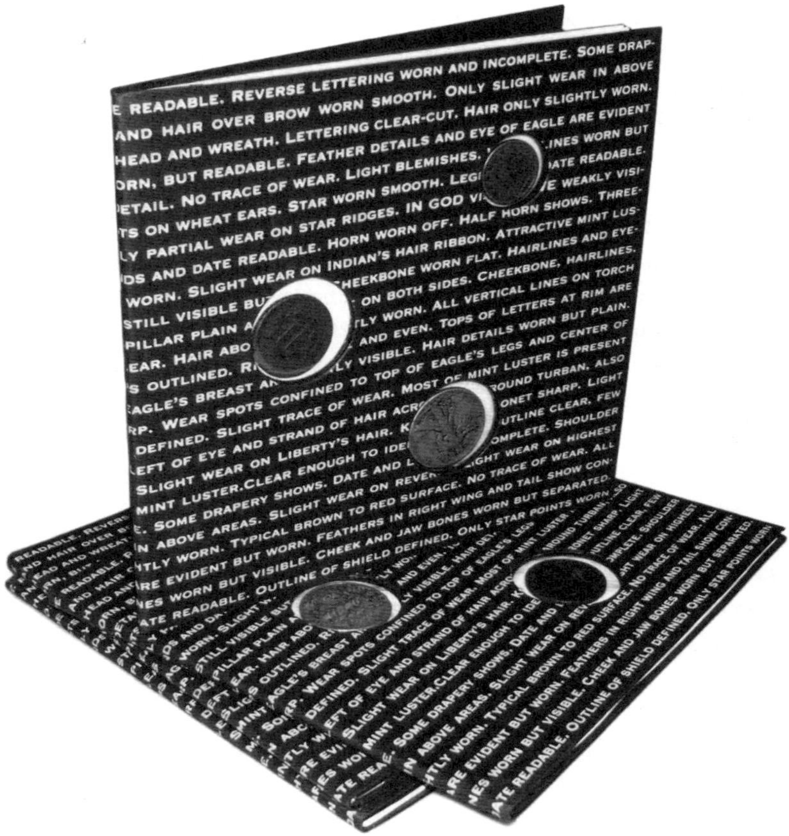

Prose and Cons books published by Les Editions Belle Haleine, 1992, edition of 18. The cover of each handmade book included three antique coins, one set of which was the trio of coins actually used in the con operation described at the close of "Mr. Entertainment's Diary." Which copy had that set was not revealed to purchasers.

Further Adventures in the Two-Party System

Originally published in Parkett, #58, Zurich 2000.

"What were the tastes of the vast majority of affluent Americans? Bauhaus and the International School were considered the leaders of design, but were Americans accepting these imported theories of Gropius and Breuer and Mies van der Rohe? The answer was an emphatic 'no'! So where was I to seek that certain style which would satisfy the hotels' guests and would represent for them their dream of tropical opulence and glittering luxury? I finally realized that American taste was being influenced by the greatest mass media of entertainment of that time, the movies. So I imagined myself the set designer for a movie producer who wanted to create a hotel that would make a tremendous impression on the viewers. Wasn't that exactly what I wanted to do when I studied architecture? So I designed a movie set!"
—Morris Lapidus*

FIVE YEARS AGO, WHEN I WAS MORE CLOSELY FUSED TO THE ART WORLD THAN I CHOOSE TO BE TODAY, I ATTENDED A DINNER PARTY AT WHICH I HAPPENED TO BE SEATED ACROSS FROM A RISING YOUNG CONCEPTUAL ARTIST RENOWNED FOR HIS SERIOUSNESS OF PURPOSE. His ascetic, and rather pious artwork, which came in combinations of just three colors (black, white, and silver) and often incorporated the writing of continental philosophers, enjoyed the respect of the right curators, especially the right European curators.

While our table waited for dessert to arrive, the rising young conceptual artist informed me that he'd have liked me to have participated in his latest multiple, had sought me out, had failed to reach me. (This was during a nomadic period when I roamed from town to town and from exhibition to exhibition, and my whereabouts were often difficult for others to pinpoint.) He proceeded to describe the opportunity I'd missed. Memory is now a bit hazy about what, exactly, his then-new multiple entailed, but I am clear on the fact that it involved collecting some physical essential—hair? blood? breath?—from a number of then-popular artists. Neither the exact nature of the material nor the exact means of their transformation or presentation matters here. What does matter—and what has stayed with me—is the exchange that ensued:

"I wish you could've participated," said the conceptual artist, orange candlelight flickering across his rimless eyeglasses.

"Yes. Well, thank you," said I, smiling, flattered. "Actually, I could easily have done so."

"Really? How?" he asked.

"You could have taken someone else's blood/hair/breath and labeled it with my name."

"Impossible! Absolutely not."

"Oh? I'd have given permission. Happily."

"But doing that wouldn't have been authentic."

"I see. Need it be?"

"Of course!" he insisted. "Of course it must!"

"And why is that?"

"The fact that I have really done this thing—this is its power."

Nostrils flaring slightly, I swallowed a yawn. "Hmm. Tell me: Didn't you only need the audience to <u>think</u> you'd acquired and processed the actual blood/hair/breath of these artists? Wouldn't that have been sufficient?"

"Not at all," replied the conceptual artist, his answer hard as a shield.

"Why not?"

"To do so would be false. It would violate the gesture's integrity."

I pensively tapped pursed lips with the flat of an index finger used to pushing buttons. "So, then: Integrity's the thing you're trying to <u>communicate</u>?"

"You are encouraging me to lie?"

Was I? "I respect that you feel the need to remain loyal to a particular model of integrity. I only wonder whether that model's still the most appropriate. In the piece you've described, for instance, frankly I can't help but detect a measure of ... nostalgia."

He tensed. "And about what, exactly, am I nostalgic?" His voice aimed for neutrality and just about found the target.

My reply, though direct, was calmly delivered. "The idea of the sacred. Specifically, the idea that in order for the audience to discern the presence of the sacral, the sacral must actually be present."

He didn't bother to hide his distaste. "In order for my artifacts to be properly charged, these things must actually be done. They are the record of how I've lived, what I've done with my life. In order to communicate that, everything must be actual."

"To communicate?" Had I been a smoker I would have exhaled concentric rings. "No. For that, they don't need to be actual."

"And why not?"

"Show business." I spoke the words as if citing an amendment to the Constitution. "This is the age of show business. In the age of show business, a good story that happens to have the slight disadvantage of never having occurred easily wins more of a response than a dull story whose sole merit is its verisimilitude. The audience need only <u>believe</u> that you've done the thing you've claimed to have done. And that, in the end, comes down to presentation."

"Presentation."

"Yep. Packaging."

"I had heard you were a cynical man," said the young conceptual artist bluntly.

I did not ask that he divulge his sources. "Am I? Gosh, I certainly don't <u>feel</u> cynical. Not remotely." For just a moment I wondered whether genuine cynics felt that way as well; the thought didn't take. "To me, it seems a hell of a lot more cynical to pretend that authenticity is still the absolute definition of truth. We're living with a much roomier version of truth now. Something—in my view, show business, but really who knows?—has expanded it. The authentic is just a subset of what feels, to us, to be truth. Truth, <u>in order to feel</u> like truth to us, now must acknowledge and include the inauthentic. You want to stick by the old integrity? Fine. I say integrity has become a material. What's cynical about that?"

This conversation has remained alive in memory, I think, because it shines strong, even light on the two kinds of integrity—classical and synthetic—that organize our culture but rarely get seated in such close proximity.

The classical model of integrity, of which the rising young conceptual artist was a representative, holds that art is produced through an existential congruence of intent and deed, that said deed is to be undertaken for its own sake, for the sake of doing it. Steeped in the faith in the human's power to act and, by acting, to change the course of events, the old integrity, which we associate with human<u>ist</u> endeavors such as art, literature, and PBS, celebrates the high degree of refinement and subtlety that can be attained through the conscious, persistent pursuit of individuation. Without the formulation of the authentic established by the old integrity, much of history—and all of modern art—is unimaginable. Existential congruence of intent and deed underwrites everything from Duchamp's readymade to Manzoni's cans of artist's shit to the latest Sensation.

Synthetic integrity, on the other hand, is concerned less with doing something for its own sake than with the audience's perception of it—or, as Andy Warhol put it, "It's not what you're doing that counts, it's what they think you're doing." (A middleman between the two integrities, Warhol upset a lot of people with his honesty.) Recognizing a basic truth about communication, this mongrel integrity propounds that, from the audience's vantage, so long as the tap dancer smiles during his performance, the sincerity of his smile is beside the point. To validate him/herself in his/her own eyes, the artist may insist on existential integrity, sure, but effective communication doesn't require it.

Method acting is not the only technique available to the actor, after all.

In works of the new integrity, whether something is "done for real," whether anything is "meant," no longer matters *so long as it succeeds*. Q: Where is the success of new-integrity product measured? A: In the marketplace, of course. Obvious example? The Spice Girls.** But you don't even need to go that flimsy. Synthetic integrity underwrites most broadcasting and most movies and all advertising and most fashion and the glossy, tossy magazines that comprise the mainstream culture. Contemporary culture. *Our* culture. Synthetic integrity has pretty much conquered the world.

A decidedly modern phenomenon, the origins of this new integrity lay not in the 20th century but in the 19th, with the invention of the camera and the phonograph. Before the camera and the phonograph (the tape recorder of its day), there was another eye and another ear that we believed to judge us. That eye and that ear belonged to a judge, also of our invention, whom we have called "God." Gradually, over the course of the century just past, the invented judge named God was replaced with invented machines that watched and listened to and recorded our actions in godlike fashion but did not judge. Neither the camera nor the phonograph are capable of judging. And as these 19th-century inventions—the camera and the phonograph (and, later, the tape recorder)—became widely disseminated during the 20th, many millions of people came to have personal, direct experience with the confusion that resulted from replacing a judging God with, instead, machines that did not, indeed could not, judge.

These machines—camera, phonographs, tape recorders—separated integrity from its representation. They proved that a) integrity has a look and a sound, and b) this look and this sound can be fabricated. This news, although disturbing, *was not itself a falsehood*. And that's why, ever since, things have been complicated.

Gradually, they remade the environment, these machines. Out of the strange new environment they created has evolved a new kind of person whose experience of existential truth can no longer be said to be wholly restricted to a simple experience of authenticity. A new kind of person for whom authenticity is _but a subset_ of what feels true. Persons for whom the experience of the authentic is derived in part from—you guessed it—the synthetic. A kind of person to whom Morris Lapidus' "movie-set architecture" is real architecture—real, for the finally unassailable reason that it is, after all, authentic to their experience.

So far as classical integrity is concerned, this _arriviste_ is mannered, neurotic. It's new money. To those imbued with it, however, synthetic integrity feels as natural as a spring morning in the Hollywood hills. They offer no apologies. Indeed, to them it's the old version of integrity that doth seem the import.

True, in the hands of the hoaxer, the prankster or the creep, the new integrity often yields frighteningly cheap stuff. Ugly and disorienting as it sometimes may be, though, synthetic integrity's emergence isn't accidental. Nor is its staying power attributable solely to the smothering presence in our lives of the purveying technology of mass entertainment (the fact that 98% of American homes have at least one television, for instance). If we human beings didn't sense something of substance in our transactions with its products, the new integrity wouldn't have lasted. And since last it most certainly has, the new integrity mustn't be _necessarily_ or _only_ cheap. Apparently, to the idea that the tap dancer need only appear to be smiling, an integrity _does_ inhere. The synthetic is not without integrity. _Plastic_ has its own integrity. That some persons among us should see integrity as a material—_this_ idea, as an idea, also has its own integrity.

A communication system that accepts the integrity of appearances, show business is informed not only by the clammy admission that we do not always tell the truth (even to ourselves) but additionally, and more positively, by the knowledge that our capacity for dissembling is part of what makes us human. By acknowledging the essential role that untruth plays in our makeup, synthetic integrity paradoxically taps into a fundamental human truth, one that the old art integrity, with its dogged insistence on absolute congruence of intent and deed, cannot reach. The classical-integrity crowd comforts itself with the thought that all those clearly inferior synthetic-integrity industries attained their dominance via bullying tactics and an avaricious willingness to do anything for a buck. Might it not be possible, though, that those industries have the power they do because they communicate a fuller (if darker) truth about the nature of human beings than does art?

Some will always maintain that art's gestural fundamentalism is its singular strength; as wise old Ad Reinhardt decreed, "art is art and everything else is everything else." In the dinner conversation recounted above, the rising young conceptualist believed in the value of existential urgency, of classical authenticity, of the iconic payoff art exists to provide. At what point, though, does this necessary faith congeal into assumption? At what point does faith, turning churchly, prevent inquiry into the foundations of the endeavor? This question, valid any time, becomes all the more so in an age of show business, when it's apparent that hewing unquestioningly to a classical model of integrity may not be a good idea, either for yourself or for the culture, since that model can't be relied upon to communicate to modern people the most powerful configuration of truth.

To modern minds seeking contact with the complex Lapidusian authenticity that is their true home, art's existential earnestness reads as, well, monochromatic. Such minds prefer a more worldly model of integrity to one that seems forever snagged on an arguably adolescent formulation of the actual, the pursuit of which leaves unexplored the wider imaginative spectrum. Children of the synthetic integrity who desire to remain true to their own experience of the authentic are entirely free to pursue their own version of truth, of course, but they should expect the pursuit to carry them beyond the borders of the art world.

NOTES

* Morris Lapidus, Too Much is Never Enough, Rizzoli, 1996, p.166.

** A slickly packaged all-female British singing group of the 1990s. Their "Girl Power" theme was designed to appeal to the pre-teenage girls, who would propel the group to stardom.

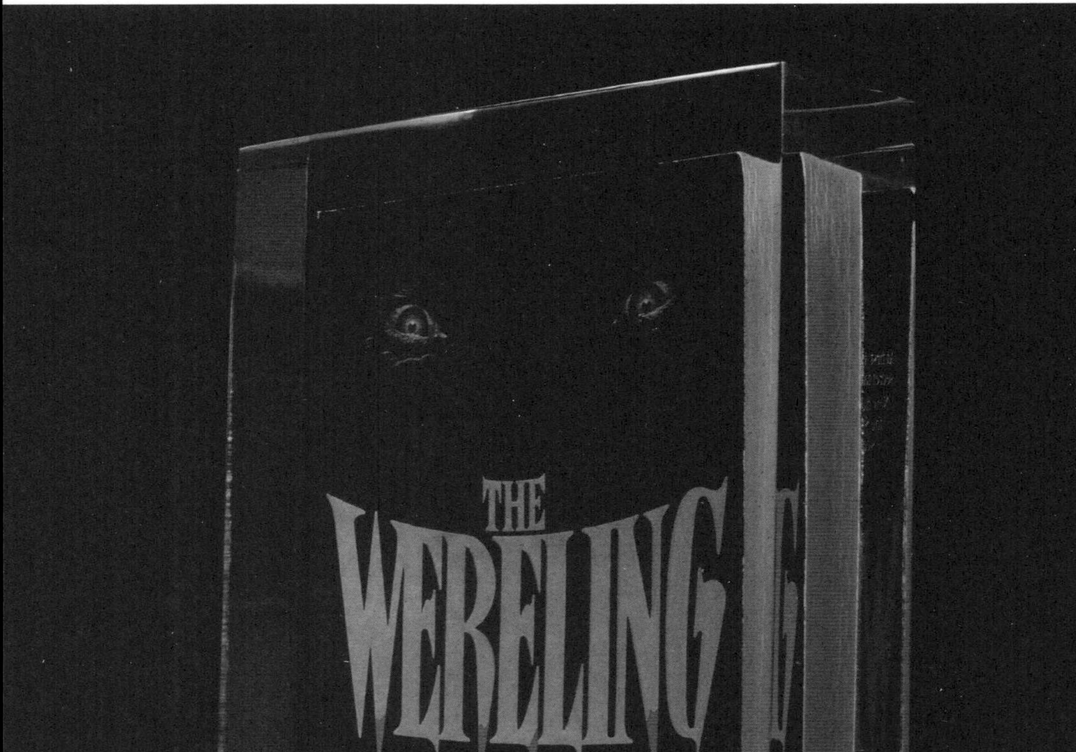

The Wereling (Book Authored by Another David Robbins), 1986
paperback book in solid Lucite block, 8" x 5" x 2"

David Robbins Goes Fishing at Loch Ness: A True Story

Originally published in Index magazine, New York, November 1997.

CERTAIN IDEAS, IF TALKED ABOUT, DON'T GET TO BECOME ANYTHING MORE THAN TALK, SO WHEN AT LAST I DECIDED IT WAS TIME TO ACT ON A NOTION I'D ENTERTAINED FOR YEARS AND GO FISHING, SOLO, ON LOCH NESS, I DIDN'T TELL A SOUL UNTIL THE NIGHT BEFORE MY DEPARTURE. With my bag packed and tickets booked, I figured it was safe to reveal the imminent undertaking, but even then I told only Iris. She did her best to take the fun out of the enterprise.

"Nessie's the ultimate in Old World breeding, of course," she said, "so certainly I can understand your attraction, but aren't you going a little far? What happens if she does show up? With you out on a boat alone? What if she fails to appreciate your little visit?"

"I'm prepared for that. I'm taking along a waterproof movie camera, so if anything unfortunate should happen and I don't make it back I'll still have proved her existence and in that way, by just the tiniest increment, I'll have restructured the world's imagination."

"Right," she said," assuming they find the camera."

Reaching Loch Ness required an early morning train from Brussels to Oostend, four hours on the ferry to Dover, and crowded trains destined for London, Edinburgh, and Inverness—all together some 15 hours of constant motion. Traveling light, I carried in my backpack but a single change of clothing, toothbrush and soap, a super-8 movie camera and film, a roll of gaffer's tape, and a small collapsible tripod.

After a night's stay in dreary Inverness I boarded a tour bus, and headed south. An hour passed and my destination came within view. The loch certainly looked mythic enough. Odd wind patterns corrugated the water's surface, beneath which shifted unsettling patches of ragged dark. Around the edge of the basin a forbidding wall of conifers grew, thinning further up to meadows dotted black and white with cows and sheep. Tonsures of mist ringed the tops of ancient hills.

At Drumnadrochit I stopped to investigate the Loch Ness Visitors Centre. Adjacent to a souvenir shop selling "I'm a Wee Monster" children's t-shirts and green terrycloth Nessie dolls, a tiny museum dedicated to the murky mysteries of the region offered pilgrims an opportunity to study ambiguous and compelling photographs, and to view a film of respected citizens—scientists, sportsmen, clergy—recounting their brushes with the beast. To my mind, the film's most convincing evidence comprised 30 seconds' grainy footage of a very large something moving rapidly across the water's surface while a motorboat gave chase bravely and in vain.

At the film's end, all visitors exited through a hall, which fed them back into the souvenir shop. There I purchased postcards featuring "An Artist's Rendering of Nessie," and posted one to Iris. Then I boarded another bus to Fort Augustus. Within 20 minutes of my arrival I'd steeled myself for the task ahead, and marched into Invermoriston Boats, "On the Loch Since 1962." I was soon wandering out toward the pier in search of my rented aluminum rowboat, clutching in my left hand a faded orange lifevest and a cork-handled fishing pole, in my right the movie camera, silver gaffer's tape, and tripod. Draped from the crook of an elbow the backpack swung in the wind.

Sublime comedy and exquisite terror correspond so rarely there's little chance to hone any practiced reponse to an encounter with their union, so I was quick to forgive myself when my nervous clamber aboard the rowboat recalled less the triumphs of

Cousteau than those of Hulot. Once the proper places had been found for all my paraphernalia, nautical and cinematic, I set about establishing a vantage point for the camera. For its perch I selected the wide crotch formed by the bow. Securing the camera took longer than I'd expected, since my hands, twitching with nervousness and cold, lent no grace to the endeavor. Eventually, the camera jutted proudly skyward, half mast, half periscope. I swiveled its lens around to face the stern, satisfied that the camera's position would place me squarely within range when the time came to film.

From a zippered compartment in the backpack I plucked the lure I'd bought at a fishing supply store back in Brussels and examined it in the moist palm of one hand. The thing had a bright red unblinking eye painted on either side of a bright yellow head of wood. Around the neck fluttered a glued-on boa of wispy yellow feathers, below which extended for all of two inches the lure's tiny body of yellow-tinted transparent rubber. The bottom third of the larval body had been shredded to create a kind of skirt. These rather luridly feminine attributes were aggressively contradicted by the lure's copper hook, which extended with deadly conviction out the front of the transparent skirt—a naked raging erection, murderously endowed. Demonic drag was the overall effect.

After tying the radiant creature on the line with an inexpert but serviceable knot, I disengaged the tangle of ropes from the pier, and began pulling on the heavy oars. The boat, uncertain of my captaincy, lurched toward open water.

As always in Scotland, there was wind, but the sky was blue, and what clouds there were portended no trouble. I concentrated on tugging away at the oars until a sudden jolt of fear, felt in direct proportion to my distance from shore and safety, froze the unfamiliar motion of my tiring arms. I gave in, 50 yards from the pier, and floated along. Sheep snickered from the hillsides.

When I felt sufficiently rested, I levered the oars out of the water and set them, blades sopping, inside the boat. With the boat's bottom wavering beneath my feet I crab-walked toward the movie-camera, aimed a trembling finger at the auto-focus switch, twisted my wrist to note the time on my watch, and flipped on the camera. It was show time. I resumed my seat, grabbed the fishing pole, and plunked the flirtatious lure into the inscrutable loch. Three minutes, the length of a single film cartridge, was all the time required to properly document the gesture.

"Cut to medium shot of the brave fisherman," I said aloud, "the constant breeze his only companion. Sunlight breaks through the cloud-clotted sky, striking the water like a searchlight." The dramatic narration was solely for my own amusement since, in pursuit of pure gesture, I'd purposely loaded the camera with silent film.

The rowboat bobbed in black water—not a fairy-tale or watercolor blue or green but opaque, secret-bearing, secret-keeping black. I craned my neck to inspect the water and found another surprise: no reflection returned my gaze. Just below the surface, slim chains of algae and broken bits of fern pirouetted to the music of the camera's whir. I allowed myself to grow vaguely hypnotized by the modest spectacle of the gyrating foliage.

Suddenly my reverie was invaded by the thought that the lure, costume jewelry adorning black velvet, might succeed in attracting the ungovernable, infinitesimal, and ineradicable possibility that a massive, thick-necked holdover from prehistory was actually circling in the darkness at that very moment, contemplating whether to surface and, by capsizing the boat, add my bones to the primordial bouillabaisse. That pale chance was chilling enough to transform the entire loch into an existential arena that admitted just myself, Herself, and the fishing line that intersected the glistening black membrane that divided our worlds.

Initially a mere prop in a facetious water ballet, that transparent nylon line became the tense center of an ontological tug-of-war. Competing for dominance were two differing claims on reality—though the contestants involved represented not so much opposing parties as positions of greater or lesser radicality on the same platform. In the running: Nessie, a sub-aqueous rumor, a mosaic of conjecture and misted sightings, versus a lightweight who liked to think that what got called "reality" never amounted to much more than somebody else's idea of a good time.

The movie camera muttered to itself. Had it been capable of recording more than appearances, it would have preserved that day a transformation sequence far subtler than any ever engineered in the cinema of horror.

Nessie won our tug-of-war, of course, there being no way for Her to lose. She'd had me where she'd wanted me—at her mercy. To claim victory, She hadn't needed to go to the trouble of actually manifesting her saurian brawn, against which I'd have been utterly defenseless. No, the ominous promise of that manifestation was by itself sufficient to make Her absolute authority over Her highly conditional reality—Her true domain—known to me, actual, felt ... The queen of the deep opened wide and swallowed me whole. Peristaltic waves drew me down, propelling me toward the bowels of a profoundly attenuated reality. All my individual attributes disintegrated. Skin, hair, muscle, bone, nerve, cell, biography, personality—all dissolved until the sole undigested thing that remained of "me" was the irreducible and impersonal human essence, a raw consciousness of life that's inseparable from any living organism. In the thick, congealed pudding of a lightless silence, that point of supreme neutrality between matter and anti-matter, my essence floated for a moment, then what little was left of me spilled forth and became absorbed into the bloodstream of another whose very existence had eluded proof.

Surfacing after that afternoon on the loch, I felt reborn, not spiritually but, like the superheroes from the comic books of childhood, as one endowed with some exaggerated and specialized power. I'd acquired a kind of double vision, seeing everything through my own eyes and those of a perfectly congruent twin who shared my name and history. No longer just myself, I was also a character based on myself, in a story that happened also to be my life. All of my actions became invested with a doubled weight, of fact and of something like fiction. The character could do things that I was too timid to do, and I contributed a certain sturdiness the character lacked. We made a good team.

That very night, my twin and I went into action. In my room at the Edgewater Inn, unable to sleep, I lay in bed watching a movie about a decrepit LA vampire who owned a theater where nothing but splatter flicks were presented. Suddenly an idea took hold, and I threw back the covers, rose from the bed, dressed, grabbed the movie camera, and headed outside.

The full moon looked like a hole punched in black paper to let the light of another world shine through. Past a patch of pines I found a tiny clearing. Dried brown needles crunched underfoot; I kicked a square meter clean of them, opened the back of the movie camera, and pried out the film cartridge. The film hadn't rewound entirely; from between its rigid black lips protruded a short, taunting tongue of celluloid. Gazing at it, I considered the distance traveled, the time, the expense, the fear endured. All of it registered. None of it stopped me. From my front pocket I fished out a lighter, flicked it to life, and touched the flame to the razzing tongue. The brown celluloid curled from the heat, then caught fire. The flame worked its way inside the cartridge. I placed the smoldering pinwheel on the ground. It fumed and popped. Black plastic bubbled in a sacrificial fire, an offering to faith. In a moment there was nothing left of the trip but a story to tell. Anyone who heard the story would have to decide to believe it, to believe that I'd gone fishing alone on Loch Ness, just as they'd always had to decide whether they believed that the old dame existed.

The fire didn't take long to burn itself out. When the brown plumes of smoke stopped, I scuffed sandy soil over the cartridge, and abandoned it to the darkness and the cold. I picked up the camera and headed back toward the hotel. Stopping in the parking lot to look up at the stars I was suddenly filled with a wonder so pristine that, had I been in a musical, a song would have been forthcoming. I wasn't, but there in the cold night air my twin and I began to sing anyway, in perfect harmony, with voices dazzlement had made small.

"There's <u>no</u> business like <u>show</u> business … "

Herr Valentin

Originally published in Art issues, April/May 2000.

NEARLY A CENTURY AGO, WITH HIS "READYMADE" ARTWORKS, MARCEL DUCHAMP INDICATED THE ART CONTEXT TO BE JUST THAT: A CONTEXT, SEPARATE, SPECIAL, AND CONSISTENT IN INTENT. The discovery that anything could be introduced into that context, and be elevated thereby to the condition of "art," was at the time an innovative and important chess move to make. More recently, however, minds less nimble have turned a supple gesture rigid. Many among us, artists, critics, and curators alike, spend entire careers smugly assuming the sanctity and finality of the context of art: Duchamp's liberating inventiveness now contributes to the retardation of the evolution of the imagination. Just on general principles, we should resist the idea that art represents the limits of our imaginations. Fortunately, we also have the example of Duchamp's lesser-known contemporary, the comedian Karl Valentin.

In the German-speaking countries, Karl Valentin (the V is aerated, pronounced as F) has long been considered as essential to his culture as Cantinflas is to Mexico, as Tati is to France. The most popular and ambitious comic mind at work in Germany in the first half of the 20th century, Valentin recorded dozens of 78s, starred in nearly 40 films and trod the boards in literally hundreds of stageworks during the roughly 40 years of his performing life.

Success on this scale is sufficiently rare that, in a way, it's not exactly surprising that, since 1959, the work of Karl

Valentin should have his own museum, in Munich; in show-biz mad America, after all, careers even a fraction as remarkable have poured the foundation for more than one star's institutional self-tribute, as vanity projects like the Liberace Museum or the Debbie Reynolds Museum impressively, adorably, risibly demonstrate. While it's true that today's visitor to the Munich site will see vintage posters advertising Valentin's stage and film work alongside photographs of the man himself, the Valentin Musäum (yes, for some reason it's spelled with umlauted "a"), founded in 1959, isn't really dedicated to displaying show biz relics from the performer's glory days. Displayed instead are artifacts of a very different sort—indeed, of a nature sufficiently singular as to distinguish the German comedian's oeuvre from that of all other performers of the era.

Karl Valentin, in addition to his considerable ability in the performing arts, also created imaginative and self-conscious objects and installations of real ambition. Don't confuse him with the show-biz variant of the hobby artist, your Tony Bennetts, your Frank Sinatras, your accomplished genre-scene painters that go with the flow of mainstream visual representation. Valentin is hardcore: a comedian who remains a comedian whether he's working on stage, in celluloid, or in wood, shoe polish, or decoupaged banknotes. Never merely visual, his objects and installations instead ping a complicated triangulation of the visual, literary, and theatrical.

Valentin termed his objects "art-kitsch." The two words don't really represent opposing ideas of valuation, aspiration or achievement so much as degrees of the same idea: kitsch is art that's managed to overshoot the mark. In kitsch, there's an over-earnestness, a pretentious over-ripeness, a sense of creativity gone sentimental on itself. The term connotes a maker who is overly operatic about The Human Experience and, at the same time, excruciatingly naive—the naïveté manifesting itself as his blindness to the work's failure to achieve that meshed groove of existential adventure, gestural innovation, and finesse that high art efficiently attains.

The producer of kitsch doesn't <u>know</u> it's kitsch he's producing: he's convinced that he's producing Art. Yet the person who willingly designates his own creations "art-kitsch" is about as naive as a Bob Mackie gown. The label that Valentin applied to his objects is tantamount to a pre-emptive strike.

"Art-kitsch": the comedian was the first to marry the terms. It's a shotgun marriage; each concept is placed forcibly into the context of the other. White glove versus white trash, they bicker continually, mocking each other, perpetually undermining the other's status. Neither the "successful" valuation system of cultural aspiration and achievement that's signified by art nor the "failed" version that defines kitsch wins out. Eventually wising up (and no doubt exhausted by the tension between them) the two lay down together and lose themselves in blissful collaboration, producing a mutant offspring.

The kid's quite the weirdo. It communicates in a tongue all its own—a sort of Yiddish, based upon, yet clearly distinct from, the signals that either art or kitsch emit. From day one, it's a fully formed third category of cultural aspiration and valuation, confident of its special status. From the vantage of this cocky, confident third position, both the concept of "art" and the concept of "kitsch" get reduced, as do all parents, to a status akin to that of a prop—logical enough, this, since Valentin is a man of the theater.

Props are generally dismissed as geeks from the audiovisual department of life, their inferiority as objects attributed to the fact that they're fake; they splash about in the shallows of illusionism; and they only exist for the purpose of propping <u>up</u> a narrative. But a classic Valentinian creation such as "Cold Steam of An Express Train Locomotive"—nothing more than a clear glass flask, half-filled with tap water—resists this sort of casual dismissal. "Cold Steam" is physically real, not merely made to <u>look</u> real. Just as importantly, it provides no narrative other than the one it generates in our imagination. Valentin consciously placed "Cold Steam" outside the protective force field of proscenium-arch illusionism. Instead, it stands on its own—oozing insubordination, nakedly challenging perception, and humming with comedy. "Prop" is a misnomer, even; <u>prop-like</u> more accurately describes a theatricalizing, concrete object that is inserted into reality without the prophylactic of narrative. It's all the difference in the world. The German comedian understood that to consign his little piece of theater—a hybrid of art object and theatrical prop—to a venue usual to the display of self-conscious imaginative objects (the art gallery or museum) would have been a bad idea. Doing so would cause it to be interpreted as art, which would obscure with static the very vibe that makes an object like "Cold Steam" hum with special life. Valentin intuited that his comic objects required another context for their distinctive hum to become audible.

Or so the evidence indicates, for in the early 1930s, he undertook to establish that context.

The site Valentin chooses for his experiment—the cellar of the Hotel Wagner—is familiar to him. For 20 years, he's been a featured performer in the hotel's basement cabaret, Wien-Munchen. Familiarity isn't the place's only virtue, though. Picture it: a vast, unfinished, subterranean realm removed from the buzz and bustle of life, a series of mostly windowless, dark, enclosed chambers lacking the usual signposts of time and place. Before very long a visitor finds him or herself tested, compromised, confused. In those sunless rooms deprived of compass and clock, the vulnerability of the senses becomes magnified, perception wavers, and what above ground has seemed solid certainty—the distinction between the real and the imagined, say, the border between theater and life—develops a case of the jitters. That hotel basement was already halfway to metaphor. In Valentin's hands, time spent there could be made to seem time spent inside the carnival of the human mind.

To fully exploit this metaphor, Valentin adapts an exhibition model—the Panoptikum—that's already been around for a while. Common throughout Europe during the 19th century, these centers of popular education were part science fair, part history lesson, part <u>Ripley's Believe It Or Not</u>, part Grand Guignol. Panoptikums presented theatrical tableaux that featured reproductions, usually in wax, of some of the more sensational aspects of life. Updating the self-serious Panoptikum for the skeptical 20th-century mind, Valentin tweaks the traditional categories—scientific diorama, recreations of historical scenes (common were scenes involving physical torture), aberrations of nature, sundry wonders trivial or grand—according to his skewed comic vision.

To help realize that vision Valentin enlists the aid of collaborators—his theatrical partner Liesl Karlstadt; the Wagner brothers, owners of the hotel; and, crucially, the academic sculptor Eduard Hammer, whose wax figures Valentin will arrange in numerous installations throughout. (Eduard Hammer's replicas were well-known, his life-size anatomical figures used as models at medical schools around the world; in fact, Hammer himself had operated the International Trade Panoptikum and Museum, also located in Munich until a fire had forced its closure in 1902.)

Valentin puts Hammer's figures—those that haven't either melted or been processed into soap—under new management. The result is Madame Tussaud's on Ecstasy, a series of installations specifically designed to confuse the senses for amusement's sake. Certain scenes of outrageous human behavior, such as a wax Inquisition tribunal, required minimal tampering to attain the desired level of weirdness, but when necessary Valentin imposes a more active hand. He freely invades Hammer's sober arrangements, stripping them of their dignity and enlivening them with the capricious dictates of his own playful imagination.

The expenditure of an impressive number of Deutschmarks gradually transforms the hotel's basement into, as a Valentin press release describes, a "grin and creep show." To make his assault on the senses even more total, the comedian signs an agreement with restaurateurs to open a tavern in the same basement. It's called, charmingly, Hell. Entrepreneur Valentin, ahead of his time, cobbled together an early full-service one-stop fun stop, a dark, disorienting Disney World, Deutschland-style.

Posters and handbills tout this odd new addition to Munich's cultural life: "The joke museum for the thinking man! A glimpse into Munich's underworld! Laughable philosophy of the century! Human mockery and stupidity in the mirror of the comic!" On October 21, 1934, the Valentin Panoptikum opens. Visitors willing to clamber down the basement stairs are treated to a spectrum of exhibitions ranging from the exquisite to the vulgar—from edifying historical events to gruesome acts of human torture and sly displays of … preserved theater.

For the dozens of comic objects and installations in the Panoptikum, Valentin concocted subtle comedies, blunt comedies, vulgar comedies, refined comedies, dumb comedies, cerebral comedies. There is banal stuff which, with the addition of a simple label, is elevated to the status of a historical object: "The Apple, From Which Adam Took The Bite," "The Jacket That Janitor Josef Maria Meier Was Wearing When He Met His Wife." Driven into a wall is the nail on which, ostensibly, Valentin hung his early career as a carpenter and became a "folksinger." Other displays betray, in varying degrees, more intervention: the "Cold Steam of an Express Train Locomotive," an empty bird's nest designated the "Nest with Unlaid Eggs," a wax child demonstrating the "Electric Nose Picking Apparatus for Kids." Here are roses that smell of gasoline and a gasoline can that smells like roses. Two umbrellas, one smaller than the other, are labeled "Father and Son." A portrait of a child is titled "Portrait of An Eighty-year-old Geezer At One Year Old." Preserved drops of "A Bureaucrat Sweat" are on view, and not far away, an "Old Box That Once Was Young" and a "Glass Nail."

Stationed all around are some of Eduard Hammer's wax figures, the more anonymous ones purporting to represent little known inventors, including "Mr. Empfenzeder, the inventor of the sponge bath" and "Mr. Rembremberdeng, the inventor of barley soup." A collection of natural history specimens is now "Karl Valentin's Zoological Garden." Included in it is the subtly hilarious "Tragic Mistake of Nature, or Camping Site for Turtles"—a taxidermied turtle climbing toward a birdhouse that's lodged in branches near the ceiling. Interspersed occasionally among the waxen and stuffed likenesses are living creatures, biological and botanical: figures that a visitor assumes to be still, suddenly move. In the Panoptikum's cinema room, there's the opposite effect: paying customers are seated next to life-size dummies.

When there are customers, anyway. Attendance is a problem. Get real: a hotel basement, filled with self-conscious objects of eccentric intent? Inaugurated in Germany during a period when freedom of expression had begun to be actively suppressed? Competing with newfangled dazzlements such as film and radio? Of course "the most original museum in the world" failed. Surely even its originality counted against it. (Despite our claims to value originality, we're not particularly skilled at identifying the real article.) Valentin's Panoptikum crashes within two months, closing at the end of 1934. The following May, the intrepid comic gives it another shot, but again it sputters, this time closing in December of 1935. Its second failure is more serious, as Valentin and his investors lose their money.

Despite the wreckage to others caused by his pursuit of his vision, the roaringly resilient and obsessive Valentin refuses to concede defeat, bouncing back less than two years later, in June of 1937, with a new version of his museum, a new partner for it (one Martin Wegmann), and a new address, Farbergraben 33. The basic concept doesn't undergo much alteration. It remains a combination horror chamber/exhibition hall offering many of the same comic objects and wax genre-representations of historical scenes. In this incarnation of the Panoptikum, however, Valentin more aggressively smudges the line between the animate and inanimate, between theater and reality. He adds a stage, performs his plays. After each evening's play he continues to perform—now, as museum tour-guide. Treating the displays as extensions of his live theater work, the comedian "explains" them, imaginatively riffs off their contents, sometimes spontaneously changes their titles, fusses with their physical arrangement, alters his intent for them mid-tour. The crowd trailing him from chamber to chamber can no longer mistake the objects before them for anything but prop-like curiosities born of an imagination perfectly afire with theatricality. On some nights Valentin behaves like a prop himself, suddenly disappearing—he's a figment of the imagination!—only to reappear minutes later, in disguise and mingling with the disoriented, now leaderless group. By amping illusionism across the board—he even intensifies the torture chambers by adding sound effects of dragging chains, groans, and screams—Valentin finds a way to more totally communicate what it's like inside his mind.

And it works! The Valentin Panoptikum finally catches on with the public. For three years the enterprise chugs along nicely. If the war hadn't intervened and shut down the experiment for good, in November of 1940, it might have lasted until 1948, the year of Valentin's departure from this vale of yuks.

Most of the 122 displays in the collection of today's Valentin Musäum are reconstructions and reproductions; few works from the original Panoptikum survived the war. It matters not; the extraordinary behaviors enacted by this giant of comedy surely dwarf niggling concerns about the contemporary museum's shortcomings. Herr Valentin widened the pool of possibilities for all creative spirits. With his proplike creations, Valentin established a category of production—the comic object—that is not between life and art, but between life and theater. A popular comedian intent on making comedy, he initiated the idea that a self-conscious, sophisticated object could be made with comic rather than aesthetic intent. If Valentin's objects skimp on aesthetic quality—and they do—it's because he knew that too much aestheticization would obscure the comedy. For him, the comedy is what counts, always.

Marcel Duchamp pointed to the existence of the art context. Karl Valentin demonstrated that a context could be invented. He invented a context for his objects, and then he signed his name to it. Upon examination, this context expands, touching and re-locating objects made by others—entertainers, artists, housewives, and traveling salesmen. The separate category of cultural production that Valentin established suggests the possibility of an alternative reading of the 20th-century imagination. His works foreground a kind of comedy—concrete comedy—that has been practiced throughout the century but has gone unrecorded.

The Dr. Frankenstein Option

The text originally appeared in a catalogue published by the Forum Stadtpark, Graz 1993.

TONIGHT I WANT TO TALK ABOUT COMEDY, BUT IN ORDER TO DO SO I'LL NEED TO MAKE A CONTEXT FOR WHAT I HAVE TO SAY. And to do that, I'll need to begin by talking about mass media.

The term "mass media" has become thinned out, almost transparent, through overuse, but the reality of mass media's power and influence grows ever more robust. Of course, mass media's impact hasn't been equally distributed; certain societies have been more fully exposed to its incessant noise and color than have others. In the US, media culture's impact on both private and public life has been enormous because we had had no strong national culture before it; there were strong regional cultures, but mass media was our first national culture. Media culture unified the country as a marketplace, just as it unified the country's imaginative life.

As it's too early in America's development for a strong alternative to media culture to have emerged, we're stuck with it. Europeans are fortunate to have a strong cultural alternative; the Old World—classical culture—is woven into European life so completely as to be nearly invisible, and though not as potent as it used to be, still classical culture serves as a kind of daily vitamin which, among other functions, helps the cultural body to resist the invasion of the mass media virus. America lacks such a vitamin, so there media culture, already the national culture, has now moved on to replacing the earlier, folkloric culture in living people's memories.

Originally, media culture was functional, offering information and, in the form of entertainment, relief from harsher realities. Its presence is now so pervasive, insistent, and inescapable, however, that it has transcended mere function; no longer simply a mirror of experience, media culture has become a considerable portion of primary experience itself. In the States in particular we must wrestle constantly with the place of mass media in our lives, because we can't separate it from ourselves. This is producing a new kind of person.

To register the progress of media culture's impact on the construction of human personality, think first of Warhol, the Christopher Columbus of media culture who discovered that the Pop personality had a specific structure that was somehow different from those that preceded it. Warhol said that if you wanted to know all about him, you had only to look at the surface of his paintings. Now compare Warhol's work to that of Cindy Sherman or Richard Prince or Jeff Koons, to name three well-known examples, all of whom sacrifice themselves to and celebrate the next level of pop, the level at which there is no separation between media and the recognition of self. We see Pop moving from the surface, a hovering presence outside us, preparing to penetrate … then it is inside us, uniting with our imagination of ourselves.

The fact that our sense of identity has become so closely tethered to media culture's structural life means that the pace of evolution of our identities depends in part on that culture's evolution. That's not necessarily bad, but it's become something of a problem in recent years, because mass media no longer seems to be evolving in a way that the audience can use.

Evidence: TV viewing is decreasing. The audience isn't getting what it wants—even if it doesn't know exactly what it wants. The television industry is concerned. They don't know what's wrong, exactly. They think that if they fiddle with the content of their programming they'll regain their monolithic audience and once again deliver it on a platter to advertisers, like in the good old days. But content isn't the problem.

The problem is structural—in fact it's infrastructural. In the earlier part of the century, mass media spurred human evolution because each new development in mass-media technology was accompanied by social invention, that is, an invention of the social: movies and radio and TV and pop music connected people to each other in new ways and provided them with a new grammar of experience that made the audience aware of itself as a specific human gathering. This may be the real reason for mass media's wild success. Unfortunately, that sense of evolution is no longer communicated because mass media has become bogged down in its own amazing success; the industry is now so enormous, commodified and professionalized that the social it communicates is wholly over-determined. The means of relief from ritual are themselves ritual, now. We go to a movie, we watch a TV show, we go to a concert, but little sense of human adventure is available to us in these because their outcome is predetermined to such an extent that, in an important sense, they are over at the same moment they've begun.

Audiences must be attended to or else they stop being audiences. Dissatisfied with rituals of relief that have gotten stuck on a particular plateau of the social, the audience for media culture's products has begun instinctively to search for ways to regain control over the pace and direction of its evolution. This search is bringing about a "silent revolution," a structural change in our relation to and use of the experience of mass media and its artifacts. Unsurprisingly, the revolution is being led by personalities that were incubated within Pop culture.

The natural product of a mass democracy of 250 million people, Pop is the expressive side of marketplace culture. Pop is democratic, aggressively so, made to be accessible to everyone. Marketplace culture is democratic in that it allows into the cultural stream anything thought to have the potential to sell. There's some debate as to whether this affords many different kinds of people a voice in the culture, or whether in order to gain entry to the culture all voices must sing (in unison) songs in the key of sales, but on the whole marketplace culture is positive, in that it allows for a wider set of aspirations—by exactly one—than had been previously allowed by classical culture. This aspiration is: entertainment, the most accessible cultural product.

Entertainment is a strange and complex idea on which to base a culture. It is also a liberating idea, because it frees people from the idea that a contribution to culture need aspire to refinement. Some people's gifts happen not to take the form of refinement; while refinement is still considered a perfectly respectable ambition in marketplace culture, if one's contribution happens to have other qualities which can show themselves to be sufficiently attractive to people—i.e., sufficiently entertaining—those qualities too will win respect. It's important to understand that, in democratic culture, the respect shown toward these other, less refined qualities is in no way ironical. The respect shown is real respect.

This democracy of virtues—what I term horizontal culture—is the basis for the cultural life of modern America, and it's a fascinating and radical concept. It's equally fascinating and radical that an entire culture should be based on the idea that the human quality known as "genius" should be required to compete for respect, as a quality, against other, arguably less ambitious qualities. Of course, genius is celebrated in American culture—so long as it is also successful. Genius is not at all a prerequisite to success, however, and success is what counts. Success matters more than what you did to be successful. That, too, is democratic.

Please hold in your mind this idea of a marketplace culture in which the human quality of genius must struggle for respect against other human qualities, while we consider another question.

What is the most pop thing of all? The answer: emotion. Rich or poor we all have emotions—which is why it's entirely natural that pop be obsessed with emotion, because everyone can be reached at that level. So TV is obsessed with laughs and drama, movies with laughs and thrills and drama, pop music with love, lost love, found love, endless love … Pop music is either about love, or about pop itself: "Rock Around the Clock." "We Built this City on Rock and Roll." Warhol could handle pop about pop, because to him pop was about the idea of pop, but he never figured out how to deal with the fact that emotion is the natural subject matter of pop culture.

Now bring these two ideas together. Adding pop's obsession with emotion to marketplace culture's idea that anyone should have access to the powerful distributive systems of mass media so long as they are successful yields a problem with the quality of representation of emotional experience.

Think about how emotion is represented in pop culture. In order to package emotion so that it can be sold to as many people as possible, pop culture first simplifies, then amplifies emotion. Take two recent musical examples, both from Whitney Houston. Whitney had a hit called "I'm Every Woman." Simplification and amplification. Her next hit was "I Have Nothing." Simplification and amplification par excellence. And what range she displays! From everything to nothing! No wonder she's a superstar! Of course, it is really no range at all, because in the simplification and amplification of both "I'm Every Woman" and "I Have Nothing," emotional subtlety—the complex and difficult personal nature of emotional experience—undergoes a kind of plastic surgery which smooths away the ugly and confusing and rewarding demands of an authentic emotional life. Though that plastic surgery is occasionally performed by a master, a genuine artist who has survived the challenge of winning a place in the market, it is more usually the case that it's done by an "entertainer" with a modicum of talent but plenty of ambition, a wall of amps—and a cultural guarantee of unrestricted access to mass media.

Simplified, amplified emotion is a misrepresentation of emotional experience—or to use simpler language, it is a kind of lie. This would not be a problem were there something to balance against it and cause it to be seen as a lie. For millions of people, though, nothing in the culture offers a strong enough contrast to do this. There is perhaps another way to prevent the lie, but it's hard to argue that access to mass media should be restricted, because the only way to restrict access is by engaging the State, and we do not want to involve the State in our imaginative lives. So we are stuck with the difficult consequences that result when a sprinkling of geniuses and a horde of less ambitious people have access to media culture's obsession with emotion. The less ambitious people win control of the culture, because the deck is stacked: Pop is built for and defined by accessibility, and fewer people have been trained to connect to works of genius. John Cage never found his way onto Top 40 radio. Thus the simplified/amplified misrepresentation of emotion gets repeated day after day, year after year.

This repetition has turned out to have significant impact on the creation of personality. Drawn to truth, the human organism eventually acts to shield itself when it detects a lie. But in this instance the protection comes in an exceedingly complex package. On the one hand, the person who senses the lie about emotion offered by pop culture comes to distrust mass media—but he or she also distrusts emotion, which has been poisoned, polluted, by mass media's portrayal. For people so affected, emotion cannot be experienced apart from the chain of associations that lead back to mass media's exploitation of it: personal emotion leads to thought of media emotion leads to disgust with media emotion leads to disgust with personal emotion leads to rejection of personal emotion. And then things get really complicated because it is impossible for people to do without some connection to emotion. Imagine wanting to have nothing to do with love.

A tough problem which, it would be nice to say, is neatly solved by unplugging oneself from mass media, or by going back to some more trusting and natural experience of emotion. But the first is difficult if you live in the modern world and the second is impossible because no "natural" state had ever been part of the experience of these particular human organisms. Instead, what remains is the queasy, mistrustful relation to both media culture _and_ emotion.

This unfortunate situation describes the experience of millions of people, at least in America. The American writer, George Trow, has even coined a simple phrase to describe this kind of person: "the cold child." The cold child is disconnected from feeling but has learned to treat the disconnection as a kind of joke in which, we might say, he considers himself as "referring to" the human. The idea that a person should "refer to" the human is not such a new idea within the liberal humanist tradition, having appeared a hundred years earlier as the metaphor of the Frankenstein monster, the synthetic person pieced together and unequipped to handle feeling. But it is a new idea that people should actually see themselves this way.

Cold children are interesting, in part because they are a new kind of person and in part because they not only sense the damage to their relation to emotion but are fascinated by its structure. And a great many people have been convinced that it is fascinating: the cold child has managed for some time to hold the West in the thrall of his/her fixated gaze upon the structure of his/her relation to emotion. Think, for example, of Punk, which I believe to be the most important cultural configuration of recent history. Many cultural moments since fall fully within the shadow of the configuration of personhood established in and expressed by Punk. To understand why, it's necessary to say something about (of all things!) the readymade.

Duchamp's readymade objectified the construction of reality. The readymade made it clear that an imaginative person, lacking the power of the state, still had the power to construct reality—because reality was a construction. Duchamp's readymade was evidence of what could accurately be termed the decentralization of reality. Fifty years later, Warhol's work further contributed to reality's decentralization by demonstrating that the cultural environment was itself a construction that could be treated as a readymade. Warhol spent the rest of his life profiting from this insight and its politically radical subtext, which said that in a media culture, personal empowerment depended on seizing the means of reproduction. More evidence of reality's decentralization turns up a few years later when the conceptual artists of the 1960s and 1970s discovered that specific social, political, and economic systems could also be considered readymades, and so treated as material.

Brilliant as these various gestures were, they were all generated by the view that the readymade was outside of us. Punk changed that. Punk said that one's emotional life could also be, in fact for many people actually was, pre-fabricated, fabricated by others, received, i.e. a readymade. Punk said that your feelings were not your own. For better or worse, Punk put quotes around feeling—for better, because it signaled a wish to regain emotional autonomy; for worse, because it meant that an entire generation of cold children had developed a mistrust of and an ironical relation to both emotion and the vehicles by which it was communicated in industrial society.

In Punk we find the first flowering of the metaphor of the synthetic person, the metaphor of Frankenstein, at the level of the social. In Punk it is manifested in its simplest and most accessible form, that of fashion, a "look." It's no coincidence that the look of Punk was the look of Frankenstein and Dracula, the look of the synthetic life and the undead. It is the look of the cold child who, beneath the impassive surface, shares the monster's need to revenge himself against life.

Punk has faded, but the quotes around emotion have remained. Since Punk, the ironical, distrustful, disconnected relation to emotion has pervaded American, perhaps Western, culture, and it has gone much deeper than just a "look"; the disconnected relation to emotion has reached the level of the expressive. There is commentary on this experience. There is Cindy Sherman. There is Richard Prince. There is a band in New York called Utensil, which plays only covers of New Wave songs: an ironical attitude toward irony. And there is the conceptual expressionism of Jeff Koons, the post-therapeutic Frankenstein, for whom the solution to the Frankenstein problem lies not in terms of trying not to be Frankenstein but in the social power acquired when one says "I am Frankenstein but I am not angry." In Koons' world there is no solution to the synthetic emotional life because there is no problem—or rather the problem is fun. This is, in my view, a fairly common American schizophrenia, and it's the case that in America Koons does not stand out in such sharp relief as he does in Europe. But Koons has earned an undeniable cultural power because he saw correctly that the integrity of the synthetic was integrity nonetheless, and then went about identifying himself as closely as possible with that integrity. There is a real achievement in that.

As much as Koons should be respected for his own solution to the Frankenstein problem, there is another option, of course, which is to not be Frankenstein at all. I think that it's possible to exploit the quotes around emotion towards other ends, to create something that is not expressive, admittedly, but is personal and possibly authentic all the same: The Dr. Frankenstein Option.

I am myself a cold child. Pop culture defined and limited my experience until I went to university where, exposed consistently to non-pop culture, I began at last to consider it strange that my childhood and adolescence had been passed transfixed by glowing screens and hypnotized by an endless broadcast of three-minute love songs. It was then that I discovered most of my memory was pop memory, and that much of my life had been spent negotiating and embracing the synthetic.

Well into my adult and professional life, I remained typical of the cold child. I was "interested in the idea" of the cold child, amused by the "problem." But for some reason I could not sustain my fascination; though I had the damage, I had a negative opinion of it. Instead of learning to play in the ruins of self, as many artists of my generation have done, I wanted actually to evolve toward a condition that could in some way be described as "improved." Not that I had any illusions. I don't believe that it is possible to ever lose the synthetic core—once a cold child, always a cold child—but I do believe that other layers can be added which are not as synthetic. However, as the cold child mistrusts feeling, the new layers can only be added in a cold way. Here the coldness of ideas comes in handy. Thinking can lead the cold child into tests of logic that make it impossible to remain fascinated by the damage. After all, imagination, when taken seriously, leads one places.

Taken together, the desire for a path away from the synthetic core and the repeated applications of doubt about its virtues created a small space, a little perspective, a distance sufficient to enable me to understand that the story of the cold child wasn't necessarily tragic. Why not? Because any person who thinks he has to *try* to be human is deeply, inextricably involved in comedy. When I formulated that idea, I broke the cold child's loyalty to his damage and replaced it with something that, while unformed, was alive and authentic.

One of the really big human inventions, comedy can be difficult to handle. The comic's is such a complex role to take on because comedy isn't only an imaginative enterprise whereby we reconcile the irreconcilable. There's more to it than that—or at least there can be. The "medium" for comedy isn't paint or film or music or writing, the medium is us, what we do and the way we do it, and the fact that its currency is human behavior gives comedy the capacity not only to propose but to embody an alternative physics of human and material relations.

That promise of an alternative physics is based on a naked disrespect for reality; comedy, after all, "makes fun of" the world as we know it. Comedy represents a positive kind of destructiveness, which, in its most extreme forms—in the grotesque, in cynicism, in black comedy—communicates disrespect for life itself. We are right to be disrespectful toward life, in a way, because life eventually does us in; comedy is our complaint about that neat and murderous arrangement. With characteristically playful perversity, comedy camouflages this critique of death as a critique of life.

Given this complex structure, it's not difficult to understand why comedy's ambitions should take their toll on those who agree to further them. Certainly it's the case that many comic personalities end as victims—frustrated, angry, embittered; this happens partly because life doesn't like to be toyed with (it will have its revenge), but partly too because the traditional relation of the Fool to the King leaves the Fool powerless, and childlike. Peter Pan was wrong: In reality, it is a drag never to grow up. Looked at psychoanalytically, the King's mature phallic power forces the Fool to the margins, where he chooses either the role of the eunuch or that of the satyr, the hypersexual role. Either position at first signals and then maintains the Fool's ineligibility to rule.

Now, I'm sure you can see that, for my project, it would have been lunacy to add these frustrations to the already damaged condition of the cold child. To avoid doing so, though, I had somehow to remake or transform the Fool's relation to the King. I had to make the Fool's role substantive, else his relation to the King's power could only be pathetic. Put another way, I had to make the Fool's role large or it would surely make me small.

Once I'd identified what needed to be done, through trial and error I found a way to make comedy large enough to challenge the King's power: instead of performing comedy as a character, acting out a make-believe situation before a movie or TV camera, I would do it as a real person, as myself. Because, frankly, if you want to encourage an evolution of the synthetic core, you cannot maintain an ironical relation to experience; authenticity, the extreme congruence of word and deed, is crucial to the project's success. Everything must be real. Thus the kind of comedy I have in mind is better described as "the comic life." It is a lived comedy, a comedy of action, a nonfiction comedy that yields objects and images and concrete gestures.

This concrete comedy is not so much an expressive activity as one that treats reality as a material; the objects produced through this activity do not share the art object's concerns for metaphor, analogy, description, and compression. It is a question of doors versus windows. I prefer doors.

Comic objects have a performative relation to reality. Located somewhere between a prop and an art object, comic objects parallel in certain ways the readymade's relation to reality. The readymade was powerful because it was nonfiction, an existing object, to which "nothing" was done; Duchamp, converting no mass yet an enormous amount of energy, exploited without mercy the stubborn claim on reality maintained by that object. He exploited the object's integrity and, by doing "nothing," identified himself as closely as possible with that integrity.

This was such a powerful act that we are still talking about it almost a century later. As the object's hold on reality refused to budge, our perception of it—and of him—had to. The readymade was performative, a prop on which perceptual change turned. Comic objects explore a similarly performative relation to reality—though with a crucial difference, in that comic objects aren't readymade. They must be constructed.

Though I named Concrete Comedy and made it a self-conscious activity, I did not invent it. Concrete Comedy appears to be a 20th-century phenomenon, which is manifested in both the context of art and the context of entertainment. Its beginnings, in both contexts, date around 1910, with on the one hand, Karl Valentin, an entertainer who also made objects, and on the other, Duchamp, who worked in the art context but who thematized the question of the artist's seriousness. In the 1930s, there is the work of the American comedian Robert Benchley, whose short comic films included strange props made specifically to be filmed. After the War, there is Piero Manzoni, who treated the body as a conceptual gesture machine, and Ernie Kovacs, who performed self-consciously live comedy on live television; Kovacs usually ended his program by declaring "It's Been Real." In the 1960s there is a great deal of activity that might be described as Concrete Comedy. A playful, aggressive attitude toward reality is the rule. It was the era of LSD, which taught millions that consciousness was plastic. There is Warhol, interested in a different kind of plastic. There is the Swedish artist Fahlström, who in 1966 organized a demonstration on a New York sidewalk in which people carried picket signs displaying large photos of Mao and Bob Hope. There are the Diggers in San Francisco and, nationally, the Yippies. There are John Lennon and Yoko Ono, who introduced a kind of global comedy in actions like the Amsterdam Bed-in and Bagism and the full-page ads in The New York Times. As that decade turns the corner into the 1970s there is the enormous comic presence of Marcel Broodthaers, who invented the insincere object and who exploited the idea that personality, too, was a kind of context.

Thus the kind of nonfiction comedy I had decided to pursue for personal reasons was, in fact, in a tradition of comic action. A history existed—but that history hadn't been written, so there was no context for the interpretation or appreciation of this activity. The only context in which the fruits of nonfiction comedy could be considered as self-conscious, contemplative objects was the art context. There the superego of art suppressed the comedic id, with the result that the comic object's performative relation to reality was misplaced and their unique and peculiar power lost. In order to have this work read the way I intended it to be read, then, I have had to consider the problem of context.

We have inherited the idea that if something appears in an art gallery, it must be art. That may have been a discovery in Duchamp's day, but by now it has become a hindrance to creativity rather than an aid. Surely it cannot be beyond our abilities to "write" new "software" for the "hard-drive" of the gallery space. If we are going to be creative, let's be creative. Let's not be so afraid to make something that isn't art. There will always be plenty of slaves to the superego of art—a fact that should free the rest of us to risk the pursuit of new territory! Actually, this pursuit is almost an obligation, if we take seriously the idea that, at this point in its history, art, the widest cultural aperture, is less about the invention of pictures and objects than about the invention of behavior. Art wants us to have that kind of permission. But art didn't expect, I think, that we would end up inventing behavior that included but was not limited to art. That's turned out to be very confusing for art. Because if you end up inventing a behavior that includes but is not limited to art, what is the relation of art to one's behavior?

Comedy is a behavioral enterprise that freely trespasses contextual borders. It might take the form of a film, a stage work, a book—it might be an object. Invariably, the comic object straddles two contexts—the history of art and the history of comedy. A comic object, though, is never quite an art object, or else it is always "art-plus"; either way, we cannot begin to define the nature of this object by referring only to a single, existing context. The question of this object's identity can only be answered by referring to both contexts of interpretation, or by referring to a third, invented, hybrid context that has been spliced together through what might be termed contextual genetics. Similarly, the behavior that produced such an object can only be understood either within a multiplicity of contexts, or as a single, invented context created through contextual genetics. In short, properly locating the comic object in the world requires us to imagine into existence a new context of human endeavor.

The most efficient site of construction of any invented context is, of course, the mind of the audience. Construction—by which I mean the education of the audience into the vocabulary and aims of Concrete Comedy—has been underway for several years now.

So far I've found three ways to instantiate a context for Concrete Comedy. All three employ the strategy of "deadpan" to different ends: I began as a photographer, and "deadpan" is the "photographic" version of comedy. Identifying as closely as possible with the integrity of deadpan, I try to present my comic structures in such a way as to suggest that, instead of justifying their reality to you, you feel as if you must justify your reality to them. These objects have no doubt about the reality they mean to construct.

The first strategy involves the literalization of the imaginary site. This is an ongoing, portable project called The Institute For Advanced Comedic Behavior. The Institute is based on a well-known comic device, that of parodying institutional forms. I "broke ground" in 1992 with a small book, the Foundation Papers, and have continued the construction in gallery and museum exhibitions and magazine pieces.

A second strategy involves generating an imaginary context with each exhibition. An example of this is The German Re-Unification Public Sculpture Competition, which I installed at Galerie Nagel in Cologne in 1991. With this strategy, the objects in the exhibition refer first to the invented, comic context; in the same moment that the objects in the exhibition refer to the invented context, they invent it. The audience cannot interpret the objects without "passing through" this invented context—an approach that effectively interposes a "non-art" context between the audience and the gallery.

These first two strategies are fun, but as of this writing the third means of addressing the problem of context has been the richest and most radical. In the third, I "write a program" for an individual object; by "scripting" a comedy that takes place in real time and real space, then dipping the object in it, I can program the object's imagination of itself. In other words, I create a prior history—a memory—for the object, which it cannot "forget," even when, eventually, it is shown within the art context.

Strange things happen when I "script" comic scenarios for these objects, because in order for the object to have an imagination of itself other than art, it has to be born into a context other than the art context, which means that the object literally must be shown first in some physical site other than the site of the art gallery or museum. Not only is this non-fiction comedy, then, but site-specific, nonfiction comedy.

An example of this, <u>The Ice Cream Social</u>, was presented in January of 1993 in Manhattan. The germ for this event was in an abstract painting I'd wanted to make—pink and brown dots on a field of white—that was based on the logo of a company, Baskin-Robbins (famous for its "31 flavors") which owns a chain of ice cream shops throughout the United States and Europe; by making the painting, I'd sought to confuse a corporate identity with my own, through the "Robbins" link. I hired a young artist to make the painting, so that, like the company, it would be the product of a partnership. Then I sought and obtained permission to install it, in a Baskin-Robbins Ice Cream Parlor at 23rd Street and 1st Avenue. On the cold winter night I'd scheduled the event, 30 of my friends showed up to eat ice cream, see the painting, and hear a poem I'd written for the occasion. Three video cameras made tapes of the event, which culminated in my recitation of the poem, spoken from behind the counter where the ice cream was dished out.

Where the clock strikes 31,
Players conspiring in the enjoyment of enjoyment
Unfurl the pink and brown of the Insupportable
Against animal virtue's blooded tribes
To savor the Ice Cream Social,
Cold, licking sweet, always melting and,
Empty of all save their pleasure in it, sticky enough.

A fertile experiment, The Ice Cream Social is a prototype for future ventures into the absurd, because certain of the structures it contained may be extracted, and repeated.

1. Physical frontiers have limits, but perceptual and behavioral frontiers can be renewed, extended. The 30 people who attended the event cannot think of the building where it occurred—nor, for that matter, any Baskin-Robbins Ice Cream Parlor—in the same way; I've "signed" the architecture! Thus The Ice Cream Social demonstrates that when the playful, disrespectful id of comedy is unleashed in a controlled, crafted way in an existing, psychologically neutral site—a readymade site—that site is remade through an ecology of perception.

2. It happened that the memory that was to be instilled into this particular comic object—the abstract painting—required the attendance of other people. Those who attended the Social knew the behavior appropriate to an art opening, and they knew the right behavior for an ice cream parlor, but no one—including myself—knew how to behave at an ice cream parlor at which there was scheduled to be unveiled an object that did not aspire to the condition of an art object. When I interviewed my guests afterwards, many who'd attended said that they'd been slightly uncomfortable because they'd not known what had been expected of them. In fact, nothing had been "expected" of them: as the function of The Ice Cream Social wasn't predetermined, its outcome was unknown. By applying comedy's disrespect for reality, the social rituals maintained by the context of the art gallery and the context of the ice cream parlor were canceled; offered in their place was another social, a new reason for people to gather, one where people "did not know what was expected of

them." It is not unreasonable to conclude, therefore, that far from merely producing a commentary on experience, site-specific, nonfiction comedy has the capacity to create experience itself. This is The Dr. Frankenstein Option, so named because it is not dissimilar from creating life itself: "purpose and outcome unknown." And as with any good science experiment, it can be repeated: first we employ comedy's disrespect for reality to kill off the old social, then we splice together a few of its parts to invent a living social, thereby reanimating the audience's evolution.

3. The idea that comedy's playful disrespect for reality can be used to liberate us into a self regard sufficient to reinvent experience is attractive because it encourages us in the belief that we, each of us, has the power to create reality. Reality is not only a construction, reality is the construction of reality, and anyone may have a hand in that construction. The Ice Cream Social stood not as an alternative reality—it did not oppose anything—but rather as an additional reality, an ambition far, far wilder.

Additions (and for that matter, alternatives) to reality are specific; they distinguish themselves from some prevailing configuration of reality. They have a certain character and not another.

The configuration of reality proposed in The Ice Cream Social has a specific character. It is an entertaining configuration, one consistent with the vernacular thrills which years of exposure to media culture have taught us to appreciate. However, unlike most media moments, The Social isn't just entertainment for entertainment's sake; the audience's pleasure is not its final goal. Rather, its entertainments function as a point of origin, from which the audience embarks together on an evolutionary journey toward … well, something as yet unnamed.

My friend Ann Bobco described The Ice Cream Social as "a TV show without the TV." Yes, exactly. Using the term "post-media" to characterize such an event suggests too strongly a rupture, a break, when it would be wiser to indicate a continuum. We need another term, therefore, one with a lighter touch—

perhaps "après-media." An après-media era struggles to its feet, and when it gets there, it promises to be at least as complex as the era of media hypnosis was, for we are that much more complicated now. To hold our attention, to satisfy, more complex configurations of experience will be required.

The Ice Cream Social entertained by splicing together a number of cultural contexts, high and low—painting, television, architecture, theater, poetry—in the interest of a single, if densely textured, goal. Its aim was to invent experience, which is not necessarily the same thing as being concerned to create culture. Instead of putting biography to use as a material in the production of culture, The Ice Cream Social used culture as a material in the production of biography, thereby suggesting a fundamental reversal of our ideas about the value of culture. Downgraded is the idea that one participates in culture in order to maintain the culture. Upgraded is the idea that one is free to disrespect cultural conventions in order to invent a meaningful life. This is proper. Culture will always disappoint us. It cannot save us. We have to save ourselves; culture only adjourns the meetings at which we determine how that might be accomplished.

Long live The Social.

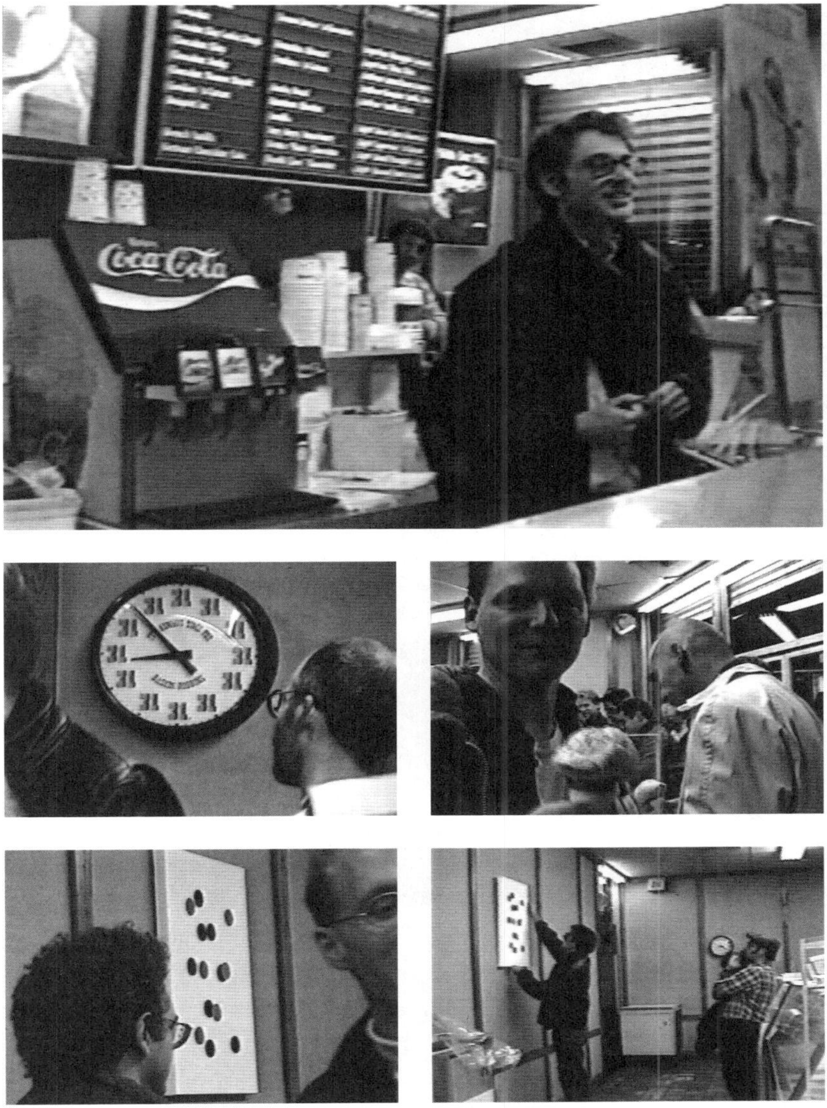

The Ice Cream Social, New York, 1993
video stills

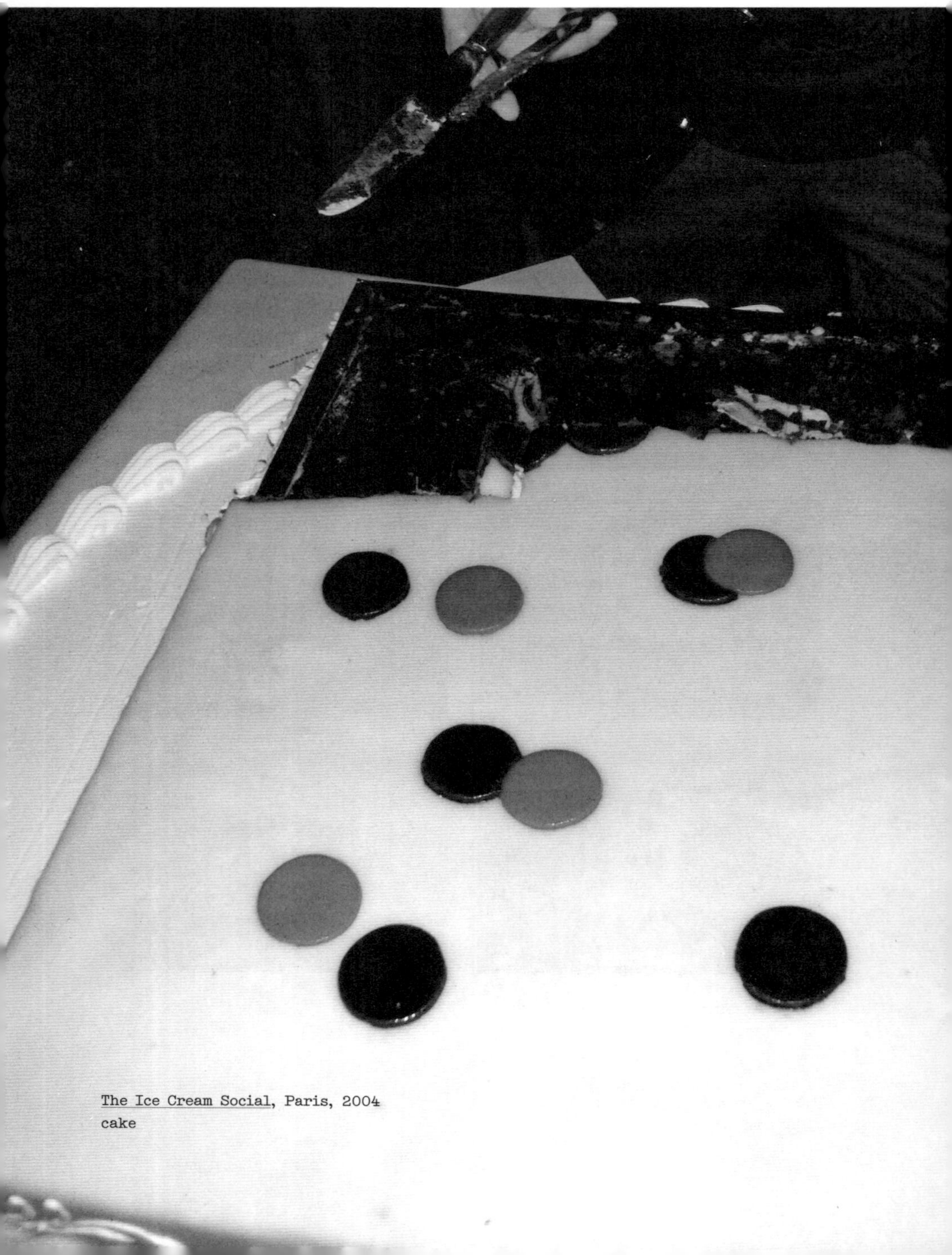

<u>The Ice Cream Social</u>, Paris, 2004
cake

Untitled. Exactly.

Catalogue essay for A/drift, Bard College Center for Curatorial Studies, Annandale-on-Hudson 1998, an exhibition curated by Joshua Decter.

YOU'RE SITTING IN THE CONTEMPORARY ART MUSEUM CAFE TALKING THE KIND OF SHOP THAT CAN PROMPT A GUY TO DECLARE, AS TONY JUST DID, "C'MON, WE BOTH JUST WANT TO BE GREAT AMERICAN ARTISTS." You respond that, no, you don't care about being a great American artist, you want to be a great American imagination. He gives you a "what an ego" look but you meant what you said. If you're going to be a modern American then you treat the culture that raised you—entertainment culture—with the respect due to a parent, and that means you take it seriously enough to reflect in your own behavior entertainment's refusal to privilege forms. Do that, and sooner or later you'll evolve a way of working that avoids, ignores or resists the kind of hierarchization of experience necessary for designating things art, so get ready to kiss your art career goodbye, since to freely trespass between media and projects and, most crucially, contexts with an entertainer's unconcern for cultivating or protecting an iconicity of production puts you closer to Walt Disney than to Walter De Maria.

No one takes entertainment this seriously in order to protest against the art establishment. It's not part of some strategy of critique. Nor do you do it to prove you've got the Picasso fecundity thing so bad you couldn't possibly restrict your brilliance to one medium or one context of endeavor even if you wanted to. Nope, you do it because you have to. You do it because you were raised by the radio dial and the television remote. You do it because not to let entertainment's liquidity penetrate the very structure of your endeavor is downright _un-natural_.

Prolonged exposure to show biz did a number on what it is you want from culture, what it is you use culture for. Show biz winkled a wedge into whatever you understood of the old integrity-based model of endeavor called art, that good old absolute congruence of word and deed, eventually succeeding in separating _integrity_ from _the appearance of integrity_. To entertain, the appearance of integrity will do; the smiling tap dancer doesn't have to mean it, he just has to look like he means it—a truth nailed 30 years ago by another great showman, Warhol, when he said, "It's not what you're doing that counts. It's what they think you're doing."

The integrity- and the appearance-of-integrity-models satisfy different sets of needs, but for some reason neither, in its purest form, manages to fully satisfy you anymore; either you've overdone the consumption of both art and entertainment or you're just a new kind of person. Whichever the reason, in pursuit of new life-forms (in pursuit of life) you take to experimenting with mixing the two models together, in different proportions, to gain different effects. So impure are certain of the resulting blends it would be difficult and unfair to characterize them as art (as unfair to art as to the hybrids concocted). You're not making art, you're inventing exerience, one part show biz, one part art, one part huh? Experience—for yourself, for others if they want it. Culture isn't an end in itself, not anymore; it's a material to be used in the pursuit of personal adventure. Let others take their personal stories and process them through imagination's alchemy to make culture (what's popularly known as "expressing yourself"), you'll exploit culture's elastic properties in order to invent biography.

Maybe you do it because you don't see any other way to have a life. Maybe you do it because you're the type who's addicted to pioneering. Maybe you do it because you'd been stung once too often by your naive faith in culture, watching as in trend after in-trend of beloved cultural moments turned on you or disappointed you or sold you back your affection. You needed some way to protect yourself against the romance of the notion that 'tis culture will save you. A dry-eyed approach that demotes culture to "something to do" (as Paul Westerberg sang to sum up the Replacements' what-the-hell attitude towards rock) fits the bill.

Could be you favor the invention of experience over the invention of art because you've been trained by television characters to think it natural. Television characters have experiences, but within the context of the show it doesn't matter whether those experiences add up to art or to much of anything else; they'll be back next week. Now, remove the TV cameras. Isn't that how you approach your own life? You want experiences, but you've not scriptwriters so you have to do everything yourself. If the experience you invent happens to further or maintain an existing context of interpretation or field of endeavor—"art," "literature," "theater"—fine, but you've too much work to get done to wait around to find out.

So. Not an artist anymore. Not an entertainer either, though, since you're exercising too much control over what you're making and how it's being presented. An "imagination" is the description that fits. An imagination, definition unfixed, one part art, one part entertainment, one part huh?

Finally it's more American to be a great American imagination than a great American artist because in the end the designation isn't up to some museum, it's up to everyone else; those in the audience decide for themselves what it was you gave to them. And if they all decide that you weren't a great American imagination, well, it doesn't really matter, does it, since you'd have found a way to be free during your lifetime to make what you'd wanted to make, art when it was art and not-art when it was not-art, and therefore had had full access to your own mind. And isn't that kind of person exactly the kind of person you'd wanted to be, all along?

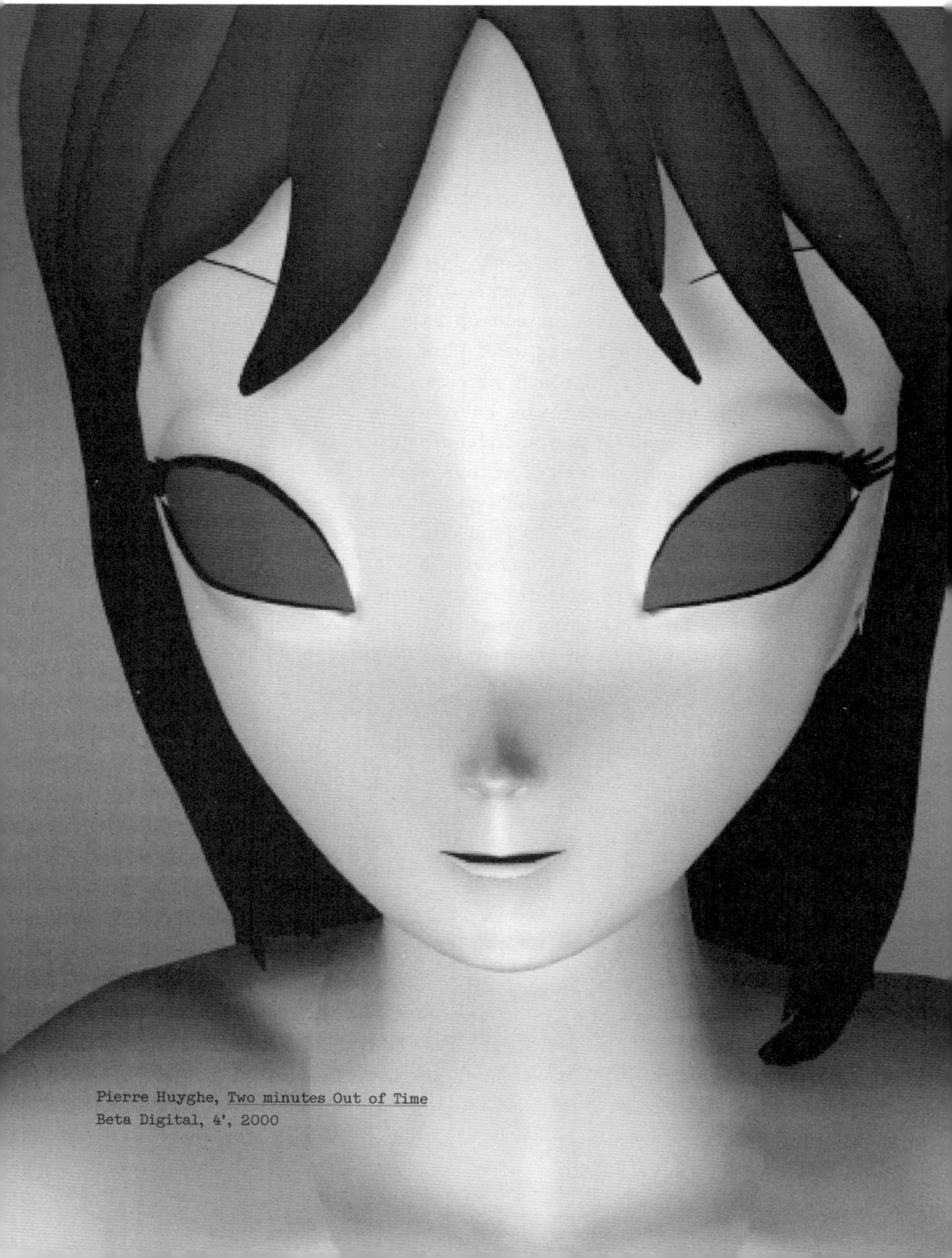

Pierre Huyghe, Two minutes Out of Time
Beta Digital, 4', 2000

Warm Science Fiction

Originally published in Pierre Huyghe, a monograph by Le Consortium, Dijon/Van Abbemuseum, Amsterdam, Les Presses du réel, 2003.

MISE-EN-SCÈNE 1

THE NATURE OF ADVENTURE HAD CHANGED. In capital and province alike, a shift in people's relation to synthetic experience—to movies, television, pop music, advertising, magazines, books, fashion, design: all the modes by which industrialized mass culture delivered itself—had gradually acquired force. During the long years of agrarian living, of toiling in the fields and drawing water from the well, and, later, in the earliest years of clock-punching and modern nation-building, contact with synthetic modes of communication had accounted for only a tiny portion of experience. After plowing the fields and chopping wood you'd sit down to read Virgil by the fire. In time, however—the nations now built, the humming electromagnet of the city pulling people away from farms and villages, the division of labor ever more ornate, the hours for leisure increased, the economic importance of leisure gaining heft—the duration of contact with and exposure to the forms and formats of synthetic experience expanded, coming to fill more and more of a day. Unascertainable, the precise moment when the scale tipped—folk critique liked to hold television responsible—but afterwards it could no longer be said that synthetic experience merely performed as a reflection of or commentary upon experience. Rather, it now comprised a significant portion of human experience.

A recurring, prolonged interaction with the forms and formats of synthetic experience became, henceforth, the primary experience of countless children. Once each generation so imprinted had negotiated their entry into maturity, they (correctly) identified the realm of synthetic experience as a site where an essential part of their evolution would continue. This recognition of their historical coordinates, i.e., their inheritance, displayed an impressive degree of self-possession. They were not to be people who would toil in the fields under the hot sun, after all, and they knew it. They would not be leading revolutions against tyrannical kings. They were not destined to tame any wilderness.

A relation to wilderness was part of their birthright nevertheless. (The children who had been shaped by prolonged exposure to synthetic experience understood that, too.) A hundred years prior, the physical frontier had closed and another, perceptual frontier had opened. Knowledge of the change was implanted, deep, in gene or psyche. Since life devoid of the ancient, wilderness-taming, frontier-exploring energy was life too small to be borne, some means of re-assigning that energy had to be found. Again, success: the children of synthetic experience identified a proper re-assignment of the old adventure energy. Instead of wilderness taming, they'd be directing adventure energy toward wilderness creation. The kids who had been formed by prolonged exposure to movies, TV, and pop music decided that their inheritance fronted a perceptual wilderness that could be perpetually renewed through their own, active engagement of synthetic experience.

Adventure had, then, a new address. Millions of children, proceeding by instinct, now pursued adventure in the plastic perceptual space established in the forms and formats of synthetic experience. They willfully evolved via such vehicles as "being in a rock band" or "working in advertising," by "publishing a zine" or "making movies," by "building websites" or "designing clothes." Of course, the creation of communication artifacts was nothing new. Frontierspeople had always produced handiwork. A frontier wife in a cabin on a wind-scoured Nebraska prairie in 1884 created impressive needlework. The difference now was that, following the invention and dissemination of cameras, recorders, and computers, the needlework undertaken on the new, renewable frontier had the capacity to create fresh synthetic experience for hundreds, thousands, not infrequently millions of other people.

Culture's status underwent a transformation. The classical reason once given by noble souls to explain their participation in cultural production—namely, "to maintain the culture"—receded to a point, nearly, of inconsequence. A noble and elevated sense of responsibility to the achievements of the past suffered demotion. Promoted in its place was the idea of culture as a tool, a mule, something put to work to create autobiography; "culture" became entirely personalized, a dimension to be explored for purposes of adventure and willed, directed evolution ... Culture moved out of the mansion on the hill and settled into your basement, your garage, your home office, your den.

Using culture as a space for personal adventure and evolution provided many people a path to a necessary sort of freedom, and those adventures which they could make for themselves often were exhilarating; through them coursed life genuine and unrepentant. That culture-making also became deeply stained with the attributes of comedy was a price they were willing to pay.

JULES VERNE VERSUS BALZAC

The renewable wilderness is highly accommodating. As it is of course an utterly human proposition, it accommodates an adventure-set as varied yet as individuated and specific as we are. A child of synthetic experience who decides to exploit the plastic space of the renewable wilderness in order to project and live through (to take one example) elaborate private mythologies that mix an aesthetic derived from 1930s film musicals together with motifs from televised sports, will encounter no resistance to his plans, here.

But fantasy projections and the creation of elaborate private mythologies are just one application of adventure energy—and a rather obvious one, at that. The exaggeratedly bold demarcation that fantasy-projections lay down between reality and the imagined holds greatest appeal for the self-dramatizing existentialism of youth. Let's all dress up like pink mermaids! Fun!

And without question, it _can_ be fun. More likely, though, today we're not all going to dress up as pink mermaids. More likely is that, right after we take this call, we're going to watch _you_ dress up as a mermaid. Apart from the joys of bearing witness to the radical exercise of personal freedom (transacted within the safety zone of aesthetics), what's in it for us, exactly, your dressing-up like a pink mermaid?

The question can reasonably be asked because, although a good and (at times) necessary strategy, aggressive exaggerations of adventure energy (such as the creation of an elaborate personal mythology) are frequently underwritten by, ironically, an essentially conservative, _privatized_ notion of freedom. Privatized notions of freedom don't inquire into the condition of freedom so much as assume and exploit the fact of it. Sometimes this is to marvelous effect (it must be acknowledged), but something important is sacrificed in the pursuit, also.

What's lost is a particular and useful tension. The pioneer who explores the renewable wilderness of synthetic experience doesn't entirely _lose contact with_ the demands and rewards of the quotidian, after all, but occupies the two territories _simultaneously_. This dual citizenship—adventuring in the synthetic, and selective involvement in the everyday—is a privileged condition that also happens to throb with the tension between the overlapping domains. The frontier's border runs right through us. The tension plays out nowhere but in us. The renewable wilderness, although hugely accommodating, has an appropriately human limit—namely, what change we can imagine, what change we can accomplish, and what change we can bear to undertake. Fantasy projections and the creation of elaborate personal mythologies sacrifice, then, the tension between adventure and _reality_, between freedom and constraint. They sacrifice, in short, the reality of freedom, as freedom plays out not in the interiorized space of the individual imagination but within the finite, actual, and seriously legislated public life of any society. Freedom is only rarely screamed in the streets. More usually the exercise of it is negotiated, finessed, secured by operations covert as well as overt—maneuvers of a greater subtlety than pink mermaids are able to pull off, generally.

So it is that another sort of imagination, preferring to activate the rich, constant, painful tension that exists between freedom and constraint, eschews the limitlessness of the fantastic in order to foreground the complex infrastructure of everyday reality. So it is that another sort of mind does not costume itself as a pink mermaid but instead locates an advertising billboard near a construction site, hires actors to pose as construction workers, photographs them at the site on a weekend when the regular workers are absent, prints this photo and sticks it onto the billboard, and lastly makes a second photograph of the construction site that incorporates the new billboard (_Les Affiches_, 1992). So it is that another sort of mind, wishing to apply adventure energy to the quotidian, arranges for a male pedestrian to walk an exercise treadmill, which is set inside a glass vitrine mounted in the truck-bed of a vehicle that traces that same pedestrian's daily route (_Trajet_, 1992).

PEOPLE REQUIRE OXYGEN, IT HAS BEEN SHOWN

This latter sort of mind isn't exploiting so much as _thematizing_ freedom.

Freedom may be thematized, in positive fashion, as aspiration and possibility, or negatively, as illusion and impossibility. (Either variant is only an opinion. Think of that.)

Freedom, thematized, is a breeze carrying a germ of the Future—not a fantastic, let's-vacation-on-Jupiter strain, but one that infiltrates and infects with possibility the structure of the Present.

So infected, the Present acquires a slight fever. Three symptoms are especially noteworthy.

1. Reality temporarily slips its constraints and drifts closer to the condition we associate with dream, fairy tale, theater. To anyone who is interested in applying adventure material to the everyday, inventing ways to extend the duration of reality's temporary liberation from its awesome responsibility to itself becomes a highly attractive pursuit.

2. Reality remembers that it's a construction. (Anyone may participate in the construction process. Some thematize their participation. They are known as "public figures.") Reality is a process that continually mistakes itself for an end. Reality is a theme park with reality as the theme.

3. A certain kind of friction results. Applying adventure energy to the everyday creates friction. Willfully bringing the future into close proximity to the present is a political act, no matter how total the disguise may be. Questions of a substantial scale are bestirred. What Is and Why It Is are set against What's Imaginable and What Might Be—with all negotiations playing out before the backdrop, What Is Allowable.

The theater of operations involves no specific political agenda; the future, in its purest, thematized condition, is a minister without portfolio or agenda. (The future is <u>intrinsically</u> a critique of the present. There's no need to push it.) What critique or deconstruction may occur whenever adventure energy gets applied to the quotidian is not on behalf of either the Right or the Left but on behalf of the adventure condition itself, the promotion of which oxygenates the social realm. To the extent that there is any political platform at all, it is: Oxygenation!

Let's face it: reality needs all the help it can get. Applying adventure energy to the quotidian in the name of the future is doing reality a favor.

BIONIC LIVING

We might consider an amusing paradox the fact that in its natural state modern reality tends to the machine-like were the effects of this a trifle less tedious.

Much of what counts as specifically "modern" about modern life has been constructed and is sustained through the (nigh occupying) force of a small but very powerful set of machine-inspired abstractions—standardization, systematization, dissemination, replicability, ideas of that ilk. Part of a larger and (to our credit) not unvaliant effort to restrict the rule of chance, unify the world, and provide ourselves a measure of control over the vagaries of life, these machine-inspired abstractions have underwritten an impressive list of progressive developments over the years. Unfortunately, in that moment when synthetic experience shifted from being a commentary upon or reflection of our experience to outright comprising much of it, machine-inspired abstractions such as systematization, standardization, replicability, and their ilk got, shall we say, a little too familiar with the look and sound and feel of life itself. While their contract with us continues to assign them responsibility for reproducing and disseminating only those myriad synthetic artifacts that (through their own agency!) now comprise much of the experience of modern life—they are to make, for instance, the pop record, and also to inform the experience of listening to the pop record—the truth is that through this commissioned intercourse they have been able to reproduce their own structural life without limit and thus to reinforce their presence among us as abstractions that define life as we know it. As a result, life, in its essence, has become increasingly bionic, robotic, kitted out with plastic valves, joints, and membranes.

Well. Powerful the machine-inspired abstractions may be, but they're still abstractions. And in order to make contact with us, they require some sort of embodiment. They require, in short, hosts.

The host which has afforded these abstractions their deepest penetration into everyday life is something that we've come to term a "format." As Pierre Huyghe describes it, a format is "a frame of representation, a standard. It's not a form or an objet." The Hollywood movie is a format. The pop song is a format. The pop band is a format, as is a pop band in concert. TV news is a format. A conference is a format. An artist's retrospective is a format. The private residence on the tree-lined street, this is a format as well.

A frontiersperson roaming the renewable wilderness applying adventure energy to the everyday would do well, then, to get his hands around a format or two. For to engage a format is not only to engage a manipulable representative of the everyday, it is also to engage the host of abstractions—systematization, standardization, replicability, dissemination, and so on—that underwrite all formats. Any single format is the tip of an enormous iceberg of compacted, machine-inspired abstraction.

FORMATS AND VENUES

A "format" is one expression of an impulse toward standardization, predictability, and control. A "venue" is another. A venue is real estate that has been assigned a commercial and cultural role that has been formatted.

Capital has an active relation to formats and venues. Active, and controlling: capital usually defines its interest in these two narrowly—that is, in terms of their standardization and predictability. Capital prefers to know what something will look like tomorrow. Taken too far, of course, that preference can work against capital's own interest, since ultimately it can work against the pleasure a consumer derives from a specific format or venue. Applying abstractions such as standardization and predictability to the formats and venues of synthetic experience thus can give rise to problems.

MISE-EN-SCÈNE 2

Life-as-we-know-it, in the context of this discussion, must be defined in part by a recognition that synthetic experience also evolves, and further, that in our time it has evolved out of its classical phase. Pop culture is too essential to the health of the economy for the pop culture industries to rely for their continued success on the early, classical phase's ecstatic discovery of the radical egalitarianism represented by two, identical, full bottles of Coca-Cola. Pop culture's centrality to the economy dictates that pop-culture industries now must do everything in their power to arrange the success of whatever product they happen to be introducing. Thus in a quite real sense the continued health of the mass industrial economy depends not just on the success of today's pop product but on the success of tomorrow's—which success is built, of course, upon the success of the gesture of introducing today's. And with a steady supply of pop now guaranteed—millions of kids who identify the movement through culture as necessary to the construction of their autobiographies! And the number's growing!—the success of any one pop product depends less on its quality (its ability to attract us to it) than on controlling the environment into which it's to be introduced. Question: What is that environment to be controlled? Answer: We are. (Delete the human element and the product has no reason to exist.)

For these reasons the consumer's experience of the formats of industrialized popular culture is now, inescapably, an experience of Being Managed. Said management, which is a continual condition, plays out partly in the language of form—bright colors for children, say, and streamlined designs for urban sophisticates—and partly too in the way that information outside the frame of the form is shaped to enhance the desirability of the form: "It's cool!"

Any conscious effort to respond to the reality of industrialized popular culture now must accommodate the presence of all the support industries that prime the consumer environment for the successful, deep penetration of synthetic experiences. Tightly wrapped in press releases, publicity, and spin, synthetic experience—industrialized popular culture—has entered a mannerist period.

ONE MANIFESTATION OF MANNERISM

Go to a concert. Attend a movie. Watch a TV show. Notice how these experiences feel as though they're over, somehow, before they've even begun. They feel this way to us because capital has over-determined format and venue—mannerism, at work. There is life yet in both the format and the venue, but capitalism has so constricted their space of exploration, they have very little room to move. This constriction frustrates the application of adventure energy. And that's a serious problem, because the audience has become dependent for its own evolution on, at least in part, the evolution of synthetic experience.

When the evolution of synthetic experience stalls, it aggravates the fissure between the experience the audience needs and what the synthetic-experience industries—"the mass media," "pop," "the communication industry"—thinks to provide them. This gap never closes entirely, although sometimes it is wider and sometimes narrower. The discovery of this gap recurs with each generation, and each instance of this discovery takes a different form.

The most uncompromising instance of gap-discovery in recent years was termed Punk. Much larger and more significant than a musical style or a fashion statement, and also lasting well beyond its immediate manifestation <u>as</u> a style, Punk was the expression, by a generation, of their desire for vengeance. An authentic response to the ongoing constriction of venue and format, Punk was Angry About The Situation. A sophisticated sort of temper tantrum, Punk splashed corrosive irony energetically and haphazardly. It was a messy strategy but useful at the time; for a while, in other words, corrosive irony and anger <u>worked</u>. However, the aesthetic of revenge, of punkish anger and irony—this is now finished. Its official end came on September 11th, a day when the entire world witnessed the angry critique of Western institutions shift from inside the West to outside the West. That merciless shift in critique made the anger and irony of Punk appear as toys, as tiny aesthetic toys. "You want to see a critique of your system—infidel?" The new critique didn't mimic death, as Punk had. It <u>was</u> death. So: Punk is over, dead of embarrassment on September 11th.

SOME ATTRIBUTES OF THE NEW EMOTIONAL COORDINATES

Punk was already over by September 10th, of course; certain advanced imaginations specializing in the public articulation of complex cultural attitudes—artists, in whatever media—had already identified its close and had moved on. "We don't have time for anger or inarticulate discussion," asserts Pierre Huyghe. "Anger is a frontal reaction not a proposition. It's a located emotion. Anything that can be located is easily ejected out of the game."

The decision by certain advanced imaginations to pursue new emotional coordinates had the effect of advancing our collective response to the producer-consumer gap into more constructive and positive territory than Punk, with its stubborn investment in defect and defeat, had ever thought to offer. The exhaustion of formats and venues still registered, but the trauma of the discovery transferred now to the background. Placed in the foreground was something still forming, something distinctly without the scent of trauma on it, something that could not be easily ejected out of the game. Huyghe: "The avant-garde was based on an opposition with the previous generation, and the cycle just kept repeating itself. In order to get out of that logic and avoid producing one more rupture, a change was needed. The change came by 'doing with'—a principle of alliance and of negotiation that elevated the <u>discussion</u> as an elaboration of a non-rigid thinking (collaboration, social events) and, as well, a way to build an image ... Instead of rupture there's a play that can always change, a potentiality—a positive emotion." Given exercise here is the supple dimension of mind of a person who participates in the tradition of questioning formats and venues not to destroy them but to use them in precise experiments, the success of which risks opening an over-determined infrastructure to the adventure condition and its promise of a corresponding oxygenation of the social landscape. A positive emotion, indeed.

TWO ARTISTIC RESPONSES TO MANNERIST REALITY

An artist who seeks to render a contemporary landscape full of over-determined synthetic formats might stay on the surface of the problem, dancing around on it, making little "moves," dabbling, producing pastiches, quoting styles. The mannerist moment <u>does</u> live through such an artist, who in turn expresses it. Merely expressing the mannerist moment is some sort of accomplishment, since it leaves behind a record of the dance, but it isn't so much, really.

Another kind of artist renders the complications of industrialized mass culture using a practice marked by distilled, sophisticated simplicity. Such an artist reveals the infrastructure that promotes the mannerist condition and, by revealing it, furthers our evolution away from that condition and toward one that recalls and restates, in contemporary media and situation, something akin to classical virtues. (It is even possible that this kind of artist may rehabilitate something of the classical argument for participating in culture: "to maintain the culture.") Such an artist burns through the distracting mannerist haze using a steady beacon (achieving, in the process, another sort of deep penetration). This artist, who is in a sense from the future, looks back at the mannerist moment that his own practice has superseded. Many of us do sense that the story of Elvis Presley has contracted from a line to, today, a dot, but only a certain kind of artist is able to act on this knowledge without expressing any nostalgia for the years during which we (it seemed like a good idea at the time) lent our attention to Elvis's linear narrative.

In the work of this latter sort of artist, then, a new kind of behavior is innovated. It hasn't the character of a dance. It's not a new style or material or color that's innovated but a new behavioral model, evolved and resolute.

In order for us to see the difference between adventure and the everyday—in order to see and fully appreciate the structure of the gesture of bringing the two together (and the new structure that's been created through their synthesis)—the gesture can't be obscured with a lot of aesthetics. Consequently, the behavioral model is primarily defined by an extremely sophisticated attitude toward verisimilitude. Verisimilitude, together with an attitude toward it, will be two key components.

MISE-EN-SCÈNE 3

Whether wide or comparatively narrow, the gap between what the providers of mass synthetic experience give the audience for its evolution and what the audience needs is a constant. In this sense, it is stable.

A language gap between producer and consumer also evolves, however, and in recent years that gap has narrowed dramatically. Because of advances in technology, the individual is able, more than ever before, to "speak" in the same media-language as that of the dominant and pervasive mass media. Consider the dissemination of sound-manipulating software and CD burners: you can start a band, record it, produce a CD, distribute that. (Or, more ambitiously, you can start a record label.) Consider the website, which puts to work identical numerals and pixels no matter who is writing the code. Consider the digital video camera. The person who picks up such a camera is no longer obligated to think only of video art, and of video art's old ghetto of venues; camera in hand, they now may think "television" or "movie" and not seem to themselves altogether deluded. Consider the relative ease with which the individual imagination can have a picture book of his/her work published and distributed. (Artists barely 30 years old have large-format, possibly hardcover books on the shelves of chain bookstores—even in America. Talk about developments.)

In short, art product—the product created by the individual reflective consciousness working independently toward imaginary solutions to imaginary problems—can now in many instances look exactly like dominant, mainstream culture product—the product created by committee and corporation. And vice versa. Art product and mainstream product compete using many of the same languages. The radical similarity of the two contestants destabilizes the assumptions of each. Controlled destablization is oxygenating.

INTENT

With the language gap thus narrowed and less significant, another distinction has acquired weight. Given the unprecedented similarity of the languages spoken by artist and corporation alike, what quality is it that now distinguishes the artist? How is a hardcover glossy picture book about or by an artist different than one dispensing advice about interior decoration? Is there any difference? What is the difference between a 35mm film made by an artist and shown in a museum, and a 35mm film made by a Hollywood director and given theatrical release in a thousand cinemas?

What that difference might be, and what it _should_ be, and who decides this: the artist? An institution?—these are issues of _intent_.

One of _the_ defining attributes of life among the pioneers who explore the renewable wilderness of perception, intent can forever be remade and reshaped. Intent is information contiguous with but not confined to form or medium. Intent is _why_, and why is attitude, and attitude trumps formatting; attitude can be shaped, but it can't be legislated. Attitude has trumped format when a Pierre Huyghe is able to "speak through an existing format while saying something else. Changes in the law of arrangement may be discovered by shifting the internal parameters."

The children of synthetic experience who are blessed and emburdened with the need to pursue their evolution through the formats of synthetic experience work, with the same time and space as anyone. Only intent—their attitude toward their movement through time and space—has changed. But this makes all the difference in the world, since it yields a very different autobiography—and yielding a different autobiography, a different life, is precisely the point.

In order to pursue that particularized evolution, however, each is obligated to discover and invent some _means_ that will allow them to apply intent to time and space, cleanly and directly.

THE ANALOG WORLD

The power of any communication technology—paint, photography, cinema, and so on—is proportionate to its capacity to establish an analogue and a metaphor for the relation of human consciousness to the abstraction termed reality. Those technologies and forms that offer the fullest dimension of verisimilitude—that most completely capture the look and sound and conditions of life—will consistently attain dominance. They will define an era. The pre-eminent model for consciousness during most of the 19th century was the prose novel. Subsequent to the novel's dominance, the experience of verisimilitude, as that experience blooms in us and between us, has been captured most fully and accurately by (no surprise here) a variety of machines, specifically cameras and recorders. For much of the 20th-century, film (aka the motion picture, aka cinema) performed as the model for consciousness. After 50 years (or so) of dominance, film was superseded by another novel invention, television. Again, after 50 years (or so), television was superseded by the computer.

While these models may and do supersede each other as Today's Most Compelling metaphor for consciousness, any model that is truly fundamental remains competitive beyond the period of its dominance. Painting, for example, lives on as viable practice and powerful consciousness-analog. And as with painting, so with all the best models, all of which evolve concurrently.

Thus the appeal of cinema as a metaphor for consciousness has extended well into the reign of television and indeed beyond. (Its longevity assisted, no doubt, by the enthusiasm expressed toward the film model by intellectuals and artists, among which groups the idea of TV-as-consciousness-analog never really caught on. Television was, from the earliest days of its reign, tainted with a frank and unapologetic commercial dimension, and this single attribute, in the eyes of people who make it their business to identify and promote metaphors for consciousness, disqualified it from the highest ranks of modeling. Apparently commerce plays a minor role in defining reality.)

DUCHAMP DIDN'T THINK OF EVERYTHING.
NEITHER DID GODARD, FOR THAT MATTER.

"Life is like a movie, movies are like life": the equation stands as the populist variant, rendered in a specific medium, of a larger, more encompassing art/life dichotomy, one that was fixed in the imagination (around the same time as the emergence of cinema as a popular form, curiously enough) by Marcel Duchamp's innovation of the readymade.

Talk about applying adventure energy to the everyday! Does a purer instance of the psychology exist than in the example of the readymade? Deploying nothing <u>but</u> attitude, the readymade re-casts prosaic reality as the theater of verisimilitude. (Re-presenting reality with exactitude and without editorial, Duchamp may consciously have been mimicking the camera's capacity for deadpan. Somebody may want to look into that.) One of the great destablizing acts of the imagination, the readymade has amounted to one of the great oxygenating acts as well.

However, Duchamp didn't think of everything (the evidence of 20th-century art to the contrary). He didn't identify or touch a finger to, for instance, the competing, modern analog for consciousness that was already, in the earliest days of the readymade, budding in motion pictures. He made a few little films, but he never got around to investigating what resonant triangulations there were to be discovered by playing off the populist variant—the film/life confusion—against the more esoteric art/life confusion he so elegantly embodied.

Had he done so, he would have added to his haul. For while the film industry may be bigger, richer, and more influential than the comparatively marginal and effete art world, in a pure contest between abstractions it's film that winds up jumping through the hoops. The reason is simple and huge: art does not require any single medium—even the medium that Jean-Luc Godard once characterized as "truth, 24 times a second"—to pull off its sly, sleek, slippery, and superior contextual tricks.

When the motion picture format is drawn into the art context, art liberates for its own purposes all the conventions defining that format. "Scenario," "mise-en-scène," narrative devices such as "jump-cuts" and "dissolves," "the star," "the extra," film time and real time, "fiction" and "documentary'—these and other conventions get pried loose. Unmoored, they become materials that are no longer under any obligation to serve the interests of cinema. Mr. Warhol knew something about this, but he didn't take the next step. Scenario, mise-en-scène, et al may be lifted from film and re-applied, by art's ruthlessly concretist hand, directly to the situations of life. Film's conventions retain their particularities but all now serve a new master, one with a very different agenda.

Let's be clear: the point here is not another Duchampian, modernist exercise in "introducing into the art context ... " blah blah blah. The point is rather to deploy art to liberate powerful, objectified narrative devices so as to use these to create experience. The discoveries made by doing this may or may not be categorizable as art, finally. The person introducing these experiences into reality may or may not need to refer to himself or herself as "an artist."

THE FILM MODEL, LIBERATED: SOME EFFECTS

When the conventions comprising the film analog are activated with the express intent of setting them adrift, does this time-based, hopelessly verisimilitudinous medium still "tell a story?" What story might it now tell?

Trick questions. Actually, the term "story" has become inapt. The narrative conventions of film, activated but adrift, are no longer working in concert to sustain the illusionistic frame on which at least the popular usage of this medium commonly depends. Flickering, wobbling, the illusion-generator is now too weak to launch imagined narratives free of the gravitational pull of reality and into the self-completing orbit known as "fiction." Prevented from reaching this condition of full-on, illusionistic make-believe, "story," now grounded and weakened, is infiltrated by a host of earth-bound narratives—reality's narratives. Fiction and non-fiction contaminate each other. The contamination destablizes each category until, eventually, between them a new equilibrium is attained. The equilibrium point is determined by elements of both, but ultimately gravity weights things in favor of reality.

Pierre Huyghe refers to the effect on reality of this bi-directional flow as "fictionalizing the present." His fictionalizing process applies strategies principally derived from the illusionistic, narrative, performative cinema-analog to anti-illusionistic, not-exactly-narrative ends. Story has been dispatched, replaced by a strategic implementation of scenario which is applied not only within film and television projects but also without and, in every instance, abjuring the illusionistic demands of narrative concepts such as "story arc," "resolution," and even more radically, "author." Huyghe: "Capitalism has a fascination with story-makers. Stories that we listen to, tell, and play, stories that are signed with one name and celebrated to validate the system ... Playing with the roles created by the narrative monopoly is healthy: the narrator (the one who tells) and the narrated (the one who is listening) can be reversed or changed."

A clear-eyed, ruthless update of history painting, Huyghe's concept of "fictionalizing the present" proposes a process of picture-making that has been infused with a recognition of the opportunities that mass communication media not only afford the contemporary imagination but pretty much obligate any aspiration to identify and record the fullest truth of culture in our time. If it's history painting, it's designed with the temporal dimension built in. The Image is no longer an end in itself; this isn't about painting pictures in a skylight-endowed studio. As all pictures are, the picture-model offered here is yet fenestral, but it's now a paneless sort of frame, through which flows a narrative of some specific adventure-scenario, established in real life with real people in real situations. Whatever image is created exists in transparent relation to the situation that has occasioned its creation.

"ATTENTION IS NOT DIRECTED BUT FRAMED."-PH

Within the frame, our attention is free to take note, in no special order, of the following:

I. PAX AMERICANA

Because picture-making in our time isn't restricted to the context or media of fine art, the master-narrative produced by directly applying adventure energy to the formats which connect modern people necessarily touches upon the infrastructural power arrangements that mass-communication media daily promote, and of which they are emblematic. A work such as Huyghe's video Blanche-Neige Lucie (1997) is as much about the disadvantageous post-war trade agreements forced upon the French film industry 60 years ago (and that industry's efforts to retain its identity against the since unstoppable barrage of Hollywood movies) as it appears to be about one Lucie Dolene's description of her heroic (and ultimately victorious) battle for control over her own creative identity (as the French interpreter of the Snow White cartoon character) in the face of legal and corporate maneuvers by the Disney behemoth. (The American film Dog Day Afternoon serves as the inspiration and model for The Third Memory, another complex Huyghe project about who owns history.*)

Any single format is the tip of an enormous iceberg of densely compacted abstraction. Forms such as cinema or television are, of course, the forms of the media state, and no country has been more responsible for establishing and extending to global proportions the reign of mass media than has the United States. America is the pre-eminent sponsor of synthetic mass experience. Everyone everywhere consumes some kind of American media product. Everyone everywhere is brought closer together as a result: cultural differences are processed out. (A bad thing? We might trust people to know a good idea when they see it.) The radical egalitarianism embodied in pop product is America's most successfully exported political concept. Whether it's manifested as entertainment, communication hardware, or "information," pop product has been indispensable to establishing, extending, reinforcing, and sustaining the Pax Americana, such as it is.

The particulars of the Pax have rendered nationalism an enormously complicated affair. Under the circumstances, is "America" defined by latitude and longitude or by a culture that has infiltrated, melded with, and sometimes displaced regional identities the world over? Obviously, consciousness of existence under a Pax Americana exists most acutely in those people whose cultures have been challenged, diluted or overwhelmed by it. At the same time its foreign subjects enjoy certain of the benefits of the occupying force, they resent, not unreasonably, its inescapability. Some, reacting violently to its rule, even seek to end it. (The latter is surprisingly difficult. Who would have expected fun to be such a formidable opponent?) An artist, on the other hand, must travel another road. He or she encourages the evolution of the situation through ruthlessly pursuing the creation of the fullest possible record of the experience of human consciousness during the Pax. And the fullest possible record is made by working directly with the materials—film, television, pop music—that do so much to underwrite the monolith.

> II. SHE'S A VERY SOCIAL YOUNG WOMAN, IN THE SENSE THAT SHE REALIZES SHE NEEDS OTHER PEOPLE. SHE IS A COMPOSITE OF RELATIONSHIPS, SITUATIONS AND PEOPLE, BUT WITHOUT BEING THEIR HUB. IMAGINE A NETWORK OF RELATIONSHIPS FORMING A SELF, AN OTHERNESS. THIS IS BASED ON THE IDEA OF SUGGESTING A SET OF MODELS FOR SOMETHING WHICH IS BIGGER THAN SELF, POSSIBLE MODELS OF SOCIETIES, PROPOSING A SERIES OF ACTIONS, WHICH BRING RELATIONSHIPS TO THE FORE, AND ALTERS THEM.**

Medium, format, venue—what reason have these to exist, really, other than to extend us out toward points of contact shared with everyone else similarly extended? Media, format, and venue are prostheses for human identity. In the act of extending us, they become part of us; at the same time, through that extension we become realized.

Billions of extended identities, overlapping and connecting, establish, by their connection, new kinds of public sites, only some of which are measured in meters. Together we stroll electronic piazzas, hang out together in TV series, debate in dematerialized conference rooms ... Singular and plural continually intersect. Furthermore, as it has had a hand in forming us, the abstract condition which the identity-prosthesis creates remains active in us beyond the period of contact with any specific medium, format, or venue. "The singular in the plural, and the plural in the singular" (in Huyghe's phrase)—this is active in us _always_. Independent of the particulars (which are always temporary), the abstraction is _itself_ a prosthesis for identity.

It's a condition felt most keenly (naturally) by the children who were raised by the formats of synthetic experience. That child (and really, today who in the West is not that child?) has undergone a not unpleasant but still involuntary and continuous "out of body experience" _for as long as they can remember_. "Who we are" is based, at least in part, on who we remember being, but "personal" memory also includes generous dollops of collective memory, the official history of the mediatized environment; we're defined in part by memories of specific moments in a shared history of synthetic experience.

The "self" known, it should by now be apparent, is a self extended by media, by format, by venue—by every and any axis that comprises public space. Our experience of "self" is the experience of _managing the selves that are extended through the prostheses of media_. The physical corpus is merely management headquarters.

III. "AFRAID TO CONTACT JERRY LEWIS? WHY? WE'RE ON THE SAME PLANET."

Anyone who is evolving through the time and space of synthetic experience has plenty of company. All those similarly extended by the prostheses of media are present; the space is crowded with extended selves. We recognize our fellow travelers, and in the recognition a modicum of emotion gets exchanged. But only a modicum. The reason: people aren't media. Beyond a certain point, we resist and elude what others imagine for us, want us to be, need us to be … so we don't normally represent to each other a free space or a screen onto which another may cleanly project his imagination without hindrance. To perform that sort of service, some additional layer of artifice must be present. Another can't be only as human as we are. They must be either more or less.

The famous are (famously) imbued with the requisite artifice. Enjoying lives of scale that play out both privately and publicly, they exist apart from us while living on in us. It's the greed intrinsic to fame: we think about them, they don't think about us. As famous figures already speak to the audience, they are especially ripe for activation by the sort of adventuring imagination interested in advancing new scenarios for action and connection. "The influence that a character will spread over a work is something to consider in the construction of a meaning," says Huyghe. "Working with a politician or an entertainer yields of course different effects."

Character: public figures moving comparatively freely through public space, are not the famous, in our imaginations, next door to fictional characters? "Brad Pitt? To most of us, he might as well be Batman," says the American painter Scott Reeder. The reverse doesn't hold true, however; Batman isn't Brad Pitt. It doesn't hold true, because fictional characters lack a crucial dimension: they haven't any private life. Their lives are confined to the public sphere, where they await our connection to them and the use we'll make of them. The reality of their public dimension is the reality of an absence of any other.

A lack is an emptiness. But an emptiness is both a space and the opportunity to insert something into it. For their ongoing No Ghost Just A Shell project, Huyghe and frequent collaborator Philippe Parreno have acquired the rights to a fictional character who came complete with just such emptiness. In fact, Ann Lee, the minor manga character purchased by the pair from a Japanese animation company's commercial catalogue of "extras" meant for supporting roles in cartoons and video games, is a little emptier than most. As she was never intended to be the center of attention, her creators didn't go to the trouble of giving her definition, attributes, history ... The opposite of famous, this shell of a gal, her mopey, anxious features rendered with a few cartoony lines, arrived in the world as mere sign. Huyghe and Parreno set her wandering in a sort of moonscape, lost and lonely, "existing in the place and time of exchange with her own incertitude." But she needn't look so sad, really, as she's been blessed with clever managers. Huyghe and Parreno acquired the rights in order to pimp her to other artists, for use in *their* own projects. Over time Ann Lee's emptiness is destined to gradually be replaced by the uses these make of her. The "meaning" of the Ann Lee sign—her "personality," her "biography"—will become the uses that others have imagined for her, *and nothing other*. She is chaste, an innocent, and at the same time a courtesan without peer. She's a tabula rasa and a palimpsest of others' intentions. Compensated for her services with the currency of meaning, she'll end up a rich woman with lots of friends. There's no reason for sadness. Ann Lee has her whole past ahead of her.

Ann (herself a second embodiment of an earlier impulse/character, "Anna Sanders," incarnated in another Huyghe/Parreno production, the magazine/film *L'Histoire d'un Sentiment*) isn't Pierre (nor Philippe either), and Pierre isn't Ann. And yet they certainly mirror each other. This, because, as modern artists have done ever since there's been an avant-garde, "Pierre Huyghe" also becomes a construction in our imagination.*** Bent on thematizing the construction process through a succession of scenarios while rendering them all transparent, "Pierre Huyghe" is established as a matrix of negotiations between image, ritual, technology, fame, fiction ... The character built in our imaginations is heroic, "on our side," while steering clear of self-mythologizing. He's the product but not the point.

IV. MAKING HISTORY

Anything that lends itself to the construction of mediatized public life, as well as everything that is constructed by it—a film, a piece of architecture, an entertainer, a politician, a writer—is an axis of the prostheticized environment. Management of this synthetic environment is in our interest, obviously. Identifying our interest and acting upon it forces a democratization of the process whereby the mediatized public life is constructed.

The moment we contribute to the construction of public life we've stepped into the future. Willed evolution consciously establishes contact with the future. We are ourselves, but in the act of becoming who we will be. We are ourselves and a character with the same name as ourselves, moving in a warm science fiction.

COMEDY

Using culture as a space for personal adventure and evolution provided many people a path to a necessary sort of freedom, and those adventures which they could make for themselves often were exhilarating; through them coursed life genuine and unrepentant. That culture-making also became deeply stained with the attributes of comedy was a price they were willing to pay.

Pierre Huyghe accepts the comedic condition inherent to culture-making today and then proceeds to advance and alter that status through the creation of ambitious, responsible comedies. In the tradition of comic filmmaker Jacques Tati, Huyghe makes sophisticated comedies about the public dimension of contemporary life. A Tati who knows his Barthes, Huyghe has chosen to operate within the art context not because he adores art or seeks to privilege that discipline over all others, but rather because the art context is the stubborn context of the real, of anti-illusion, of things done for their own sake. The comedies that he constructs gain added integrity from the fact that, rather than being penned up within the frame of illusionistic media, they're assigned to play out a tough, interminable negotiation with real space and time.

Ultimately, comedy is an attitude toward reality. It is not a medium but a medium-and-context-trespassing attitude. It's pure intent, applicable to anything, anywhere. Huyghe's work is comedy because a) it's theater and b) it's theater with an ascendant emotional arc. That's comedy. He separates character, narrative, and the means by which the narrative is established, yet they don't fall apart. The spine that holds them together, despite their unravelment, is his generosity and good will—his attitude. His work isn't about the terrible tragedy of over-determination and mannerism. It is instead a comedy of liberation, and of all that might happen after. He's working to get us past the stuff we don't like about life in order to let us connect more fully with all the stuff we do like about it. Propelling his scenarios forward, he endeavors to move us past a manneristic, at times suffocating landscape, past the myriad formats of false communication, in order to identify, reveal, and recognize the genuine connections always hidden therein.

ABOUT THIS RENEWABLE WILDERNESS: DOES ANYTHING GET BUILT THERE, FINALLY? ARE SETTLEMENTS FOUNDED, OR DO THE CHILDREN OF SYNTHETIC EXPERIENCE JUST ROAM ABOUT IN IT AIMLESSLY?

That depends on the pioneer, actually.

Huyghe, to take a handy example, roams the renewable wilderness on the lookout for strategies that might enable him to fabricate the perfect neutrality of pure experience. When he confesses a desire "to suspend resolution and conclusion without denying potential drama and intensity"—what is that but the confessed desire to create experience, in its most pure and neutral state? The term "neutral" is a bit misleading, here. Experience—at the atomic level, before it is polluted with circumstance and detail—may be open and fiercely unresolved, but neutral it is not. It is positive, constructive—it's life; experience, in its most profoundly uncategorizable version, is indistinguishable from life. When we've been exposed to pure experience, we don't categorize it as "art" or "film" or "a context." We can't; pure experience resists categorization as anything other than life itself.

To fabricate, via invention and strategy, pure experience that is truly contemporary—in other words, to fabricate pure experience that has taken account of the fact of contemporary life, which is to say the fact of history, which has rendered the structure of the contemporary—this would be, then, no small potatoes.

Does Pierre Huyghe create category-transcendent experience? Can anyone? Is the pursuit itself one more comedy, albeit of a high-grade, gloriously affirmative sort? You decide. Huyghe comes awfully close to the mark. Sometimes he ends up with art that's got pure-experience-fabrication on its mind. At all times, in his work art seems just a phase, a means to embody strategy and give it legs, when what he'd really prefer is strategy without product. Ideally, even strategy would be transcended, ultimately. To simply live the imagined, without the ball and chain of criticality, opposition, categorization—heaven, no? Ah, but we're earthly. Knowing humans, a fully oxygenated landscape is probably beyond us. Fortunately, finding and making air pockets isn't. And these can sustain us, long enough for work to continue.

NOTES

* See Jean-Charles Massera's brilliant and very funny text, "La leçon de Stains," in the book about the Third Memory project.

** Pierre Huyghe and Philippe Parreno, in their magazine project Anna Sanders (The Story of a Feeling).

*** A text such as this is a double prosthesis. Pierre Huyghe is extended through a writer who has agreed to voice a response within a format conforming to the needs of a specific business context, "the art world." Pierre speaks through the hired writer. But the writer is also "speaking for" Pierre. The writer represents his own interests in presenting his own ideas; "Pierre Huyghe" is here a construction, determined to some extent by the writer's response to him, and through whose office the writer has been given a voice. Each of the puppet selves in this double act of ventriloquism is directed, however, by another self. Huyghe and the writer took a decision to trust each other even though they did not know each other beyond the person that is revealed or can be discerned in the work either has created. At the end of the ventriloquism act, money will change hands, but since the writer is not desperate for money, he is not compelled to align himself with any content or figures with whom he is not in sympathy. All of this is in the background. It is a pleasure to trust someone, of course. The important pleasure of trusting a stranger, together with the objective respect the writer has for Pierre's accomplishments, informs the theater of this essay.

Autodidact

A version of this conversation with Michael Banicki was previously published in Purple Prose, #10, Paris, 1996.

In his trusty Volvo, Chicago-based artist Michael Banicki has driven more than 300,000 miles to visit and compare thousands of small American towns, preserving his evaluations in paintings as well as assemblages.

MICHAEL BANICKI I've driven 75 to 100 separate trips, all of them originating from my home in Chicago and heading out to such "end point" destinations as Kezar Falls, Maine; Plain Dealing, Louisiana; Sisseton, South Dakota; Luxora, Arkansas; Tunica, Mississippi; Canisted, New York. I maximize every journey by "seeing" as many selected small towns along the way as I can. By now I've been to a couple thousand towns, in 38 states—having never yet seen the Pacific Ocean, the Great Northwest, Nebraska, or South Carolina.

DAVID ROBBINS What's the mileage on your Volvo?

MICHAEL BANICKI 158,000, on this one. Had it about eight years. My previous Volvo had 165,000 miles on it.

DAVID ROBBINS There's something primal about driving that taps into our emotional life in a way airplanes or trains can't. Sitting behind the wheel naturally engages classic existential questions: "Which road do I take?" or "What if I just kept going and started life over again where no one knew me?" All The Twilight Zone questions …

MICHAEL BANICKI Last year I drove from Chicago to New York for an exhibition, and while driving through Ohio I purposely veered from my route about 150 miles to go to a town called Leetonia, south of Youngstown. I just wanted to see it. I'd been thinking about that town for years, wondering about it. I drove way out of my way to get there, and once there, I had a cup of coffee—and that was all! The absurdity of being there was unbelievable. But that's part of the pleasure, of course.

These trips are a way of staying in touch with adventure, of heading off into the unknown. I'll get off work on Friday afternoon, pack up the dog, and just get in the car. And just go there. Sometimes I'll go beyond it. But it's that sense of adventure, the fact that I've never been there … and also that little tickle that on Friday you're at work, laboring away, and Friday night you're 175 miles away in a little town that nobody's ever heard of, or ever will. To be among the percentage of people who have been in that town—I get a kick out of it.

DAVID ROBBINS How do you keep track of all these journeys?

MICHAEL BANICKI I've been documenting my trips for over 20 years, though it's only in the past five or six years that I've decided to incorporate the process into art. I'm on my second atlas now, the first one having become dog-eared and coverless through use. I transcribed all the old routes I'd taken onto the newer atlas, so it's quite a complete record. In it, every town I've visited is highlighted with faded yellow or orange marker, as is the route taken. States like Wisconsin here, the whole southern part of the state has been highlighted, with just a few fingerlings of routes into the extreme north of the state.

DAVID ROBBINS What other evidence do you carry away from your visits?

MICHAEL BANICKI I rarely take photographs. I'd rather have a memory of the town. The only physical evidence I might collect is the odd postcard or a local newspaper. But I'm not there for that purpose. I just pick one up here and there.

DAVID ROBBINS What kind of contact have you with the people in these towns?

MICHAEL BANICKI Fleeting, somewhat voyeuristic contact. I have no illusions that I know them. A lot of the people I encounter there have lived in these towns their entire lives, and I'm just someone who has come by for an hour, a half-hour, to absorb the way they live, what the area is like … I come away with the feeling of having stolen a little bit of their lives.

When I arrive, I usually go up to one of the local diners or the bar and talk with whoever's in there. Sometimes the old woman next to me will say, "You know, Mine #6 is closing, isn't that a disgrace?" and then I have to admit that I'm not too familiar with it. For an instant, I'm exposed, and I think, "What in the hell am I doing here? Where am I?" A sense of displacement wells up. I'm far away from where I'm comfortable, and I know the dialogue is going to become more of a test. Driving a Volvo with Illinois plates into these small towns makes you stick out! But I'll just talk. Ask them what the town is named after. Learn that the town is the Indian word for water that swirls or Welsh for the "coal brook." Or I may ask them how they pronounce the name of the town. Is E-l-i-d-a, Ohio, pronounced El-eye-da or is it El-ee-da? Is M-u-s-c-o-d-a, Wisconsin, Muscaday or Muscohdah—the former is correct, incidentally. I tell people that I'm traveling through, liked the town, wanted to stop … I never let on that I traveled six, seven, eight hundred miles for the specific purpose of seeing their little town! I never let the people in those towns know what I'm doing. I don't say, "Congratulations, you're part of my project."

Once in upstate New York, a place called Herkimer, I stopped to look at antiques in a complex of farm buildings and I got caught in a surprise heavy snowstorm. Really socked in.

A farmer invited me to stick around until the roads could be plowed. While we talked I asked questions about the region in order to get some sense of the area's essence. When I asked what it was like up there in Graveville, 20 miles north, the old guy responded, "Well, I don't know, I've lived here my entire life and I've never been there … I've never had a reason to go there." To me that's astonishing, because as the complete antithesis of that attitude, I'm six hundred miles from home, visiting his town!

DAVID ROBBINS Just for the afternoon.

MICHAEL BANICKI For mere minutes!

DAVID ROBBINS You say you've done this all over the country?

MICHAEL BANICKI Mostly the middle part. Between the coasts.

DAVID ROBBINS Anti-cosmopolitan?

MICHAEL BANICKI Naw. Just anti-hype, but most of the hype is generated out of big urban centers. Inflation—that's what I'm against. Too much goddam lying. So you wrap it all up in twine and throw it in the river. Right?

DAVID ROBBINS People used to spend their entire lives in the same town, big or small. You've taken the mobility factor of the automobile age and kicked it into overdrive.

MICHAEL BANICKI Total overdrive—in contrast to my entire family, no member of which has ever moved from the Chicagoland area. I still live in Chicago, but now when people tell me they're from, for example, Chenengo Bridge, I've been there. When they say "I'm from Darlington, Wisconsin, do you know where that is?" I tell them "Sure, you have a commemorative war obelisk in the middle of town." It's a heartwarming thing to be on that level of communication. They're thinking how far off and forlorn their town may be, and here they are being presented with someone else who knows there's something distinctive there.

DAVID ROBBINS Had you much contact with small town life when you were a kid?

MICHAEL BANICKI None at all. When I grew up I wanted to get a look at the amenities of small town life, partly to remove the mystery of hearing about and reading about small towns.

DAVID ROBBINS But not many people pursue 300,000 miles worth of that education!

MICHAEL BANICKI In order to educate yourself you have to invent a system for doing so. I've done that. I'm pursuing the creation of a standard of personal, subjective rules.

DAVID ROBBINS What do you look for?

MICHAEL BANICKI Nuances. Does the town have a winding road, like you find up in the mountains? Is there a river or other body of water nearby? Does the town have a Federal-style municipal building? Preferably the town will be a county seat, because I like a place that has a little bit of substance to it.

The town has to have an optimum population of between 800 and 5000 people. Any larger, and it's too much of a thriving community. The stability of the town's population is another factor: I tend to like towns that are sort of on edge, sort of in trouble—West Virginia or Pennsylvania coal mining towns, for example—and one of the reasons for going to some of these towns is to plot the change in population, from boom town to whatever they are now, fading. I find them more intriguing than towns that are edge cities or suburbs or bedroom communities.

But the single most important factor is the town name. If it's an interesting Latinization of an American word, or the romanticism of the sound of towns with Indian names, or if the town has a curious origin, like being formed from the first initials of the town founders ... Primgar, Iowa, is formed that way, as is Aledo, Illinois. Tolono, Illinois—the town's name is drawn from the initials of the six town founders. Generally, the town names help me to select and determine my routes.

DAVID ROBBINS But no one quality dominates?

MICHAEL BANICKI No.

DAVID ROBBINS So finally the evaluation is based on something intangible, right? The experience itself.

MICHAEL BANICKI Right. The experience of being there, whatever the quality of the experience may have been. When you first look at a lot of these towns on the map, you can only have a conceptual view of them. You have them in your mind. After you've gone to visit them the idea acquires a sense of closure, a definitiveness; being there imprints in your memory little vignettes of each town. After, there follows the complex matter of evaluating them and placing them in order of preference—stratification. When you're finished with a rating you can close the book on those towns. You've gone through the whole process of evaluation. Given a particular grouping, a closed set of items or names or living things, there's a sort of ordering that is established. Here is the painting. Here are my favorites. Here are my dislikes. All those subjective things are little hidden jewels in there. The viewer has to ponder why any town got superior ratings compared to any other.

DAVID ROBBINS You've not undertaken all these trips just out of some sentimental view of small town life. There's something ... harder going on here. It's more about setting a range of qualities in motion against each other. You end up with a kind of emblem of the attempt to place them in relation to one another.

MICHAEL BANICKI Right. It's not important whether I even like any of these towns. I may hate them all. Whether I like them or not isn't important. What's important is that I've gone through the process of evaluation, given a grouping, a closed set of items. Even if I find that I don't care about any of them, even if I hate every entry, there's a sort of ordering that's been established.

DAVID ROBBINS But not a hierarchical ordering: 1, 2, 3, 4, 5 …

MICHAEL BANICKI No. The thing that's being created is more abstract. All the objects in the evaluation are rated in relation to one another. Which means they have to be evaluated twice. Clear Lake's compared to Jump River, but Jump River has again to be compared to Clear Lake. That's crucial. It's all a process. It's not empirical. Documentation itself isn't enough. I want to self-legitimize what I'm considering, to get involved, organize, order it. Make it important. Also, there's the matter of closure. I've been there, I've satisfied my curiosity, I can close the book on those towns when I'm finished with a rating.

DAVID ROBBINS Of course, the question remains: why have these towns been planted so deeply in your mind in the first place? Do you know why?

MICHAEL BANICKI Maybe I'm looking for the perfect place. The optimum balance of positive qualities.

DAVID ROBBINS Tell me when you find it.

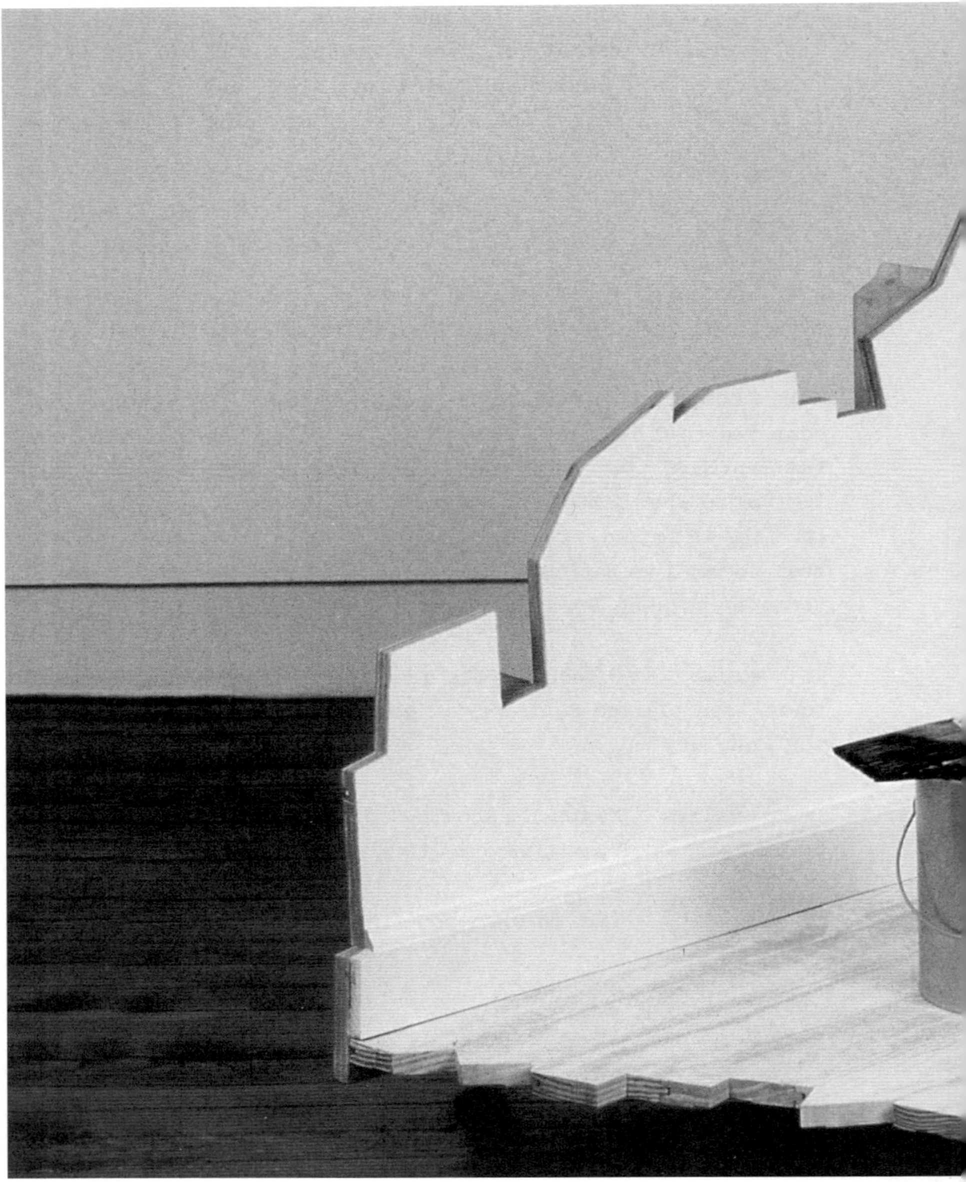

Movable Corner (Portable Dilemma), 1992
painted wood, metal, paint brush, casters, 32 1/2" x 31" x 31"

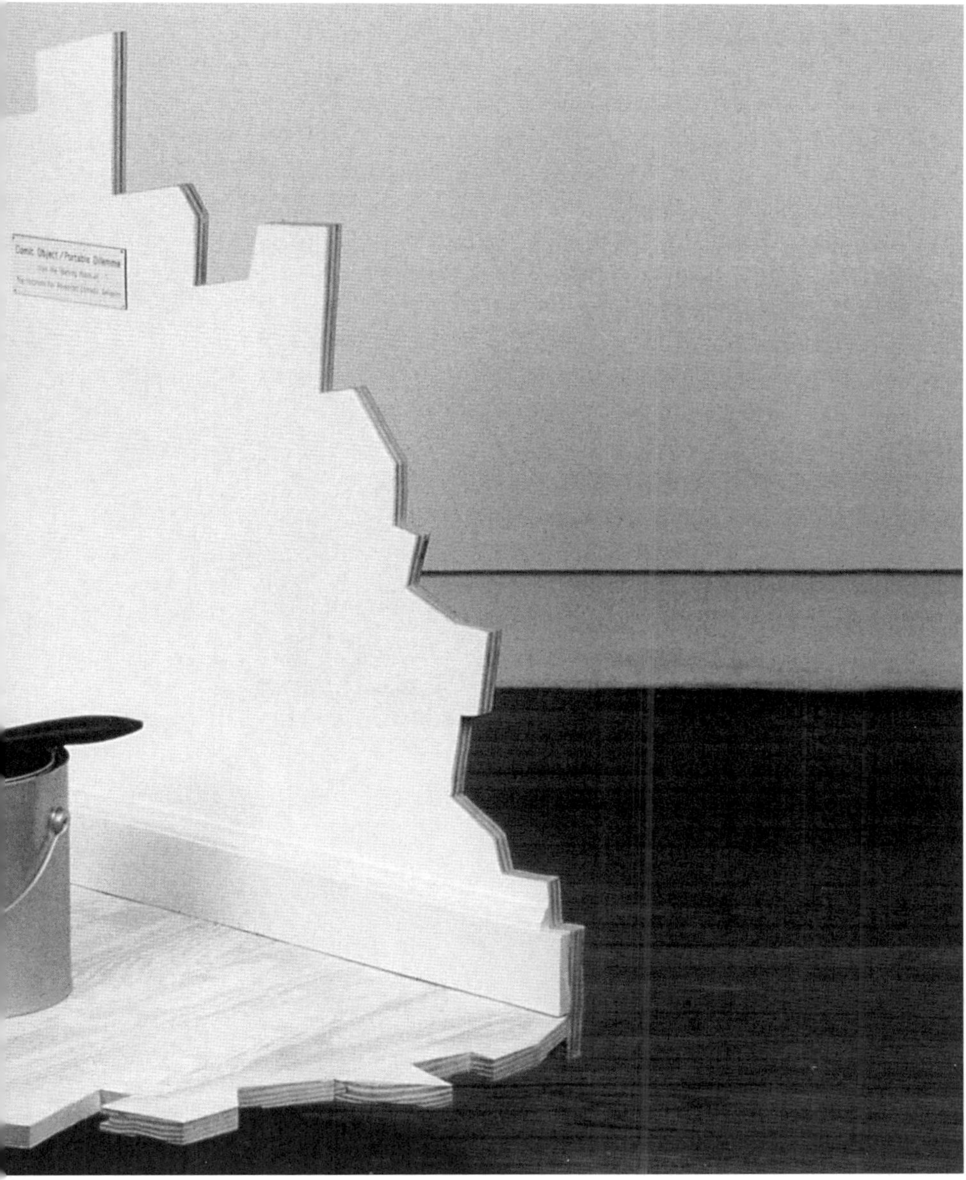
Comic Object / Portable Dilemma

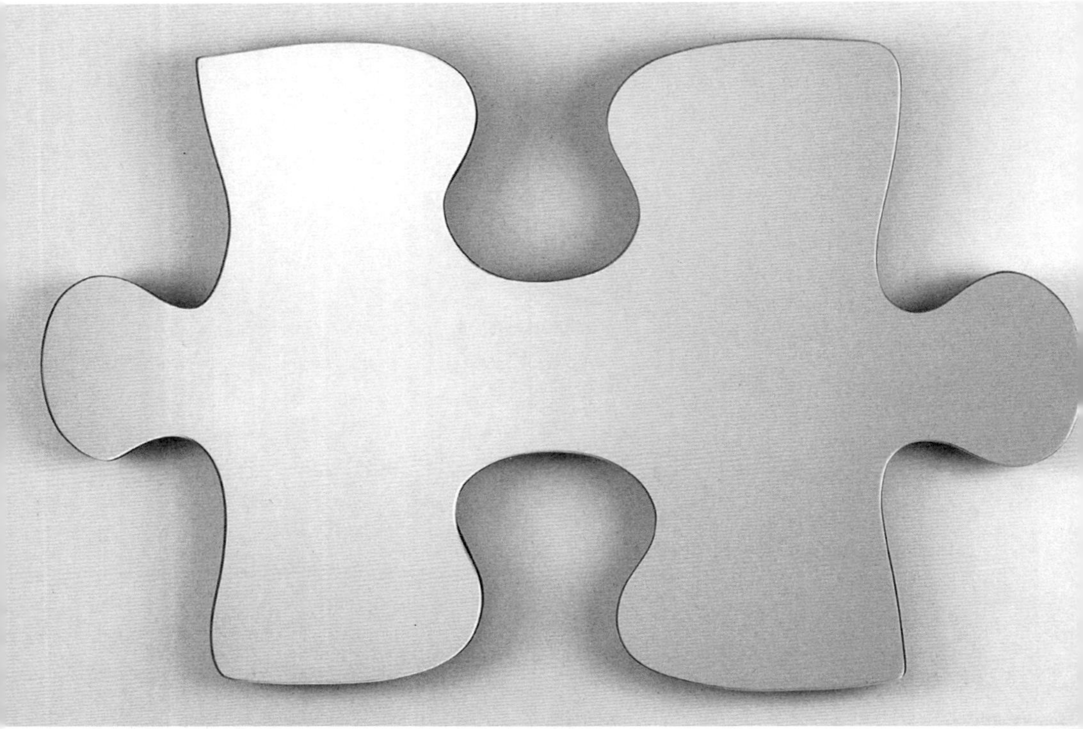

Landscape (Puzzle Mirror), 2000
mirror, 22 1/2" x 36"

The Compass Is the Map

Originally published in No Manifesto, exhibition catalogue, Galleria d'Arte Moderna e Contemporanea, Bergamo 2005.

AT THE INTERSECTION OF TWO EVOLUTIONARY TRAJECTORIES A NEW SITE FOR CULTURAL PRODUCTION IS FORMING. From seeds sown by separate and independent contexts—the art world, and the entertainment-industrial complex that produces mass culture—springs a fresh patch of wilderness and possibility. Attitudinal changes among contemporary artists, coinciding with concrete transformations in the production of popular culture, are destabilizing long-held suppositions in both fields. To a certain sort of contemporary imagination the destabilization offers an expanded, arguably unprecedented degree of freedom and opportunity.

An attempt at a topography of the new wilderness follows.

1. ADIEU MARCEL

Visual artists have long hewed to their faith in a hierarchy of "art above, mass culture below." But this prejudice has become outmoded. A good entertainer makes more of a contribution than a bad artist. A good television show is better than a mediocre painting. As a practice art has no intrinsic superiority. It is a context, perfect for some good ideas, perfectly wrong for other, equally good ideas. Furthermore, we recognize and accept that a television sitcom is as specific a form of artifice as a painting. Every format of communication delivers specific pleasures.

The independent imagination may access those pleasures by utilizing those formats. There are, in other words, respectable alternatives to art.

In the art context a core habit of mind during and since the modernist period has been the strategy, initiated by Marcel Duchamp, of introducing into the art context materials, subject matter, or concepts that had previously had their life outside that context. Countless artists since Duchamp have applied this strategy. Today, some artists would prefer not to base their work on this arguably over-explored gesture. Rather than introduce x or y into the art context, they seek to reverse the direction of the flow. They like the challenge of trying to apply to mainstream forms certain ambitions for the culture and certain attitudes toward form, process, and subject heretofore identified with the art context. They want to work as artists in mainstream forms, from a position of respect for mainstream forms. Something about this aim feels authentic to them. People are always drawn, even if a little blindly, toward the warmth of authenticity.

2. THE COLD WAR, AND AFTER

We'll revisit this development after sketching the evolution of the entertainment-industrial complex. Since it's a bigger context it receives a bigger treatment, complete with an extended metaphor.

The Cold War (1945-1990) should also be characterized as the war between Fun and No-Fun. (Eventually the American-led forces of Fun won, of course. Today that victory may have the aura of an inevitability, but during the war years it wasn't so clear. The alternative to that victory being No-Fun, we, all of us, have every reason to be grateful that events turned out as they did. Whatever else we might think about the aftermath, let's not kid ourselves on that point.) While the war was going on, the infrastructure of Fun—I refer of course to the entertainment-industrial complex of movies, TV, radio, mass circulation magazines, toys, comic books, and all the other spectacular, upbeat, mass culture product—had every reason to support the ideology that underwrote its own existence. (The Fun way of life knew a threat when it saw one, you could say.) Afterwards, when the communist forces of No-Fun were, if not outright vanquished then certainly exhausted and broken, the internal cultural dynamics of the Fun society underwent a shift. The entertainment-industrial complex freely imposed the aims, the methods, the brutal positivism of Fun without obstacle or opposition, and Fun's victory over No-Fun became fully *institutionalized*. American culture (which, to the global imagination, *symbolized* Fun) became, consequently, an extended celebration of the moment of victory, and Fun became the nation's official mainstream culture. Now only things capable of communicating a simplistic and sensationalistic positivism would comprise the mainstream. Not Wallace Stevens but *Beach Blanket Bingo*. Not Hindemith but James Bond. Not Rubens but *Charlie's Angels*. Quality? Quality was beside the point. A product might *have* quality, sure, but it could also be ineptly made or be crass yet, so long as it was Fun, still be promoted into the mainstream.

Just because this idea of the mainstream was worlds away from, say, Thomas Jefferson's, doesn't mean it was the worst idea anybody ever had. During the years of its reign the culture of Fun has offered up a great deal of pleasurable material, some of which has had the audience's best interests at heart. The culture of Fun is not entirely untrue nor utterly without insight into the human creature. Had its contribution only been limited to the recognition that, at certain moments, people want nothing more, and like nothing better, than to Do The Monkey—moreover, that they have the *right* to Do The Monkey, and *should* have the right to do it—by itself that would have been something, and really it has given us a great deal more than that. Much that has been offered up in its name would not even have *occurred* to any human being had they not felt the engine of Fun purring confidently behind them. Of course, a lot of junk has come of it too, but credit where credit is due: the people who threw this party really knew how to throw it.

How long ought a genuine cultural moment derived from real historical circumstance be extended, in your opinion? From the start of the War between Fun and No-Fun to today it's been 60 years … Can a culture keep a moment, even one derived from authentic inspiration and need, going that long? To respond in the affirmative is to suppose that a culture can keep Doing The Monkey _indefinitely_, and that there's no point beyond which the Monkey-Doing culture will suffer damage or hurt itself—two suppositions which one hesitates to endorse. I mean, Do The Monkey long enough, and you pretty much _are_ a monkey!

As with any controversy it depends who you ask. The entertainment-industrial complex, for its part, isn't entertaining any doubts. Those people are _in the party business_. They've got the theme (Fun), and they own the hall (the infrastructure of Fun). _Plus_ they've been blessed with an audience that's now been at the party for so many years, most in attendance (you understand I'm talking about all of _us_) can't even _envision_ another place to be. Add up those factors and the result will look and sound a lot like a party regardless of whether everyone present at it is in the party mood. Here artificial stimulants can help. They've never been in greater abundance—in advertising, in media, at the newsstand, on the street, right there in your hand, on your gleaming text-messaging cell phone, the one with the built-in video display.

And yet, over-stimulated and intoxicated as the audience is, some of its members are sober enough to perceive that the big party, which had begun sincerely, in an authentically-arrived-at culture's earned moment of historical truth, now celebrates something else. No longer referring to that earned moment in which a vibrant young culture discovered its power _to throw_ the party, now the party refers, instead, to that same culture's power _to keep the party going_. And at the core of _that_, anybody knows, is something distinctly un-partyish, something that's a little shrill, something imperial and professional and un-fun. Having the power to make the party not just the main cultural action but the _only_ action doesn't mean that all of the people can be fooled all of the time.

A secession movement has been afoot for a while, then. Some in the audience have been wondering whether there isn't some way to advance the party past that worn-out moment of victory of Fun over No-Fun. They're wondering whether it might not be time to make the culture of Fun behave like the parent it is rather than continue to accept the childish, irresponsible manner that has become its wearisome habit. Mightn't Fun, they're asking, be made more substantive?

It's not yet known whether any of these goals can be accomplished, of course. But they're sure of two things. First, they're convinced of the desirability of moving forward. (They think that the party should be better.) And secondly, they know that they can't look to the Fun Infrastructure—the entertainment-industrial complex—to undertake this work on its own. For one thing, the Fun Insfrastructure resists substantiveness, since it regards substantiveness as lacking in Fun. And, for another thing, the Fun Infrastructure resists self-analysis. Opacity, not transparency, has always been its game. That products of the Fun Infrastructure seem to appear out of nowhere is a crucial aspect of their magic. Why? Because if those who engineer and manage the Fun Infrastructure shared "how it's done" then you'd be in a better position to do it too, and you wouldn't need their party as much. You might even decide to throw your own party, which could be a better party than theirs. And if your party is better, then who will pay the cover charge to get into theirs?

For the entertainment-industrial complex, though, it's too late: that particular cat is out of the bag. Applied science—technology—is rapidly enabling the audience to create their own fun. Computers, video, audio recorders, all those bytes and gigahertzes and USB cords are allowing us to speak directly, economically, and with increasing skill in the language of the pop motherland. A technology gap is closing. Innovation has pried these languages free from the control of media corporations, and now any independent imagination who wants to can frame his or her ideas using formats—sit com, feature movie, music CD—that are absorbable by the entertainment-industrial complex. Instead of only consuming in an egalitarian way—which was the Andy Warhol moment, the Andy Warhol insight that the Coca-Cola that Liz Taylor or the president drank was no better than the Coke you are I drank—once again we're producing in a more egalitarian way. ("Once again"? Yes. Back in the days when the mainstream culture was literary, the production of culture was more democratic, because writing wasn't a technology-intensive medium. The 20th-century's growing reliance on machines progressively alienated the independent imagination from the mainstream culture. That trend is now being superseded by another, and the independent imagination is regaining access to the mainstream.)

These developments are very fresh, and they're sure to have a range of unpredictable long-term effects. Already, though, they're engendering a more complicated cultural politics than just simple opposition toward the entertainment-industrial complex. Long the attitude of post-war intellectuals, artists, and successive manifestations of counter-culture ("Beat," "hippie," "punk," etc.), objecting to the imbalance of power between those who owned modern communication technologies and the rest of us was, while not unjustified, attributable in part to a frustration at being on the wrong side of the lens. However, as technology accelerates the democratization of production it's weakening the Fun System's authority and, subsequently, the need for the old Us-vs-Them attitude. No one today realistically believes that television and movies are about to be banished and replaced with study groups and work farms. The media system is going to be with us in some form for as long as we live, and we know it. (Although it seems like it's been with us forever, this stuff is—amazingly—just getting started!) Isn't it in our interest to use the system to deliver less insulting, more constructive, and more sophisticated fun—fun that has greater ambitions for the culture than just garnering high ratings and doing big box office? Even a term such as "alternative culture," which made sense within the context of a particular post-war historical moment but which always implied minority status within a dominant culture, seems out of step with the current historical moment. More apt is a term such as "additional culture." As in: Don't waste your energy opposing. As in: Go ahead and build the world you prefer.

Cultural production always expresses a relation to power. Whether expressing a producer's proximity to power or distance from power, or revealing feelings of effectuality or of ineffectuality, consciously or unconsciously it will be present. No one should underestimate, therefore, the potential that is represented by the emergence of an independent cultural production that is uncoupled from anger, from frustration, from "opposition."

3. A LARGE PARENTHETICAL ...

(Before we get too carried away with indicating the contemporary situation, and certainly before we get too carried away with congratulating ourselves on how marvelously contemporary we ourselves are, a reminder that at the heart of this is an altogether classical matter, namely, how do you go about the business of telling the truth? Really, that's all that's going on here: a particular kind of imagination, configured by history in a particular way, is trying to, first, identify, and then, tell the truth about, the way it's been configured. That's all—not that that's _ever_ been a small thing!

What kind of imagination are we talking about, here, that truth telling should involve this _specific_ architecture? It is, of course, the imagination that has been imprinted with pop matter—movies, TVs, pop music, magazines, etc. Technology may have afforded this kind of imagination the possibility of articulating its truth in the most direct possible means, so that you no longer have to make a painting in order to communicate sophisticated ideas about, say, television, but why should it feel true to anyone to pursue these ends? What, in other words, is that imagination's imprinting? And in what way does it differ from the imprinting received by previous generations of imaginations?

I propose that it is a question of landscape and history—specific qualities of landscape, created by specific albeit broad historical developments. Call it the suburbanized imagination.

I and most young Americans grew up in a landscape that was neither city nor country but an amalgam of the two. Trees and Traffic—that's our experience. Before the Second World War, the suburb was primarily for the well-to-do; most people lived in cities, small towns, or rural areas. The idea that vast numbers of people would live in neither city nor country is thus, in the United States at least, not much more than 50 years old—a period that corresponds almost exactly with the Fun Epoch. The planned naturalism, the managed, neurotic landscape, the awkward in-between quality of the suburbs: for many of us, it's our primal experience of the authentic. Raised in a hybrid landscape, we are imprinted with that landscape. And just as the suburb transcended the distinction between city and country, we who are imprinted with suburban experience will naturally seek to transcend distinctions between other sorts of categories. To such imaginations, the classical distinction between contexts—between, say, the context of art and the context of entertainment—will feel less than accurate. Their purity doesn't correspond with the hybrid condition we feel inside. Neither the experience of art *per se* nor the experience of entertainment *per se* matches the synthetic condition of our experience, so neither context is ultimately satisfying. We yearn for something in-between, something with the attributes of both.

It isn't criticality that's driving the present evolutionary stage, then, but a desire to communicate personal and generational truths. That's an essential distinction from previous indie takes on "mass media," which seemed capable of perceiving utopia only through a haze of gun smoke. In the idea of building the world you prefer, a critique is *implied*. Disappointment or dissatisfaction with the status quo? It's a *given*. No need to beat that horse. No need to *mention* that horse.)

5. THE COMPASS IS THE MAP

To build the world he prefers, today's independent imagination may choose among a greater variety of media and formats than have ever before been at his disposal. As we've seen, this freedom has been granted by a combination of cultural politics and technology. Not too many years ago you couldn't make your own TV show or movie and dream of approaching a technical quality that anyone would be interested to watch, so it wasn't worth thinking along these lines but, courtesy digital technology, it now is. And, as a contemporary person who has enjoyed TV shows as well as paintings, today's independent imagination is likely less confined by internal prejudices for or against materials, media, contexts. He or she feels free to use any idea that appeals.

Thus, communication, always a matter of packaging, has never been more so. With a little discipline an independent imagination can tailor his or her output to meet the requirements of specific theaters of industry—the theater of the art system, the theater of the movie business, the theater of pop music—and deliver audience satisfaction on many fronts at once. (This is the Warhol production model, updated. Digitization of recording technologies has in effect transistorized the Warhol method, shrunk it down to the size of things that can fit into a briefcase, made it economical, portable, doable. Now we can use the Warhol production model <u>while saying other things</u>; the world doesn't need the Warhol content repeated.)

As in the past, the means determine the audience: make a painting, and that painting will travel a certain circuit; make a narrative film, that film travels another. Each route has advantages and disadvantages, and there are benefits to respecting what each has to offer. But whereas the independent imagination once had to dedicate him or herself to one route or another—everything took so much time to make!—digital technologies are letting us work more efficiently, freeing up time and enabling us to realistically develop multiple routes to the audience. To specialize in any one medium is coming to seem quaint because unnecessary.

How, though, to lend spine to that freedom? Diversity for the sake of diversity isn't much of a goal. Anyway, it's already been done, often—singer Frank Sinatra's paintings? Actor William Shatner's pop records?—badly.

Do any conditions distinguish the new independent imagination from the "cross-over" artists (successful or failed) of the past? Yes.

A) The fact that one can <u>efficiently</u> produce in multiple forms means there's enough time to actually become <u>good at</u> working at multiple forms. A campy or ironical approach to forms—i.e. "so bad it's good"—becomes a thing of the past.

B) The ability to work efficiently in multiples forms and contexts shifts emphasis to the relation between the parts. You can make a painting and you can make a TV show. But how does a painting relate to a TV show? How does the TV show relate to, say, a novella? The relation between parts is <u>thematized</u>, rendered as an aspect of the content. The relation between the parts of the project becomes part of the project.

Marcel Broodthaers initiated this way of working almost 40 years ago. But Broodthaers confined himself to a single context—art. Today the context of visual art takes its place as one among several production options.

C) Production evolves and progresses organically. It is content-driven, and uses whatever materials or media—whatever packaging—are needed to deliver the content.

D) A healthy relation with their own imagination is the most important thing that an artist, of any sort, in any field, can have. The health of that relationship must be protected at all costs. Anything that has the potential to injure it must be guarded against—and nothing has greater potential to inflict damage than the judgments of the professional arena. It's one more reason to embrace an expansion of production capacity. Doing so allows for the creation of organic exhibition models that unfold over time in a variety of forms, formats, media, and contexts, thereby bestowing on the independent imagination greater freedom from the judgments and dictates of any one professional arena. A project that plays out in multiple contexts can't be stopped by a lack of support from any one context's administrators—from the curators, the editors, the vice-presidents in charge of production who may disapprove of or fail to discern the value of a work. Why should the success or failure of a project be decided by their vision? Why give anyone that power over you?

6. A WORD FROM OUR SPONSOR

The ability to speak directly in the languages of the mainstream culture is altering the coordinates of art. If, in order to address pop subject matter in better ways than the Fun System offers, you no longer have to make a painting about pop subject matter, what is art for, instead? Given the expanded access to mainstream formats, what is art's role? Is the independent imagination, which is capable of producing in a wide variety of forms and formats, still definable as "an artist" when he or she is no longer limited by the prejudices of a context dedicated to isolating and elevating visual phenomena? Ought the standards of a single professional context apply to someone who is working in multiple professional contexts?

These questions will be answered as events unfold. Nevertheless it's important to acknowledge that it's the art context that values these sorts of ideas most highly. (An art museum, not HBO or Canal Plus or Channel 4, has sponsored my thoughts on these matters.) It's the art context that knows what to do with questions like these; that has a tradition of concern for the relation between communication forms; that celebrates the innovation of new exhibition models for their own sake; that always takes the thematization of process seriously ... While the art world may have gone show biz in recent years—with new stars introduced on an annual basis, a permanent youth cult, and the sale of the thing mattering more than the thing itself—structurally-speaking it still behaves differently than any other context. It's a zone with unique characteristics. Which is why an actor who's also a singer isn't news—both acting and singing are performances, occurring on the broad plane of show business—while the idea that independent imaginations who have been trained in the principles and habits of mind of the art context should be taking up such mainstream communication formats as a television show or motion picture is.

Although the art system is far from perfect (in the eyes of the art system, products of the imagination succeed or fail as art, a narrow appraisal that, since certain uses of the imagination are wholly unconcerned with the specific set of values that happen to be cannonized by the art system, can become tiresome) it nevertheless can claim certain advantages. Not least among them: an active interest in transparency. The art system is willing (which of course is to say willing up to a point) to solicit from its constituency a certain amount of doubt or criticality about its rituals. It regularly celebrates artists who doubt or question the theater of the art system, provided that those artists go about their interrogations in a sufficiently inventive way and/or draw conclusions that stop short of arguing for shutting down the host theater altogether. (The point beyond which the art system is not interested to go is the point beyond which almost any system is unwilling to go, i.e. the money point. The art system is not interested to tell where the money has come from or where the money has gone. This is understandable—to ask any really hard questions about the money is to risk insulting the money and result in the cessation of the money's flow toward art—but still, we have to be honest about what the art system is not interested to be honest about. By the same token—credit where credit is due—art is not only capable of taking a good hard look at itself, it undertakes to do so at regular intervals.) By exercising this will to transparency—which is a moral force, directly competing with the venality and corruption of the marketplace—the art system to a very real extent directs its own evolution. Which tradition makes it worlds more transparent than the show biz system, a congeries of opacities if ever there was one and a system that evolves only when forced to by outside forces—legislation, technological innovation, and such.

The digital revolution is enabling fine artists—independent imaginations that've been trained in a context that values and actively pursues transparency—to directly apply that training to pop culture formats. This means that the forces of transparency have at last pierced the armor of the entertainment-industrial complex. The forces of transparency are penetrating the thick opacities of TV sitcoms and narrative feature films. The forces of transparency are infiltrating the world of make-believe, of characters, plots, car chases, secret agents, cowboys and Indians, sex goddesses, zombies, golden statuettes, and all the rest of that delightful and oppressive nonsense ceaselessly lobbed at us by the Fun Infrastructure. This infiltration is just getting underway. The initial phase of it has relied on the Duchampian strategy of introducing x—in this case, mainstream films—into the art context. Douglas Gordon, Candace Breitz, Stan Douglas, Pierre Huyghe, and their like made a good start, but as future transparencists turn out original TV shows and movies, the Duchampian strategy will fade because the art context won't be as necessary a venue for these experiments. There will be real alternatives to the gallery and the museum. Transparencists will offer their creations directly to the mainstream. Expect big things of this infiltration.

7. EXTERNALS AND INTERNALS

The pressure shifts, from old questions onto new ones. No longer is a pressing question, "When will the independent imagination be able to work in the mainstream formats of the Fun Infrastructure?" We can already, right now, so a more important question becomes: "What are the differences between what you're making and what the Fun System makes?" An important question becomes, "What do you do with that DVD of your little iMovie once you've burned it?"

Getting your hands on the appropriate technology is no longer the challenge. Distribution of the products made with that technology is the new challenge. How do you get your work out?

Maybe the reason you're thinking in terms of sitcom or pop CD or narrative feature film, there at your desk in front of your computer, is that you Want In. You want the bigger desk, which you'll be able to afford if you can find a way to swim in the mainstream. That's cool, if that's your thing, if your imagination is so configured (there are people who do sincerely have a talent for thinking in terms of genre, and they shouldn't apologize for it)—and if you can stand it. (More power to you if you can stand it.) It's easier now than it's ever been. But don't forget that you've got another choice. New systems, new routes, built from new technologies, will eventually be competing with the old system. Of course, it's a little early to be thinking along these lines; only 9,000 people are working this way at present. Not until there are 90,000 people working this way will the entertainment-industrial complex feel any pressure at all. And not until 900,000 people work this way will that infrastructure be forced to accommodate them. Already, though, the independent imagination is in a position to realistically consider the question: Do you deal with the existing system or innovate another one?

Those are a few of the externals. What about the internals? In other words, just what is it that you're making, there at your desk? Are you conforming your imagination to existing formats—a sitcom, a pop CD, a narrative feature film—because these formats deliver specific experiences to an audience and you like what they deliver? If you're choosing to work in these existing pop formats, there must be something specific about them that you like, no? Or is it only that you've had the imagination for any other approach programmed out of you? You've got the tools to use these formats, now. What about them—exactly—do you want to use? And what do you toss? What will you put in place of the discards?

And suddenly there it is, right in front of you: a wall. The ability to work in the forms of the mainstream brings you up against a question you've never really thought through, and now you're heading straight for it. How isn't the question any more. How can we make our own TV, produce our own movie, have our own music label—how has been solved; you can make your TV show, produce your movie, release your pop CD. Go ahead and do it. The question, now, is WHY? Why do we want to work in these forms? What do you hope to achieve or bring about by working in them? Do you want to work in these forms just in order to connect to your childhood? The dream of revolution dies hard—are you still thinking to give it another try? Are you doing it just to get rich? What other reason than these can you envision?

The future is embedded in Why.

8. UNTITLED

The 20th century was dominated by the analog, cinema. "Life is like a movie ... " people said. Why did they say it? Because the words felt true. Cinema has since been superseded, first by TV, and TV in turn by the computer—in fact today multiple analogs, from the distant as well as the more recent past, overlap and compete. Yet none dominates as a metaphor for life the way that cinema once had. The computer may currently be the most mind-expanding popular technology but it is somewhat lacking in metaphorical oomph. "Life is like a computer?" "Life is like ... the world wide web?" Well, no, it isn't, really.

Some people still say "life is like a movie," of course, but if they do it's mostly from habit. The truth is that we haven't found the metaphor for our time. It could be that our time actually lacks any corresponding metaphor ... This is more interesting than sad.

9. CONCEPTUAL ART FOR THE MASSES?

In place of the classical opposition between city and country, the suburbanized imagination envisions the creation of cultural product—activity, gesture, and artifact—that is both/and, or that is in-between. It looks for, demands, and creates hybrids, blends, mongrels ... Art? Entertainment? How about High Entertainment?

It's one possible direction. High Entertainment suggests categories confounded. High Entertainment takes the openness to concept and the drive toward refinement, which is traditionally associated with the context of fine art, and combines it—somehow—with the mass appeal of entertainment. "Somehow": there'd be more than one way to accomplish this, since there are many points of contact to exploit. Which is not to say that a High Entertainment is an infinite set. Many things it might be but it isn't just anything. We can sense distinguishing characteristics and consistencies, and identify these.

High Entertainment acknowledges the historical fact of modern mass culture. Rather than argue against it, High Entertainment seeks to use the condition, to make the culture more interesting, more attractive, more honest, and healthier.

High Entertainment doesn't scorn the mainstream. It respects the legibility and accessibility of mainstream product—without showing the particulars (this or that product) of the mainstream too much respect. High Entertainment product enjoys the game of trying to reach as many people as possible while being not wholly defined by that game.

High Entertainment takes the spirit, the sophistication, and the ambitions for the culture associated with fine art and does away with the specialized languages and narrow concerns of the art context, in favor of accessibility. You shouldn't need to have gone to a special school to enjoy High Entertainment. At the same time High Entertainment treats you as though you have a brain in your head.

High Entertainment rejects both the specialized, exclusionary, academic language of the art context and the formal complacencies of mainstream entertainment—the worst of the two worlds.

High Entertainment—it might be what you get when independent imaginations trained in the principles and habits of mind in the art context take up mainstream pop formats like TV, movies, and pop music ... How does someone with an art mind-set go about working directly in mass media?

Exactly what High Entertainment is, we don't yet know. We will proceed from the belief that not all categories of imaginative production have already been discovered. To assume that imaginative output must be assigned to known categories and contexts is to contaminate the evolution of the human imagination with something inorganic and bureaucratic.

In order to find out what High Entertainment is, we must make it.

10. BON VOYAGE

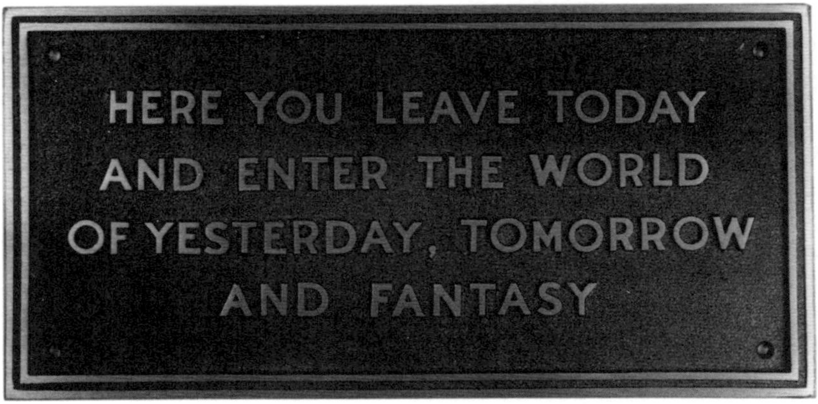

Prop, 1988
bronze plaque, 6" x 12"

High Entertainment: Curtain Up

This text, written in 2005, is previously unpublished.

In our time the vast, congested world of image-makers is organized around two poles. Around one pole gathers the sort that pursues Refinement, while around the competing pole cluster creative minds that have adopted Accessibility as their mantra. Most usually, the refinement-oriented image-maker, aspiring to offer complex and ambitious communication product, has, after surveying the cultural terrain, identified the art world as the realm best suited for the exercise of their talents and the pursuit of those aspirations. They apply themselves to making art—paintings, sculpture, and the like. Given the difficulty of engaging the production economies of the mainstream popular culture, not to mention the low-ish aspirations for humankind often conveyed in the wares offered by the aggressively Accessible mass culture, anyone's decision to enlist in the smaller and more specialized realm of art is understandable. Yet a decision of that nature doesn't exist in a vacuum. Repeated decade after decade by thousands of first-rate creative minds it accretes and forms a pattern. And in the shadow of that pattern substantial questions mushroom.

What, one wonders, have been the consequences to the *whole* culture of a flow of first-rate intellectual and creative ability away from the mainstream, decade after decade? Is it not conceivable that the flow of ability and aspiration, opting always for the same course, cutting a channel ever deeper, has actually worked to perpetuate the divide between the art culture and the accessible, popular, "entertainment" culture (the very divide, of course, that made the refinement-seeking mind feel it had no realistic alternative <u>but</u> to enlist in the art world!)? Furthermore, doesn't this continual, dependable, <u>predictable</u> flow of first-rate intellectual and creative ability into the specialized realm of art effectively <u>guarantee</u> both the marginality of the art culture and the generally low aspirations—sex and money, sex and money, sex and money—of the (now global) mass culture? Aren't both cultures weaker for that division? And doesn't the wholeness of culture—society, if you will—suffer for it?

There is, I'm saying, a sort of brain drain at work in contemporary culture, enacting a pattern so long established we don't even question it let alone imagine that it might be corrected. This brain drain configures our culture at deep structural levels. It underwrites a tired theater wherein a comparatively small art world looks down on the mainstream culture while, for its part, the popular, mainstream culture, self-charged with entertaining The People and thus feeling somehow "obliged" to find repellent not only the elitist economy of fine art but the very principle of exclusionism that a culture of refinement feeds on, represents, trades in, and promotes, walls itself off from the formal, material, thematic, and attitudinal questing that defines the fine artist in the modern era. In truth, the rules of this theater are held in place more by the players' vanity—in the case of art, the need to feel oneself superior and special, and the need for an association with exclusivity; in the case of the mass-culture, the illusion that one is speaking for The People, and "giving people what they want"—than by any condition intrinsic to either the media or the venues through which the refined and the mass cultures communicate with their respective audiences. Unchecked and unchallenged, the tired theater has settled in for a long run. Surmising that their sensibilities and interests will never be accommodated by the baldly mercenary machinery of the entertainment culture, refinement-seeking minds flock en masse to the art world, while minds geared to the valid and not un-virtuous goal of seeking to communicate in forms that are understandable to the largest possible audience sponsor, in the name of that audience, a suspicion of intellect and a fear of experiment. With each sticking to their own kind, who can be surprised that professionalized ghettos of thought and sensibility have been the result? A few individuals prosper, the ghettos thrive as ghettos—and the wider culture continues to be less than it might.

Good news! A counterforce has been unleashed, one with the potential to inject plenty of brightening fizz into this stale arrangement. Advances in technology once again are restructuring the culture. This time around it's the digital revolution that's disturbing entrenched social patterns right and left. Independent imaginations have been enabled to work directly, efficiently, and economically in the forms and formats of the mainstream media culture. The kids are pointing cameras and microphones at things and creating their own entertainment—movies, pop music, and TV-culture-influenced videos. They're burning these onto DVDs and CDs, uploading them, downloading them. Which means they're able not only to create in mass-media formats but, crucially, distribute them as well. This marks a new stage as, previously, corporations had had a stranglehold on the technology needed to communicate via the language of the mainstream media culture they'd been instrumental in establishing. In transforming this long institutionalized imbalance of technology, the digital revolution has handed this society the tools, and the opportunity, to reverse the persistent brain drain as well.

Exactly what it'll mean to have an entire generation of independent imaginations pointing cameras and microphones at things and creating their own movies, pop music, and TVesque video without obligation toward or concern for the apparatus of the media state—and keep in mind this will be the first generation to do so, not the last—isn't clear yet. Already, though, this freshly-minted phenomenon, coined only yesterday morning, is destabilizing both the context of art and the context of mainstream media technologies—the anti-intellectual "entertainment culture"—by indicating a realizable middle-ground between the two.

"High Entertainment," I've taken to calling one sector of the emergent middle-ground. Drawing upon the better aspects of both worlds, High Entertainment will combine entertainment's accessibility with art's experimentalism and bent toward form-discovery. Here I hasten to emphasize that High Entertainment really *is* entertainment. It *isn't* art, insofar as it doesn't share visual art's fixation on the complex issues surrounding representation, visual art's obsession with articulated interplay between form and content, visual art's propensity for criticality, or visual art's narrow historicity. Anyone who expects to read High Entertainment according to the rules and codes maintained by the visual art system, as manifested either in its professional or academic wing, can expect to be disappointed. High Entertainment "fails" as art because it's not trying to *be* art. High Entertainment is entertainment, and wants to be, but it is entertainment that shares something of art's ambitions for the culture—of art's ambitions for *you*.

High Entertainment is where some of art—or rather, some artists—will be going.

Writing about that destination is, at this stage, mostly a predictive operation, but it isn't entirely or only that. I base my thinking in part on my own evolution, and on identifiying the different, quite real thought- and sensibility-waves I've felt as a result of making the kind of work this essay means to delineate. Something of the character of the coming High Entertainment can be known. The essay that follows may be predictive but it isn't science-fiction.

ONE DVD BURNER, ONE VOTE

While the idea that an artist might, say, make a painting one month and a movie or TV show the next has been around since Andy Warhol, that production model had rarely been explored after he'd invented it. To do so was, for a very long time, "too Warholian"; real artists, looking to make their own mark on art history, will always seek a personal model of production. Today, though, producing in both traditional "fine" and contemporary media forms is easily and efficiently executed—one no longer need go to all the trouble of being Andy Warhol in order to use the production model he'd pioneered—and consequently it's becoming much more widespread. (That Warhol had become the boy or the girl next door was, incidentally, the news brought by the film <u>American Beauty</u>.)

The new recording and computing technologies are so good, and the results they produce so closely resemble the real thing (I refer not to Warhol's production but to the top-notch audiovisuals that media-corporation-owned technology offer an audience) that the quality gap between the kind of media work made by an independent imagination and that generated by the likes of CBS, Warner, and Disney—a gap until recently positively grotesque—has become negligible. The close of that quality gap means that an independent imagination who opts to think in terms of film or video (whether for all or only part of their output) is now <u>that much closer</u> to having his or her work absorbed by the gigantic systems of the mainstream culture. Thus an independent imagination is no longer restricted to thinking in terms of gallery or museum but may now consider communicating via DVD distribution, website, theatrical release, even (gasp!) broadcast.

Are the distribution and evaluation systems of the mainstream culture prepared for this? They are not—not by a long shot. Do they welcome it? They do not. But it'll happen anyway. As imaginations that have been trained in other traditions (including some conversant with the culture of refinement) increasingly produce in mainstream formats, gradually the existing distribution systems will feel the pressure. (The systems that have long been in place for distributing and evaluating pop culture are already starting to groan from change, and the new era I'm describing has just begun!) If today 12,000 (to choose a number) independent imaginations are producing in formats absorbable by the mass culture, before long 120,000 will produce in this way, and then 1,200,000 ... The existing systems will have to accomodate it. Eventually they'll see the commercial advantage of doing so. It's only a matter of time. And even then the independent imagination will still have real, practicable alternatives to the corporate production and distribution system.

To this phenomenon (which, as I've indicated, is only just beginning) a swarm of questions attach themselves. For what sort of movies and "TV" does someone trained in, say, the vocabularies and history of fine art make, exactly? How will they be different from, and how the same as, the movies and TV that are produced by the official entertainment culture? Is the independent imagination in question just "making art with digital technologies," or have they perhaps some obligation to respect the integrity of forms and formats that, designed for the mainstream, have their own history? (A TV sitcom is just as specific a form as an abstract painting, after all.) What, in other words, is the relation to the mainstream of an artist able to work in mainstream forms and formats? Need that artist's mainstream production—a movie, a "TV show"—be integrated with their "fine art" production, in the manner of a modern artist like Warhol? And what if that independent imagination chooses to work exclusively in mainstream media formats, and distribute their work independently? If they aren't bound either by the production rules of the entertainment industry or the rules of presentational logic maintained by the art system, what is that independent imagination's cultural location? Are they an "artist" or an "entertainer"?

For some of you, questions such as these are waiting just around the corner.

WHAT IS ENTERTAINMENT, ANYWAY?

On the periodic table of culture, entertainment is assigned a lighter atomic weight than art. Entertainment's structure, however, is as specific in its own way as art's.

Set aside the question of media for the time being—when it comes to communication, some medium is assumed to be involved—and focus on the consistent underlying structure of the entertainment transaction. Entertainment's structure is binary. There is 1) a maker (the "entertainer") and 2) an audience. It is an aggressively audience-centered model—which is to say people-centered. The entertainer is free to do "anything" to entertain an audience. Delivering pleasure to an audience is always the goal but the method of accomplishing this is wide open. Additionally, proof of a given method's effectiveness is instantly available: something either "entertains" or it doesn't.

This minimal, binary structure of entertainment may be attributable to the fact that, usually, entertainment is defined by the actions of a performer; to be entertained, an audience really needs nothing more than a proficient, entertainment-minded human standing in front of it. Although its presence isn't required, a human performer is the basic integer of entertainment. Audience members will relate to that human performer with a directness that something made of, say, wood, paint, or bronze does not permit.

Entertainment has a certain directness in its genes, then. Art, by contrast, is inherently indirect. In art, there's 1) a maker (the "artist"), who bounces a creative signal off 2) an imaginary abstraction (termed, broadly, "art") to reach 3) the audience. Art's structure thus has three parts, with the satellite off which the signal is bounced going by a number of aliases—"art" being one, "history," "meaning," and "discourse" others. While the audience still receives the signal, it does so indirectly, and secondarily. The satellite, Art, always receives the signal first.

"Something either 'entertains' or it doesn't ... "—entertainment's binary structure seems to be simpler, yet it masks a complex, ancient transaction. What, after all, does it mean to be "entertained"? What do we feel, really, when we feel "entertained"? What are the qualities of this sensation? How is it induced in human beings? The fact that each of us has experienced "failed" or "bad" entertainment—i.e. entertainment that didn't entertain—clearly indicates that it's a specific sort of enterprise, and a specific sort of experience.

If there are many ways to entertain, many methods, many means, a constancy nevertheless courses through them all. The constancy may be described as a sort of vibration. Entertainment is a vibration created in humans by humans for the sake of pleasure and delight. Question: Need a vibration be justified? Let's go further: Is it possible, even, to justify a vibration? Music may be a useful analogy here. Consider the pleasing electric guitar note. What justification is required of that note beyond the pleasure it's bringing you? Absolutely none. The entertainment vibration is similarly beyond, or before, justification.

Entertainment is to be accepted, then, as a large, significant, and mysterious human event, the exact nature of which can never be identified. Therefore to be able to do it and do it well should be—and is—sufficient. To delight others is enough. Such additional validation as elevation to the condition of Art bestows isn't required.

High Entertainment proceeds, then, from a belief that to entertain well needs no additional justification. High Entertainment pursues, and then alligns itself with, the entertainment vibration.

DOING THE MATH

Movies, TV shows, and pop music are mainstream communication formats, the communication formats of the mainstream. Since the masses—artists included—are able now to work efficiently and independently in mainstream communication formats like movies, pop music, and TV-like video, an obligation, likely new to their lives, falls to them to develop their thinking about the mainstream.

It's an obligation that's especially complex for artists. In the modern era art has aggressively set itself apart from the mainstream culture, and revelled in its separation, its difference, even its marginality. High Entertainment doesn't participate in this tradition. High Entertainment doesn't scorn the mainstream but accepts the mainstream as an interesting condition of modern culture. Any imagination that has the intention of participating in modern cultural life negotiates, after all, with the idea of the mainstream. Your work either becomes part of the mainstream or it doesn't. You want to be part of the mainstream or you don't. Regardless of a given individual's attitude toward it or the fate of that individual's own cultural production, the mainstream is a presence. Like "entertainment," a large and mysterious entity, the mainstream is a powerful force within modern culture.

We take that force for granted. And yet what, really, is the mainstream? Why is there a mainstream, i.e. what is it <u>for</u>? What purpose does it serve? <u>Who</u> is it for? Is the idea of a mainstream a universal, appearing in all cultures? Is a mainstream equally important to all cultures, or is it more important in some? (It could be argued, for instance, that the concept of a mainstream plays a much more important role in democratic societies than in royalist.) Has there been a mainstream as long as there's been culture, or was there a stage at which the idea of a mainstream became more emphatic? Is so, what brought about that change?

Sorely underdeveloped as Mainstream Studies are, certain of the properties of the mainstream may be identified nevertheless.

The mainstream is comprised of communication product—manifested in format as well as intent—that is defined by its legibility and accessibility. Legible by, accessible to whom? <u>To as many people as desire access to it</u>. Considered mathematically, this is simply remarkable: the scale of entity X (here, the mainstream) is determined by the number of people who acknowledge it!

The mainstream is, then, a game of numbers, a game of scale. Adults are known to be attracted to games of scale; attempting to enter the mainstream is one of the games that adults play to pass the time in adulthood. (Of course, not all work does well to seek the scale of the mainstream. Some work is meant for an altogether different scale of culture—smaller, more intimate scales. In its heart of hearts, though, our time isn't so interested in work meant for scales smaller than the mainstream—a serious mistake on the part of our culture, perhaps, but there it is.) What makes absorption into the mainstream desirable?

For one thing, it is <u>the</u> big game of our time. For another, it can be immensely lucrative; the mainstream is a big market. Absorption also symbolizes history's acceptance of your ideas.*

In order to enter the game that the mainstream represents, the particular communication product seeking absorption must restrain any criticism it might have made of that consortium of forces which sees to it that the mainstream continues to flow and irrigate. That restraint is essential, for (what amount to) political reasons. The forces that feed and maintain the mainstream are, it should be obvious, capital and the power that controls capital. Communication forms that rely on a large capital investment—movies, TV shows, pop music among them—will be more obliged, therefore, to restrict any criticism they conceivably might have leveled. <u>They are designed, in other words, to not reveal all that they know.</u> The limits to truth-pursuit and truth-telling that these communication forms impose on themselves keep them in the shallow end of the pool, and it's this, survivalist's willingness to remain in the shallow end that, at least in part, defines these works as "entertainment." (In view of this we might logically wonder what reward the audience for the mainstream gets out of the arrangement. They have contact with the entertainment vibration, of course. And they get a steady supply of product, pitched at a certain level of professionalism. But perhaps more importantly than either of these, their contact with that product delivers <u>contact with the mainstream</u>. "Entertainment" is the means by which an important modern abstraction—the mainstream—stays a part of their life. <u>For some reason</u>, that contact is desirable. Just why, exactly, isn't clear. Members of the audience gain a sense of their time, of course, but a sense of one's time can be derived from many alternative sources. Other than the rewards listed above, it really is a bit of a mystery why the audience doesn't revolt.)

High Entertainment enjoys a different relation to the restraint that conventional entertainment imposes on itself. Anyone who can shoot, edit, print, and distribute their own movies and TV shows will not be bound to restrain themselves in the way that classical entertainment media product has been. Thus in High Entertainment the mainstream can be treated as more of a concept, or as a material to be used. High Entertainment, in other words, respects the *idea* of the mainstream, and the legibility and accessibility of mainstream product, but without having too much respect for the *particulars* of the mainstream—this or that product. A High Entertainment product enjoys the game of trying to reach as many people as possible while, at the same time, knowing that it is a game, rejecting being wholly defined by the terms of the game.

In High Entertainment, mass media communication formats *may or may not* be used toward "conceptual ends." Does that then mean that High Entertainment is some sort of "conceptual art for the masses"? I'm hesitant to endorse that interpretation. "Conceptual art for the masses": how is the phrase (and the idea it suggests) in any way distinguished from plain old mass culture, or advertising, or marketing? Don't we *already* have "conceptual art for the masses"?

US OR EVERYBODY?

Any mainstream product, in order to be a mainstream product, must satisfy one condition. It must be *accessible*, to as many people as may care to access it. The weight of that single criterion is enough to restrict the extent to which any mainstream entertainment product may retreat into or be based upon any specialized language. Mainstream formats, which seek to be understood, accepted—in a word, consumed—by as many people as possible, utilize *specific* languages ("A TV sitcom is as specific a form as an abstract painting") without resorting to *specialized* languages.

Specialized languages are divisive. They divide the audience into those who know that language and its codes, and those who do not. Since the dawn of the modern era, art has relied extensively on the acquisition of specialized language. You either know the history of art, and consequently why that blue mark placed just so on that wall is significant and meaningful, or you do not. Theoretically, anyone who is interested to can learn the specialized language of art. But it _must_ be learned. Art in our time has posited itself as a form of _research_. That's yielded many interesting things, to be sure, but a research model isn't the only way to discover experiences that human beings will value.

High Entertainment eschews the use of a specialized language. The audience needs no specialized language to understand what it is experiencing. High Entertainment _revels_ in the challenge of being understandable to everyone.

DISCIPLINE PROBLEM

High Entertainment shouldn't be taken, therefore, as only working changes on entertainment. The destabilizing forces unleashed by digitalization also challenge artists' habits of mind.

The model of art in which contemporary artists have, for a long time now, been trained—as a system for organizing imaginative output, by now so widely accepted as to be beyond question and, thus, academicized—goes something like this. First, the artist creates a given work. Let's call it Work A. In time, Work A is followed by a Work B _which in some respect pursues the implications of or otherwise responds to Work A_. Work C then follows up on the implications of Work B, and so on into the future. The progression, which is designed to identify, make legible, and develop a body of meaning over time, might be written as A (A)B (A)(B)C … By means of this progression the artist works up their fascinations into a _sustained lather_. That sustained lather is their art.**

It's a perfectly good model. High Entertainment has no quarrel with it. Yet the model that's active in High Entertainment happens not to hew to it. In High Entertainment, the independent imagination _has no obligation to pursue the implications_ of _any_ given work in a next and subsequent work—or, for that matter, _ever_. High Entertainment isn't "working on" anything—anything, that is, other than delivering pleasure to an audience. It does not proceed according to a scientistic or investigatory model. In High Entertainment there is no imaginary problem, and thus no imaginary solution to it.

Sustaining the lather requires discipline. In fact art is discipline; it's the saying No to almost everything in order to more emphatically say Yes to a very few things. High Entertainment doesn't participate in that tradition. High Entertainment doesn't require the maker to do the same thing twice, or to find and develop <u>any link at all</u> between Work A, Work B, and Work C. High Entertainment doesn't finally reside in a fascination with form, and so has no responsibility to form. It is (in this sense at least) wildly, disturbingly undisciplined and brazenly ahistoricist. (Caveat emptor: Any reader who feels that High Entertainment is the right approach for them should be forewarned that the rejection of artistic discipline, perhaps more than any other quality of H.E., will be looked on with maximum disfavor by the art context. If it's an art career you're seeking, it might be wise, therefore, to consider creating your High Entertainment under a pseudonym.)

High Entertainment has, then, a <u>discipline problem</u>. So far as I've observed, though, just as much bad or unnecessary or tired work as good has resulted from the habit of privileging artistic discipline. Which observation suggests to me, and may suggest to you too, that an independent imagination has just as good a chance of making good work by abandoning altogether the discipline celebrated by the art system.***

VIVA EXPERIMENTALISM

Art is comparatively unbound by conventions of method and of result. Artists are forever experimenting with what art is. So much so, in fact, that art, in our time, has become identified—to a fault, some could say—with the idea of <u>form-discovery</u>.

High Entertainment applies the principle of form-discovery to the creation of entertainment. Every last one of the conventions and tropes of mainstream entertainment product—genre, plot, story arc, character, acting, the "star," length, format, the relation between editorial and advertising, <u>everything</u>—may be pried open and subjected to experiments. These experiments might dissolve them. While there's no rule <u>against</u> using the conventions of entertainment (sometimes they're entertaining!), they can also be disregarded completely, as if they'd never existed, so long as the new form discovered is entertaining. With regard to method, structure, and content, the independent imagination can do anything he or she chooses, so long as the experiment a) does not rely on a specialized language (since that would be art) and b) it activates in the audience that mysterious twaa-aa-aang of delight.

MEANING IS JUST FINE, IN ITS PLACE

By abandoning the artistic model of discipline (in its way a courageous act, incidentally), High Entertainment de-activates an important tool of meaning-making. But does sacrificing art's singular capacity to frame and sustain unique existential narratives subsequently reduce High Entertainment to a condition of outright "meaninglessness" as well? When "meaning" is not directly the point or the focus of a thing, is that thing then "meaningless"?

Young or developing artists, who are in the thick of the anxious business of carving their lives into time and space, are especially sensitive to the presence of meaning. They require and demand it. Once you've done some of that existential self-definition work, though, meaning has a funny way of becoming less important—or at least less insistent and central. Life, which is rather bigger than meaning, teaches that meaning has its limits, that it isn't the be-all and end-all, that meaning is just fine, in its place.

Imaginative work that is less emphatic about meaning is not, then, necessarily wrong, inappropriate, or bad. Of course it's too early to ascertain the exact relation of High Entertainment to the production of meaning, or how it may go about that task differently; a new category of imaginative work that doesn't behave according to the rules of either art or conventional entertainment product must be allowed to live and breathe in order to establish why we ought to value it. I don't know how High Entertainment will configure meaning. I do know, though, that if we have to be able to identify meaning in order for something to be meaningful, as a species we're in deep trouble, imagination-wise.

ADULTHOOD REVIVED?

A large percentage of the adults who work within the entertainment industry toil at inventing products that can be consumed by people younger than 18.

May I say what I really mean here? Thank you.

Our popular culture is principally dedicated to finding ways to take money from children. Easy to fool, children are the most vulnerable demographic in all of consumerland.

Correspondingly, as a person ages they'll find fewer popular entertainment products that are designed to recognize and celebrate such subtleties as the adult mind is capable of apprehending.

It's possible that High Entertainment, which is more than open to being in the subtleties business, may be more the cup of tea of mature sensibilities.

OPACITY AND TRANSPARENCY

The entertainment culture promulgates opacity. The entertainment industry does not want you to know "how it's done." It does not want to reveal its secrets. It prefers that you have no other role than that of consumer. It is, and wants to be, opaque. It is alligned with and invested in the forces of illusion. The digital revolution, which has placed mainstream media formats into the hands of the masses, therefore stands as a direct threat to some very lucrative traditions.

Art in the modern era has been a vastly more transparent enterprise. Art in the modern era has consistently been willing to reveal and to put on display, as part of the show, much of the system that presents it, and, by so doing, to stimulate and direct its own evolution. This "transparency principle" is derived from a surprising source: P.T. Barnum. Barnum, the greatest showman of the 19th century, understood that the audience is just as entertained by knowing how a trick is done—its conceptual dimension, in other words—as by the trick itself. This insight, aggressively and inventively applied over the course of his long career, establishes P.T. Barnum as America's first conceptual artist. In view of this claim it makes sense that the art world, not the entertainment industry, should have made the most active use of Barnum's discovery.

High Entertainment, intent on adapting certain of art's ambitions to the mainstream formats of media, is free to make greater use of transparency than does conventional entertainment product. It's not <u>required</u> to do so but, because it is made and distributed by independent imaginations who have no obligation to the mass entertainment state, nothing <u>prevents</u> it from doing so. As did master showman Barnum, the High Entertainer acknowledges that truth-telling, engaged in the course of displaying the system, can itself be entertaining. The entertainment context—show biz—continues to work hard to maintain and protect the lucrative opacity of its conventions, of course. But the opacity that characterizes conventional entertainment product may be dissolved in High Entertainment. This need not involve a deconstruction per se but rather the conception and enactment of new, less suffocatingly dishonest positions.

STAR MAKEOVER

In the current climate of cultural destabilization the old concept of the star, so long with us, so worn thin, has been handed a rare chance to evolve toward something more interesting and illuminating.

Stars of the mass entertainment culture that we daily negotiate are always opaque representatives of industry mechanisms. The conventional show biz star does not and perhaps cannot reveal or speak to the workings of the system that presents them without putting at risk his or her own position within it; whatever analysis of the show biz system that the star may have been required to undertake in order to achieve their stardom remains opaque. Anyone who cannot make their peace with the machinery, in other words, cannot become or remain a star. But because they must remain an opaque indicator of the mechanism that presents them—a mainstream indicator of access to the mainstream—the star's function narrows to, really, tragicomic dimensions. Does today's conventional entertainment star represent any values, really, other than access to the machinery that presents him or her as a star?

Anyone who is inclined to ponder ways in which entertainment might be changed for the better would do well, then, to give serious thought to the idea of the star—what the star is for, how it performs, what it delivers to an audience ... Why? For starters, it's easier for a person to change than a system. And, more specifically for our purposes, the sheer impossibility of defending against an individual performer's decision to alter their own behavior—<u>who they are interested and willing to be</u>, in other words—effectively renders "the star" the most vulnerable part of the existing entertainment machine. The idea of the "star" becomes a prime site for the formulation of new, less oppressively dishonest positions within entertainment culture.

High Entertainment, which will be made and distributed by technologically-enfranchised, independent imaginations who aren't required to swear fealty to the media state, thus creates an opportunity for the old concept "star" to be outfitted with new, more useful functions. The concept of "star" may become, to give but one example, a portal through which the forces of transparency infiltrate the mainstream.

MEMO FROM OUR STAR LAB

1) Imagine what a system, context, or culture needs.
2) Be that thing, either through real actions or by creation of a persona.

FREEDOM FROM SYSTEM

High Entertainment is neither art nor conventional entertainment. Because the digital revolution has enabled independent imaginations to choose and control their own communication platforms (DVD or download), a class of concept-oriented, image-based subtleties that had previously been assigned to the art context, the art system, the art world, now may reach the public by other means. To a High Entertainer the art system is superfluous. Add to this the fact that today's technology-wielding independent imagination may work in the media favored by the mainstream culture without any obligation to produce in the manner sponsored by the media state, and it becomes clear that a stunning degree of <u>freedom from system</u> has just landed in the lap of the modern person.

Just now, at the beginning of this new era, that kind of freedom is a weak muscle—real, but so absolute and novel that one hardly knows (High Entertainment? What the hell is that?) where to begin. But it will become stronger with exercise.

POLITICS

"A lackey of the corporate state," "an opiate drugging the masses"—these are among the accusations regularly leveled at entertainment. From a certain perspective all the unflattering characterizations are accurate; popular entertainment in the age of mass media has indeed become a tool wielded by the powerful with at least the <u>aim</u> (the success varies) of distracting the masses from applying their energies to mounting any concentrated and sustained challenge to the status quo. It will not be news to you that those who own and operate the media state aspire—conspire, too—to control and influence the public mind, partly by feeding us certain kinds of information constantly, and partly by denying us alternatives to that diet. Any conscious adult has to find this an insulting and scary situation.

Come the revolution. Meanwhile, the empire of the corporate remains with us. We accommodate it not only because we've convinced ourselves we must (talk about effective propagandizing!) but also because aspects of it work to our advantage. Who wants to manufacture their own toothpaste? You? Moreover, and looking past the practical, certain attributes of the business civilization's communication wing—a.k.a. the media state—have been known to flat-out _delight_. The Beatles, to draw an example from the hat. The Beatles made life lustrous for just about everybody. And if we accept that The Beatles have worked to the general advantage of human beings, then don't we also have to recognize that, objectively considered, any society (it happens to be our own) that's consistently able to come up with Beatles- or near-Beatles-level phenomena (as ours is) must also be getting something, some very basic need of the citizenry, consistently right? I think we do. And if _that's_ the case, if the pleasures that our popular culture intermittently deliver are signs that this society is getting something right, then there must be more to entertainment, lackey of the corporate state that it is, than only its damnable opiating function. Entertainment may have become a tool designed to confuse and distract the masses but surely it isn't _only_ that. (A vibration basic to human experience, entertainment, let's not forget, predates just about anything you could name. Corporate empires and their dispiriting shenanigans are, actually, quite late to the game in question.)

Politically speaking, shame doesn't _automatically_ inhere to entertainment, then. Which assertion, I'm aware, conflicts with a notion of progressivism favored in recent decades by intellectuals and the artistic avant-garde. Post-war artists and writers have consistently been among those lobbing sophisticated critiques at the media state. Here I hasten to say that we have benefited from their efforts, unquestionably. Even if the attacks they've mounted haven't succeeded either in reducing the will of the media state one iota or thwarting the exercise of its power, they _have_ taught many of us how to identify propaganda in its subtlest forms and maintain a healthy distance from its effects. They've liberated many of us from the state's control—surely their aim in the first place, at least in part.

From the perspective afforded us by the digital revolution, however, it's hard not to feel that the vigor of their opposition must have been fueled, somewhat, by a frustration at having been denied access to the powerful, seductive, bedazzling communication technologies of our time. (Artists and writers are in the communication business as well, after all.) When something has a grip on you but you're not allowed near it, fascination can twist into resentment.

But if it's really progress you're looking to bring about, there's more than one way to set it in motion. Happily, the High Entertainer—born further along in the evolution of technology, more media-empowered—needn't define progressivism in the same frustrated, oppositional terms of his or her artistic forebears. The media state underwritten by business civilization may be with us from here on out but the digital revolution has modernized and, in the course of modernizing, *altered* the independent imagination's relation to state power. New opportunities make for new politics; the fact that you and I can now communicate in and distribute mainstream formats without any obligation to the existing media system means we neither have to sign up with *nor* do battle against that system's corporate overseers. The independent imagination is now less beholden to *any* ideology. If we don't need to enlist in the opacities, distractions, and lies that characterize corporate media to proceed with our work, neither is criticality of corporate media the thinking person's only respectable alternative. Media-enabled, the High Entertainer needn't—actually, *can't*—divide the situation so neatly as Us and Them, insider and outsider.

In this sense, the digital revolution has cleared a space for innocence to take hold, a new beginning, a fresh start. The High Entertainer has been given an opportunity to work from that historical rarity, the clean slate. What might mass entertainment freed from corporate ownership look and sound like, actually? When you don't have to serve power in order to communicate in the means previously controlled by the corporate state, how exactly will you use your independence? How safe will you play it? How imaginative will you be? Free of the strictures of system, what form does communication take? The independent imagination's relation to power becomes, clearly, something to be defined anew ...

Informed by these factors, the cultural niche I've been calling High Entertainment is in a position to sponsor a transfusion of ethics into the entertainment we consume. Less obligated to rely on the bullshit of show biz, it is free to talk about the world in another way. Whether reality will fulfill the promise of theory is open to question. Many of us would welcome a new, ethically-charged, more honest sort of entertainment. Let's be careful here, though. Let's not hope for too much. This isn't a crusade, it's an opportunity. High Entertainment may deliver on it only by introducing a better—here translated as more entertaining—class of lies. But even that will be an improvement.

POST-ART

Why do I argue for a High Entertainment? To counter the brain drain, and because history has arranged for this cultural moment to come into existence; what I've been describing really is taking place. So far as embracing full on the opportunity this moment represents, though, this I do for reasons of my own.

When I began as an artist, 20 years ago, making artworks and exhibiting them in galleries and, in time, museums, art was to me a wonderful way of exploring both the world and what a person could be in the world. Through art I applied myself to the world and discovered my sensibility.

That sensibility (it turned out) had from the start big dollops of entertainment culture in it (obvious from the title of my first solo exhibition—The David Robbins Show). Too big, perhaps: the art context, as steeped as I was in it, was always an uncomfortable fit. Nor did the art world hesitate to let me know that it felt the same way. Regardless, I soldiered on, during my years in the role of "artist," making some interesting things and, I think, some interesting discoveries too, for myself and hopefully for others.

All the time, though, my sensibility pointed toward and yearned for an imaginative Elsewhere. I became increasingly dissatisfied with the narrowness of art as a formulation of the imagination. This will sound preposterous to many people, I'm aware, given that art offers and represents extraordinary behavioral freedoms, but in "making art" I found an ultimately enslaving formulation. How so? In art, you can do, yes, anything you want so long as you're willing to have it end up as art. That isn't real imaginative freedom, in my view. Inquisitiveness of mind will carry you past art, and apparently I love inquisitiveness of mind more than I love art. In the final analysis I prefer not to be a slave to any proposition that isn't of my own creation—even to propositions, such as art, that have resulted in a lot of wonderful things. (I don't expect to convince any artists of my argument, of course. Art in the modern era is a faith-based exercise, a surrogate church: you believe in it or you don't. Ultimately, I found, I'm simply not a believer. Anyone who is a believer will not understand my discomfort, but that will have to be their problem. Indeed, when it comes to faith, that's always the catch: there's no room for doubt.)

Unwilling to be who art—and the art system—asked me to be, I let my imagination gradually evolve away from its earlier emphasis on deriving adventure from intensive explorations of the visual and material realm. Eventually, my personal trajectory intersected with the digital revolution, which, god bless it, provided a way out of identifying my production as "art" without also having to give up the abilities and sensibility I'd developed through being an artist.

This cultural moment holds special promise, then, for anyone like me who, rather than introducing things—materials, subject matter, concepts—into the art context (a strategy that seems to me to have been the work of modernism, and a habit of imagination left over from modernism), prefers the challenge of pushing certain ambitions for the culture and certain attitudes heretofore associated with the art context in the direction of the mainstream. My ambition isn't to get video art shown on a television program or channel. My ambition isn't to write into my screenplay a character who's an artist. My ambition is to make "television shows" or "movies" for popular consumption—and, equally, to find out what those will look and sound like. I may succeed or I may fail at this "High Entertainment" business but, whatever the outcome, as a challenge it now strikes me as more interesting than making more Art—and more appropriate too, given my sensibility. Fortunately, the mainstream culture has evolved to a point where it's on the cusp of accommodating entertainment made by people whose thinking has been shaped in the art context; that gap too has narrowed.

High Entertainment is for me, then, a post-art condition of mind; I worked through my art fascination and arrived at something that's clearly informed by art training and art thinking but doesn't play by art's rules. What I make from here on out may yet be interpreted as art—it's still personal, invented communication, after all—but if so that interpretation will be supplied by the audience, not by its maker.

For some of you, an idea such as High Entertainment will represent the right path. You get it. (The kids, with their cameras and their microphones, get it, I can tell you.) You may not be ready yet to accommodate or pursue its promise, you may have to work through your fascination with art and its possibilities before you can become comfortable with the state of mind and the kind of production that High Entertainment represents, but in your gut you recognize home in what I've been describing.

That's great. Be forewarned, however, that your acceptance of a role vis-à-vis entertainment may require you to admit something about yourself that you may prefer not to hear. You may discover that, as it turns out, you do not have an artist's commitment to form, an artist's identification with media or material, an artist's obsessions or an artist's discipline. Everyone isn't meant to be an artist. And if you aren't? What are you to do with your perfectly good ideas? Suppress them because they're not art? Nonsense! Get to work! Understand your difference and articulate its place in the scheme of things.

From the number of galleries and museums dedicated to exhibiting contemporary art, and the quality of work that's shown in them, art looks to be in pretty good shape. At least there seems no shortage of people adept at fashioning refined, ambitious, well-made, challenging art objects. The intense competition is eliciting strong work. Art's in good hands. What's not in great shape is the entertainment culture. And that's the other reason to embrace the promise of High Entertainment: the condition "entertainment" is in.

Glance at the Sunday TV section of any newspaper in any American city: for every Seinfeld, every Six Feet Under, every Sopranos there are 20 degrading, peurile sitcoms, ten grim police dramas featuring twisted killers tracked by wise-cracking crime units, and a dozen crassly Darwinian reality programs. It's difficult to believe that adults could stand to imagine, write, and shoot the sorry line-up weekly offered. "But TV, with so many channels, must fill so much airtime," you argue. "Inevitably some of it has to disappoint." According to that argument mainstream movies, responsible for only two hours of your time, ought to really be delivering the goods, yet your ten-dollar ticket practically guarantees two hours of witless dialogue, teeth-grinding sentimentality, gadgetry, and gore. That complaints about the entertainment business are longstanding doesn't diminish their relevancy. Let's cut to the chase: In seeking to reduce risk and, by so doing, guarantee the lavish lifestyles of the people who run it, a once-inventive industry has drifted into a cynical attitude toward its audience that does life no favor. Because it has enjoyed a lock on the mainstream culture for as long as anyone alive can remember, the entertainment industry's assumptions about what constitutes "entertainment" have gone unchallenged for too long. Those assumptions have been free to rot, and rotting they, at long last, surely are. We've all learned to be ironic about the tragic phosphorescence emanating from popular culture. Thanks to the digital revolution we no longer have to be.

The zone now forming between fine art and popular art can be explored in many ways. If this discussion of a High Entertainment has emphasized recorded media at the expense of object production, it's due to the fact that the power struggle is playing out in recorded media, not objects. Certainly, though, the concept of High Entertainment—i.e., works and artifacts that retain fine art's complex ambitions for the culture while eschewing the specialized language of fine art in favor of mass accessibility—can be manifested in games, toys, fashion, public sculpture, books, hoaxes—indeed in any product that has contact with the public.

Accommodating the notion that one could, in the image business, offer a sophisticated and ambitious sort of production, in nature independent from the existing art and entertainment systems, requires mental discipline. Even if you like the idea of a High Entertainment, in order for it to exist you have first to believe that it can. Some of you will resist this. Without even knowing it, you may be someone who operates on the assumption that all categories of imaginative endeavor have already been identified, and that the best we can do is fit our sensibilities to these known categories. (The ostensibly wild and wooly art world—of all places!—is full of people who hold this view.) But that's like declaring that all scientific discoveries have already been made. Entire, subtly differentiated categories of imaginative endeavor are still to be invented. High Entertainment, a term that, at the very least, denotes categories confounded, might be among them.

The idea that all categories of imaginative endeavor haven't already been created and identified is an essential one, but it lives only as a result of belief in it. (Here's <u>my</u> church.) It takes time to get comfortable with the idea that a High Entertainment might exist. It takes time to get comfortable with not categorizing something as "art" just because it's more satisfying than run-of-the-mill entertainment. For a new category to take hold, you must <u>let</u> it take hold. This requires mental discipline—the discipline to say no to tradition, the discipline to hold the door open to allow an unknown future to enter the room, the picture, your life, and to take shape. High Entertainment is, just for starters, a mental exercise in structuring the new.

NOTES

* Speaking of history: the concept of the mainstream occupies quite interesting, even unique temporal coordinates, actually. The mainstream can be likened to the concept of "the present"—the mainstream too is huge, invisible, stable, and constant—transposed into cultural terms. The mainstream is a continual Present Tense, embodied in the language of culture.

** Art expresses and reveals the involuntary self, the maker's deepest psyche, which is beyond his or her control. Romantic individualism aside, is every psyche one that ought to stand so naked? Not based on my experience they aren't. Some involuntary selves are just not healthy enough to have a public life; without meaning to, some psyches poison the atmosphere.

What we generally categorize as "entertainment," a more limited enterprise, generally promotes and stands for a cheerier view of life. Art can be a bummer, after all, and still be quite good art. Yes, entertainment is narrower, but is this more restricted range automatically a bad thing? Mightn't we acknowledge that, really, for the good of the audience, some people's psyches ought to be swimming in the shallow end? One can already envision the ad campaign: "Some people shouldn't go very deep—and with High Entertainment, they don't have to!"

*** For some of you, accepting the idea that "to entertain" is okay will be the primary challenge. You've got "entertaining" ideas, but you think you ought to want to be aligned with the goals of art. Entertaining? Instead of "working on" a real or an imaginary "problem"? Rather than working on finding a solution to that problem? It goes against everything you've been taught. The academy, which is full of smart people, some of whom come up a bit short in the imagination department, has in our time succeeded in harnessing the imagination to the idea of "the problem." (It is one of the few clear successes of the academy in our time.) Play, says the academy, should be infused with utility. There's a lot of good in that idea. A lot of good has come of it, at least. But utility can be defined in many ways. Exposing other people to the uncategorizable: isn't that a form of human "utility" too? To keep alive human values like wit and charm, at a time when the world seems hell-bent on snuffing out those values, doesn't that count as "utility"?

Utility, in other words, is just dandy so long as you don't also hold that its nature be identified in advance.

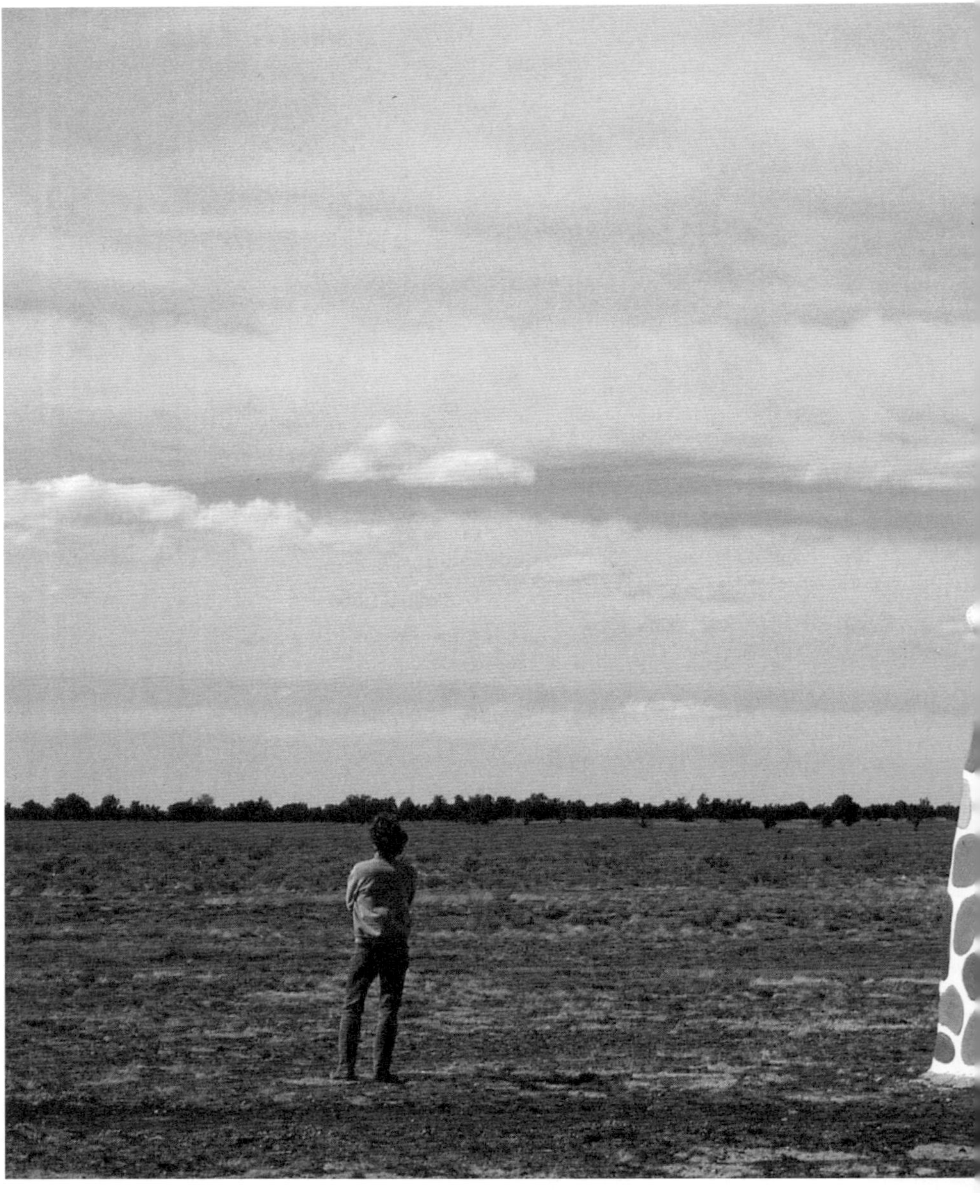

The Frontiersman, 1987
Cibachrome photograph, 30" x 40", edition of two

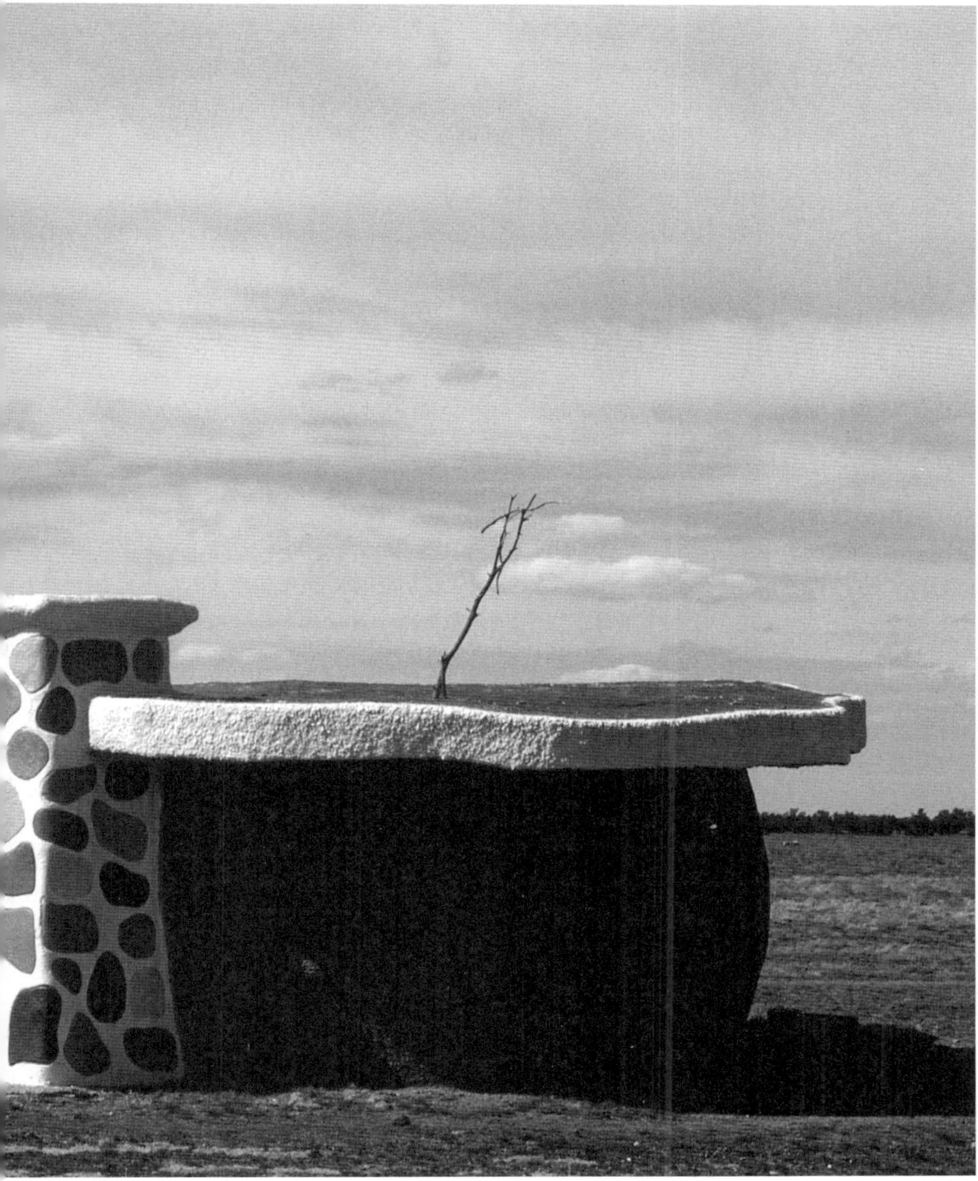

Edited by Lionel Bovier & Fabrice Stroun

Editing and Proofreading: Clare Manchester
Design: Gilles Gavillet & Fabian Monod
Design Concept: Gilles Gavillet & Cornel Windlin
Headline Typeface: "Number Two," designed by Martha Stutteregger, Vienna
Cover: photograph by Armin Linke, Milan (www.arminlinke.com)
Print: Musumeci S.p.A., Quart (Aosta)

ACKNOWLEDGEMENTS:
Michael Banicki, Elein Fleiss, Randi Hopkins, Hudson (Feature, New York), Pierre Huyghe (© Marian Goodman Gallery Paris/New York), Gary Kornblau, Thomas Lawson, Armin Linke, Allan McCollum, Hans Ulrich Obrist.

ISBN 10: 3-905701-02-2
ISBN 13: 978-3-905701-02-9

PUBLISHED BY:

JRP|Ringier
Letzigraben 134
CH-8047 Zurich
T +41 43 311 27 50
F +41 43 311 27 51
E info@jrp-ringier.com
www.jrp-ringier.com

IN CO-EDITION WITH:

Les Presses du réel
16, rue Quentin
F-21000 Dijon
T +33 3 80 30 75 23
F +33 3 80 30 59 74
E info@lespressesdureel.com
www.lespressesdureel.com

DISTRIBUTION:

Switzerland
Buch 2000, AVA Verlagsauslieferung AG, Centralweg 16, CH-8910 Affoltern a.A.
buch2000@ava.ch, www.ava.ch

France
Les Presses du réel, 16 rue Quentin, F-21000 Dijon
info@lespressesdureel.com, www.lespressesdureel.com

Germany and Austria
Vice Versa Vertrieb, Immanuelkirchestrasse 12, D-10405 Berlin
info@vice-versa-vertrieb.de, www.vice-versa-vertrieb.de

UK
Art Data, 12 Bell Industrial Estate, 50 Cunnington Street, UK-London W4 5HB
info@artdata.co.uk, www.artdata.co.uk

USA
D.A.P./Distributed Art Publishers, 155 Sixth Avenue, 2nd Floor, New York, USA-NY 10013
dap@dapinc.com, www.artbook.com

Other countries
Idea Books, Nieuwe Herengracht 11, NL-1011 RK Amsterdam
idea@ideabooks.nl, www.ideabooks.nl

POSITIONS 4
David Robbins

This book is the fourth volume in the "Positions" series, dedicated to artists' writings.

The series is directed by Lionel Bovier and Xavier Douroux.
Associate Editors: Christophe Cherix and Fabrice Stroun.

Also available:

John Miller, The Price Club. Selected Writings (1977-1998)
ISBN 10: 2-940271-05-4
ISBN 13: 978-2-940271-05-4

Thomas Lawson, Mining for Gold. Selected Writings (1979-1996)
ISBN 10: 2-940271-22-4
ISBN 13: 978-2-940271-22-1

Mike Kelley, Interviews, Conversations, and Chit-Chat (1986-2004)
ISBN 10: 3-905701-00-6
ISBN 13: 978-3-905701-00-5

New releases 2006:

Liam Gillick, Proxemics. Selected Writings (1988-2006)
ISBN 10: 3-905701-01-4
ISBN 13: 978-3-905701-01-2

Vito Acconci, Notes et essais critiques (1970-2004)
ISBN 10: 2-940271-62-3
ISBN 13: 978-2-940271-62-7